Music-Cultures in Contact

Musicology: A Book Series

Edited by **Hans Lenneberg**, The University of Chicago, Illinois

This book is part of a series. The publisher will accept continuation orders which may be cancelled at any time and which provide for automatic billing and shipping of each title in the series upon publication. Please write for details.

Music-Cultures in Contact

Convergences and Collisions

Edited by

Margaret J. Kartomi

and

Stephen Blum

Gordon and Breach Publishers

Australia • Austria • Belgium • France • Germany • India • Japan • Malaysia • Netherlands • Russia • Singapore • Switzerland • Thailand • United Kingdom • United States

Published under license by Gordon and Breach Science Publishers S.A.

Gordon and Breach Science Publishers S.A.
Postfach
4004 Basel
Switzerland

Simultaneously published as volume 2 of the Currency Press series *Australian Studies in the History, Philosophy and Social Studies of Music.*

British Library Cataloguing in Publication Data

Music-Cultures in Contact:Convergences
and Collisions. - (Musicology: A Book
Series, ISSN 0275-5866;Vol. 16)
  I. Kartomi, Margaret J. II. Blum,
  Stephen III. Series
  781.6

ISBN 2-88449-137-6

CONTENTS

PREFACE

Why and how does change occur in musical culture?

There are many possible answers to this question. Change is often engendered by contact between two or several impinging cultures, sub-cultures or classes within a culture. This is the kind of change that is the focus of this book.

The effects of contact range from the making of minor adjustments within existing musical styles, such as the small-scale transfer of discrete musical traits from one music into another, to the creative transformation of whole styles and of the ideological and music-organizing principles on which they are based. Creative transformation, which may be termed syncretism, synthesis or transculturation, normally occurs as a result of convergence between cultures over a prolonged period of contact. Such convergences may result in an influx of new musical ideas, organizing principles and repertoires. They may result in a greater level of individual and corporate creativity than before, or an increase in the total amount of time and energy spent by a group of people on music-making. Moreover, when two or several disparate groups are forced to make sense of each other's ideas and practices, they may feel the need to develop new habits of discourse about music or even new methods of teaching music. Thus it is that whole styles, repertoires, genres, pedagogical methods, extra-musical meanings com-monly attached to music, the manner of theorizing about music, and even the way a group dresses or behaves at musical events may change as a result of convergences in contact situations.

Conversely, contact may result in collisions or clashes between imping-ing cultures, as when a conservative community rejects an alien music, when colonial overlords suppress an indigenous music, or when the music of a dominant class is given priority over minority musics in a society or education institution. Partly or wholly unfavorable results may ensue from such collisions, for example, the loss or abandonment of whole works, genres or concepts, or a severe reduction in the total amount of energy spent on creative music-making in a community. Other kinds of musical impoverishment, such as the loss of instruments, orchestras and other cultural goods, may ensue as, for example, after a war. Alternatively, the energy generated by such collisions and conflict may result in new creative achievements which have a partially or wholly positive effect on the musical health of the society in question.

Authors of articles in this book deal with a range of situations involving two, three or several cultures in contact over a considerable period. Together, they pose a number of questions. What are the initial and the sustaining impulses for change in works by single composers or in whole repertoires of works, as the case may be? What are the sociomusical results of the convergences and collisions between impinging cultures? What happens to cultures which exist in relative isolation over time? How can contact influence intellectual traditions and habits of discourse about music and the manner of teaching it? Does the hierarchy of music in music schools reflect the hegemony of power relationships in society? How do impinging musics in such schools converge or collide with each other? What happens in a culture which, for economic reasons, deliberately aims to create a mass-oriented music to appeal to peoples of mixed cultural and class backgrounds?

Authors in Part I of this book discuss cross-cultural perspectives on selected genres of performance. Stockmann investigates two contact situations, one of which is the convergence between the yoiking song tradition of the Sami of Scandinavia and Western popular music, resulting in the syncretic creation of Sami pop music, and the other the collision between the disparate psychologies of orally oriented Sami musicians and outsider scholars when forced to meet in the field and undertake scholarly discourse. Thus, Stockmann brings up the pertinent question of how a highly literate researcher should go about examining a primarily oral culture whose people barely read and write. Clearly, the initial impulse for musical change in both cases is extra-musical, i.e. social and economic.

Petrovic, investigating a case of three-way contact and convergence, comes to a similar conclusion about the impulse for change. Tracing European and Asian musical elements in the "ancient singing" of isolated, mountainous regions of the Central Balkans in Yugoslavia, she concludes that the Asian contact was dominant, that it resulted in creative synthesis, and that the initial and sustaining impulses for change were extra-musical, i.e. war and migration. Mazo, on the other hand, investigates a culture which has had very little outside contact. In her study of wedding laments and choruses in the isolated eastern Vologda province of Russia, she finds no evidence of change in the musical and verbal structures, breathing, posture of singers, context of performance, and local evaluation of performers from the nineteenth century to the present.

Sometimes contact can intensify the characteristics of a national musical style. Thus, in Keller's study of Italian folk ballads and lyric songs, contact with other European and Middle-Eastern cultures has resulted in the creation of syncretic musical forms that have retained an intrinsically Italian character. Extra-musically induced contact has resulted in an enrichment of the culture as a whole.

Sometimes, however, collisions with other national groups become the motive force for the development of a new national style, as in the case of Croatian opera. Due to political collisions and upheavals in the nineteenth century, Blazekovic writes, Croatian composers aimed to create a distinctly Croatian operatic form which expressed a fierce nationalism. They chose libretti which revived the corporate memory of Croatian historical events and folk tales. Audiences recognized them as allegories of the contemporary Austrians, Hungarians and others. Thus, sociopolitical collisions were the initial and the sustaining impulse for the development of Croatian opera.

Schechter's paper, on the other hand, describes the convergence between two initially colliding parent cultures—European Catholic culture and Andean harvest rituals, cultures which resulted in the syncretic development of the Corpus Christi and Octave in Andean Equador. Schechter concludes that the initial impulse for the change was socioreligious.

Discussing the results of culture contact between the Vietnamese and the Chinese on the one hand and the Vietnamese and the West on the other, Lê Tuân Hùng isolates two cases of musical synthesis. One is the music drama in South Vietnam, where a large number of Chinese live. Another is the Vietnamese-Western synthesis marking some new compositions in Vietnam. Lê shows that the impetus for musical change as well as the maintenance of existing styles in Huê and amateur music of Vietnam between 1890 and 1920 was sociopolitical. He delineates multiple responses to this three-way contact, including the grafting of non-indigenous extra-musical features onto indigenous music-technical conventions, the rejection of non-indigenous traits, the adoption of non-indigenous traits, the abandonment of pre-existing traits, and the simultaneous development of multiple musical styles.

The last three papers in Part I of this book refer to recent developments in or the effects of mass-oriented musics. Isolating a recent case of musical contact between urban and rural populations in Tamilnadu, India, Venkatraman points to the syncretic development of a third style, i.e. modern popular music, which is mainly propagated through the medium of film. A synthesis of Brahman Karnatic music and folk music of rural areas, this music attracts both rural and urban audiences who thereby learn about each other's musical styles. This mass-oriented film music was initially developed for economic reasons, as musicians worked to produce music which could appeal to as wide an audience as possible.

In his study of musical syntheses in Papua New Guinea, Niles draws attention to three converging forms: a new form of religious music resulting from the impingement of Western (mostly European) mission music on traditional Papua New Guinea music, a new form of popular music ensuing from the contact between the Western pop media (cassettes and radio) and the traditional music, and a new form of traditionally based music resulting from the interaction between disparate groups of Papua New Guineans meeting at cultural shows and competitions. The initial and sustaining impulse for change was largely religious and socioeconomic.

Tracing the history of urban Fijian musical attitudes and foreign influences before and since 1960, Saumaiwai shows that the impulses for change were religious, educational and political. The initial impulse for the new musical synthesis developing in the 1960s was religious, when traditional Fijian music converged with Methodist hymns and anthems and new songs for school children combined traditional and Western ideas. After Independence in 1970, the impulse for change was more consciously political, as the government developed a policy of encouraging cultural exchange between ethnic groups. In the 1980s, on the other hand, a political change in the village chief government system together with increased consumption of Western popular music on the media resulted in a marked decline of interest in the traditional music in urban areas.

In Part II of this book the authors shift the focus to contact in educational and government institutions. Sumarsam's paper refers to convergences and collisions between Javanese and Dutch intellectuals which stimulated the growth of gamelan theory among Javanese scholars in the twentieth century. Javanese intellectuals were subjected to Western-style education provided by the Dutch colonial government. In some cases this contact between intellectual traditions and approaches resulted in a synthesis of Javanese and European music-theoretical ideas, while in others there was either a collision or no interaction at all.

Alter also discusses changes in intellectual practices, but in his case these changes resulted from contract between Hindustani and Western music-educational ideas and methods. In the late nineteenth century, the single teacher-pupil teaching method of the courts was replaced by Western-style music school education, which used music notation and resulted in the awarding of degrees. In the 1960s, however, music teachers returned to the single teacher-pupil method, while retaining the music institutions and associated educational ideas. This convergence of traditional and imported educational practices is seen as a favorable synthesis of both worlds.

Confining his discussion mainly to contact situations in schools of music of the 1980s in the American Midwest, Nettl argues that here the "central classical repertoire" is supported by the cultured middle class and is kept quite separate from other more "peripheral" European music (e.g. Medieval, Baroque, experimental, folk and ethnic), thus creating a hierarchy. The various majority and minority musics practiced in the schools are not lost or abandoned. They converge, he argues, only in so far as some students and staff attend performances of different musics and some study world music. Mostly, however, they collide with and repel each other; each warily guards its unique characteristics and strives to maintain its purity, thus rejecting any synthesis.

In her historical study of Chinese-Malay contact in Malaysia, Tan Sooi Beng concludes that Malay and Chinese cultures which converged creatively in pre-colonial times have diverged recently due to the growth of racist policies and that modernity and Western influence detract from this.

The impulses for change resulting in the birth of the Australian bush band, Smith argues, were primarily sociopolitical and ideological. The band came into existence as the result of a marriage between Irish folk music and Anglo-Australian folk music during the folk revival in the 1970s.

Noll's paper compares the processes and results of rural-urban culture contact in musical networks and institutions of Western Ukraine with those of Eastern Ukraine, concluding that the rural and urban musical networks converged in both regions to create a new repertoire for consumption by both urban and rural musicians and audiences. The initial and the sustaining impulse for change in each case was the social, economic and political motives of urban State officials. However, the aims differed: in the Western areas the main purpose was to establish and maintain national Ukrainian identity, while in the East it was to establish both national and supranational (Soviet) styles. In terms of state ideology, the results of contact were favorable, for the new styles did not result in the loss of the old village music.

Pasler's paper is unique in this collection in that it investigates the results of culture contact in the works of individual composers, i.e. contact between two French composers, Roussel and Delage, and Indian music around 1910. The Indian-inspired compositions for Western instruments by Delage are not just "superficial impressionism," she writes: they represent a unique personal style inspired by the timbres, tunings, forms, rhythms and — especially — performing techniques of Indian classical music. Roussel's works, on the other hand, are inspired by Indian folk music. The composers' use of Indian elements is explainable by the hunger for escape and the aesthetic of exoticism in France at the time. The works of both composers, she argues, are successful creative syntheses.

Margaret J. Kartomi

INTRODUCTION TO
THE SERIES

The Gordon and Breach Musicology series, a companion to the *Journal of Musicological Research,* covers a creative range of musical topics, from historical and theoretical subjects to social and philosophical studies. Volumes thus far published show the extent of this broad spectrum, from *Music and Its Social Meanings, Musical Life in Poland,* and *Witnesses and Scholars: Studies in Musical Biography* to *Metaphor: A Musical Dimension.* This editors also welcome interdisciplinary studies, ethnomusicological works and performance analyses. With this series, it is our aim to expand the field and definition of musical exploration and research.

Synthesis in the Culture of Scholarship: Problems in Investigating and Documenting the Archaic and Modern Styles of Yoiking by the Sami in Scandinavia

Doris Stockmann

Introduction

Sound recordings have been widely used to make oral musical traditions known to scholars, students, and broader audiences who are interested in the world's musics — for example, the music of the Sami in the most northern parts of Europe. Musical 'editions' of this modern type, which are listed and reviewed in journals, are presented with differing degrees of verbal interpretation (depending on whether the editors have commercial or scholarly aims). These range from mere lists of items or brief notes to descriptive booklets accompanying the recordings, which may include musical examples in notation.

There is no reason, of course, to question the necessity and importance of this kind of editing practice in principle. All of us know that ethnomusicology would not have developed at all, or not as it did, without recording techniques. Sound, film and video recordings are the primary source materials for music research on oral traditions, whether involving tribal, folk or popular music, while any kind of notation is secondary and interpretative, and includes subjective judgment on different levels. This is quite the opposite from research on Western art music, where composers create the primary sources that even today are mostly written, or at least include written advice.

Musical Culture of the Sami

To discuss Sami music is to discuss yoiking, a special vocal practice which in the Sami language is called *juoi'gat* or *juoi'kat* (there is no phonological opposition between *g* and *k*). This is the traditional way of singing among these subarctic people who are spread over four different state territories in northern Europe: Norway, Sweden, Finland and Russia.

Anthropologically, the Sami, who originally lived more to the south in Finland, are different from all other European peoples since they arrived in prehistoric times from Central Asia, adopting a Finno-Ugrian language type some 2000 years ago, from which time they were pushed more and more to the north. Culturally, and with respect to their way of life, they belong to the arctic populations influenced by the ecological conditions of this area. Hunting, inland and coastal fishing, and nomadic or semi-nomadic reindeer herding are basic to their subsistence. Different combinations of subsistence activities (including some agriculture) have led to the distinction of three groups: the so-called Sea-Sami (who settled in the coastal areas and now have mixed Norwegian and Finnish blood), the Forest-Sami, and the Mountain-Sami. The latter have emerged within the last two centuries from the Forest-Sami group. They are engaged in far-reaching migration (mainly to the mountain areas) with huge herds of reindeer, which was unknown before the nineteenth century. Although practised by only a small part of the population, this kind of reindeer herding has built up the image of Sami people abroad, and it is also very important for Sami music as one of the main poetic topics of the yoik (*juoigos* or *juoikos* in Sami).

Yoiking is one of the most archaic musical styles preserved up to the present time within the boundaries of Europe. It is a more or less improvised non-strophic type of singing, using special vocal techniques on short melo-rhythmic motives with several types of sequence and pattern repetition. It consists mainly of solo performance, and probably has its roots in shamanic recitation, which played an important role in Sami rituals and beliefs before Christianization but has since been totally extirpated. There was also some kind of ritual group singing (which we know about only from written sources) and, more recently, a quite different, more occasional way of 'singing together' at family and neighbourhood meetings, including recording sessions, annual feasts and weddings. Only in our day has another kind of group singing developed, with the 'new wave' of Sami pop music. This is a mixed kind of music-making with instrumental accompaniment (mostly guitar or accordion but also other instruments or groups of instruments) using tonic-dominant chords and major-minor flair, together with some yoik motives set mostly to recently created poems. It is oriented toward controlled chorus-singing in a Western style, a style that was never significant in the older tradition, though neighbouring folk musics influenced the traditional yoik style to some extent. There has been an emphasis on stage presentation for audience appeal within the new pop wave, of course, and this may include solo singers who perform traditional yoiks in a fairly traditional style. This new musical practice, initiated by young Sami intellectuals and well-accepted among the younger generation, seems to be a major factor in articulating the current problems of Sami life, encouraging people to become aware of their own identity and to struggle for their cultural as well as economic survival. (One indicator of the growing self-consciousness is the replacing of the older name Lapps or Laplanders – invented by foreigners and involving a negative meaning – by the people's own name Sami, a concern shared by other minorities who are involved in the same kind of problems all over the world.)

In recent decades, at least in some regions, the traditional method of yoiking has begun to disappear. Strongly attacked by the missionaries, it had long since become a kind of underground activity, practised secretly within the family environment and the *sii'das* (i.e. the Sami neigh-bourhood and working groups during migration). It has therefore been difficult for interested foreigners to discover. Fundamental changes in lifestyles and modes of work have weakened the practice of yoiking, but there are still areas where yoiking is a living tradition. The cultural differentiation of the Sami, which influenced the development of different musical styles, has also affected their investigation. The large region presently inhabited by Sami people (together, of course, with Norwegians, Finns, Swedes and Russians) has a population of about 35,000, to take the lowest number available from 1987 official statistics of the four countries. This relatively small population is scattered over a vast area; nearly two-thirds (63%) of them live in Norway in the so-called Finnmark area, or along the coast. About one-quarter live in Sweden, and less than 12% in Finland and Russia (around Lake Inari and on the

Kola Peninsula). Some of the latter, the Kola and the so-called Skolt-Sami, are Orthodox Christians, while all of the others are Lutherans.

One may distinguish three main language areas, building up a kind of half-circle around the so-called north calotte of Europe: an eastern, a central and a southern area, each further divided into sub-groups. The central area includes the large Norwegian Sami group that speaks the northern idiom. Linguists are divided as to whether there are nine or ten sub-groups altogether; formerly there were eight or nine. The linguistic differences are so great that distant groups cannot communicate with each other, and, to make the situation even more complicated, ortho-graphic differences have emerged in the written language. Many Sami have difficulties in writing their own language, due in part to a longstanding lack of relevant education. As a rule, however, they are bilingual, using the languages of their respective state territories fluently.

Documenting an Oral Musical Culture

The linguistic diversity and orthographic difficulties created further problems in deciphering and transcribing yoik texts, for both the Sami and others. Thus, a very valuable LP disc series was published in 1969 with an informative booklet but without texts or musical transcriptions. Produced by the Swedish Broadcasting Corporation, its contents were collected in 1954 by Matts Arnberg and Håkan Unsgaard together with the Sami nomad teacher, writer and editor Israel Ruong. Encouraged by Ernst Emsheimer, and with linguistic help from Ruong, I started to transcribe these materials around 1970, but because of political developments in the 1970s could come back to this task only in 1985.

In the meantime, Karl-Olof Edström completed a thesis on aspects of Sami musical culture, concentrating mainly on the available historical sources but including some detailed musical transcriptions as well as a short analysis of examples from the 1954 recordings, though still without the Sami texts (Edström 1975).

In 1961 Ernst Emsheimer and Bo Sommarström had made recordings among a group of Forest-Sami in northern Sweden (Udtja region), but, as often in the history of yoik collecting, no transcribing or edition followed. So I included this material in my work concerning the texts (which, unfortunately, had not been written down during the field trip). I was assisted by a Sami woman who formerly lived in this group and knew all the singers as well as the yoiks, and later by the Sami linguist Susanne Kuoljok-Angéus (University of Umeå). Some years earlier the ethnographer Sommarström had made a field trip with some students, among them the ethnomusicologist Robert Günther. Günther transcribed and analyzed the music of a few yoiks recorded on this trip and published them in 1965 in a preliminary report. No subsequent instalment has appeared.

Since the 1940s in Sweden, the more developed recording techniques that replaced the phonograph had been used systematically by Björn Collinder and the Archive of Dialectology and Folklore Research in Uppsala, mainly for documenting the various Sami languages within Swedish territory but also including examples of yoiking (see the editions by Grundström mentioned below). It soon became clear that yoik transcription would be a difficult and very time-consuming job. This had not been anticipated by two collectors who notated two large collections from the beginning of the century. The first was collected in Finnmark and other regions of the North Sami by Armas Launis, a Finnish scholar and composer who made the first serious attempt at thorough analysis and classification in his edition of 1908, but who wrote down most of his very short, schematic notations in the field, thus omitting much information that could not be obtained this way. The second collection was made between approximately 1910 and 1930 by Karl Tirén, a Swedish railway officer, amateur musician and admirer of Sami life and music, who made several field trips throughout the Sami areas of Sweden and part of the Sami areas of Norway, recording mainly by means of a phonograph. It was not until 1942 that the materials were published; they appeared in *Acta Lapponica,* a series of the Stockholm Nordic Museum, and included transcriptions which often incline to a Westernized interpretation by using inadequate bar norms or key signatures. Tirén made no attempt at musical analysis or classification of his large collection. Thus the available transcriptions of the old recordings need to be rechecked before further analysis and classification can be undertaken.

Two smaller editions of yoiks from the Lule and Pite districts in Northern Sweden, published by the outstanding expert in the language of that area, Harald Grundström (1958, 1963), also lack analysis. This material was collected and transcribed by the Finnish folk music researcher Otto Väisänen (who also notated the music in a Westernized schematic way) and Sune Smedeby. The singer who performed for Väisänen came from a family of skilled yoikers, telling his life story in what one might call a complex 'yoik composition' comprising both narrated and sung passages.

A similar item was recorded and subsequently documented on film by Matts Arnberg and his colleagues in the southern language area. However, the soundtrack for the film had to be taken from the former recording as the yoiker himself could not remember the whole composition.

One should, nonetheless, think about how to document the traditional yoiking practice on film and video recordings, perhaps in the way recently shown by Hugo Zemp in his excellent film on 'Head Voice and Chest Voice' in Swiss yodelling. Zemp's film uses a melographic presentation of the three partly crossing voices that are typical of the yodel tradition. At the beginning of the century, Evgeniya Linyova used a similar method for Russian vocal polyphony, though only in print (St. Petersburg 1904-09). Zemp's yodel melogram in his film runs along with the singing, adding bar by bar to the developing scheme. His trick for presenting the changes from head voice to chest voice, and vice versa, is to separate the two areas of pitch by a horizontal borderline through the staff system. A similar device would work well with some of the Sami yoik dialects, which divide the total ambitus into a main area, where a full voice dominates, and an upper, or lower, area that is touched only by side-slip tones. It is not by accident that yodelling and yoiking have sometimes been compared. Zemp told me that he arrived at his apparently simple solution only after long preparatory transcribing as well as electro-acoustical research on special passages.

To my knowledge, electro-acoustic devices have been used to facilitate the transcription of yoiks only by Eliel Lagercrantz in 1966 and by Ingmar Bengtsson and team at the Musicological Institute of Uppsala University in the late 1960s and 1970s, using a melograph or basic frequency writer. Using materials from the Uppsala Archive, Anikó Bodor investigated some yoiks of the Pite region in northern Sweden, attempting to learn how to improve her aural transcriptions by obtaining information from the electro-acoustic device called 'Mona'. Working at different levels, including sound formation, frequency stability and change, and time unit variation, she found that Mona was useful in transcribing an improvised yoik style. Thus, the notation of a personal yoik concerning the singer's father could be noticeably improved, while for another rather stable type of yoiking the method yielded almost nothing. Bodor also experimented with an intermediate solution between staff notation and melogram, but did not refer to this attempt in her paper of 1974. Nor did she carry out her intention to do electro-acoustic research on about 100 unpublished yoiks held in the Uppsala Archive. Yoik research at the Uppsala Archive ceased after the death of Harald Grundström.

In the edition now under way, I plan to include some electro-acoustic studies, especially on the complicated South Sami yoiking styles, and I also hope to include at least some of Bodor's unpublished materials in order to show the 'historical stages' of research and their results. The electro-acoustic approach to special aspects of yoiking may help us gain a better comprehension of its sound and of some of the structural features involved.

In any case, I intend to present all of the notations or melograms with the respective sound recordings. This is necessary today to make the work with notations more effective. The purpose of an edition, in my opinion, is not to put as much as possible down on paper but to select carefully relevant examples, or groups of examples, of styles, genres and topics. An edition may include several notations of the same item in order to show the variety of interpretation, ranging from purely orthographic differences and those involving spatial presentation of formal order to the subjective decisions concerning metre, rhythm or intervallic structure.

Other recording activities and research in the northern and eastern territories include Lagercrantz's collections among the Sea-Sami from 1928 until the 1960s (1968) and Irina Travina's recent edition of Kola-Sami materials from the Murmansk region (1987), which provides a few fairly detailed transcriptions of whole yoik performances. Two further works demand brief consideration here: a monograph on the Finnmark yoik styles by Andreas Lüderwaldt (1976) and an attempt at analysis of the *leu'dd* of the Skolt-Sami by Ilpo Saastamoinen (1987).

Around 1970, Lüderwaldt (a student of Kurt Reinhard in Berlin) made recordings in Kautokeino and Karasjok, both central settlements of the northern Sami. His thorough investigation included some earlier materials of this area, collected by Dieter Christensen, Wolfgang Laade and Wolfgang Munser. He obtained fairly convincing results in his analysis, concentrating on the rather stable giusto-style of yoiking common in this region, which is mostly pentatonic within a rather large ambitus.

Saastamoinen, a Finnish musician and composer, was highly attracted by the archaic yoiking styles of the Skolt-Sami who have lived since World War II in the northeasternmost corner of Finland (formerly on the

Kola Peninsula). Saastamoinen studied a special kind of one-tone recitation of epic texts called *leu'dd*. He made a thorough transcription and analysis of only one example, unfortunately without paying attention to the textual layout. The example shows a type of tone-level variation, using an upper or lower minor second vibrato on vowels of long duration (as happens quite frequently in the recitation of Siberian shamans) and a rhythmically highly variable (but, nonetheless, somehow predictable) motivic structure, namely different combinations of two-pulse and three-pulse tone groups at very high speed, together with a continuing 'wave movement' of tension and detension that has an effect on the actual note values.

According to one of the first yoik notations, by a Swedish musician at the end of the eighteenth century, a similar kind of vocal technique on a one-tone level seems to have been known formerly, too, among the southernmost Sami groups, who, in general, are considered to have preserved more of the older stylistic strata than have the northern groups, although the traditions have vanished almost totally in the meantime. The item mentioned was notated by J.C.F. Haeffner, *director musices* in Uppsala, from some Sami musicians of the Härjedal district, in a quasi-compositional way. Haeffner's notation, at least in some passages, shows characteristic features of the yoik style (Haeger 1955:148f.).

One of the main future tasks in the study of traditional yoiking and its dialects will be to investigate the secrets of the different kinds of formal structure. Simply by listening to recordings and reading notations one learns that the motivic structure of the yoik is one of the most important features of its melorhythmic layout. Alica Elscheková, in her classifications of European folk melodies, has used the term 'motivic form' to denote a certain type of non-strophic melody that occurs mainly in the strata of ritual and children's songs. They must be distinguished, and classified separately, from the great bulk of strophic melodies. Thus, the basic principle of structuring used in the yoiks is widely known, but nowhere else in Europe has it been developed and individualized to such a high level of formal variation. The virtuosity and creativity of good yoikers who are able to 'play' with this structural model, employing all of the vocal techniques available, can be really exciting as well as musically convincing. These vocal techniques include switching from a throaty to a normal vocal style, moving from a low whisper to full dynamic level, and use of gliding and swinging tones in the ornamentation.

Functions of Sami Music

What are the functions of Sami music as a whole? Besides yoiking, the traditional repertoire includes signalling for herding, hunting, fishing and transportation, partly by the use of instruments or, better, sound tools. These include bells for the leading animals in the flocks and for driving with reindeer and also, as I learned on a field trip in 1986, several beating tools as well as blown pieces of birch bark, fish scale, etc. These are known mainly to elderly people. The Sami did not develop any elaborate musical instruments, apart from the now extinct shaman's drum, which is more a ritual than musical instrument. However, they are highly sensitive to the different sound qualities associated with their lifestyle and modes of work as developed over the centuries. This is true, at least in part, in the case of yoiking.

While mimetic and gestural accompaniment to yoiking was once rather frequent, dancing has never played a dominant role among the Sami. When dancing occurred in the past, for example during annual fairs, they used and still use common Scandinavian tunes and European instruments such as violins or accordions. Thus, it is not surprising that nowadays young Sami like to listen to modern pop and rock music for pure entertainment, walking around with their radios and cassette recorders in the evening just as young people do elsewhere in the world. Nor is it surprising that the new wave of Sami pop music attracts them, since in several ways it tries to bridge the gap between Western influence and the traditional heritage of yoiks and yoiking.

Yoiking, in the traditional way discussed here, is said to be an art of remembering, of memorizing by recalling to the performer's mind certain situations, places, human or other beings that are connected in one way or another with the singer's life. Quite often, yoikers do not use an explicit text: they use only a few key words along with many improvised syllables of different sound qualities according to their vocal techniques and the idiom of their area. However, singers always have a certain topic in mind. The topic provides the reason to start and stop the singing; the yoiker stops when he/she has reached the desired emotional state, a special kind of 'primer effect' (as biologists call it). Moberg observed and described this effect very well in his unpublished field notes concerning a father's yoik of one singer: 'She sang with closed eyes and apparently became touched; the memory of her father obviously grew stronger and stronger under yoiking'.

Intonation in traditional yoiking is highly influenced by this very effect. Quite frequently during singing, the pitch level rises more or less continuously, ending a third or fourth (or more) above the initial level. This feature seems to indicate a warming-up of the idea or mood associated with the yoik. (This aspect cannot, however, be shown in staff notation; it can only be shown by graphic abstraction, or verbal indication, or electro-acoustically.)

Finally, since the traditional life and work of the Sami are characterized, in part, by loneliness, their music-making very often occurs in isolation as well, but – as one soon learns during field work – it is a 'lonely' kind of music-making with highly social implications. The yoik repertoire of one singer may be a sung genealogy, ranging from the personal yoiks of the singer's own generation to those of his/her parents, grandparents and great-grandparents on one hand, and children and grandchildren on the other. An individual's social network and positive or negative relations in it may be reflected in the types of melodies used, for example, for a neighbour, a comrade, or another member of the community. Mocking yoiks, or yoiks which children fear (such as those about predators that attack the flocks), frequently occur. Some complex yoik compositions combine narrated and sung passages and tell a singer's whole life story. Singers, who are more often than not separated from each other by their kind of work, try to realize their 'social ties' by yoiking about the native environment: the mountains, lakes, herding places, animals, or even the mosquito girl who helps to drive the flocks faster, and about family members, neighbours and friends who may be far away or dead (for whom one is able to search by yoiking their personal tunes). These yoiks mediate the feeling of belonging to a local social group in its continuity from a known past to a not yet known future. Thus yoiking has served in the past, and to some extent still serves, as an essential part of Sami life.

Although it seems premature to predict what fate the future may hold for the still living yoik dialects and traditions, we may make one prediction: the Sami themselves will decide, on several levels, how to go on with their music. In the not so distant future – since they already have their own linguists – there will be Sami musicologists, as well, to study their deep-rooted musical heritage from inside. Until then we may do our work to the best of our abilities, because we need knowledge of this musical culture for the benefit of a general theory of music.

References

ARNBERG, Matts, Israel Ruong & Håkan Unsgaard
1969   *Yoik* (7 discs, RELP 1029, Sveriges Radio Records, accompanying book). Stockholm.

BODOR, Anikó
1974   'Analys och Beskrivning av Lapska Jojkar med utnyttjande av "Mona", En "Case Study".' Uppsala Universitët (unpublished).

EDSTRÖM, Karl-Olof
1975   *Den Samiska Musik-Kulturen.* Göteborg Universitët.

GRUNDSTRÖM, Harald & Armas Otto Väisänen
1958   *Lappische Lieder, Texte und Melodien aus Schwedisch-Lappland,* Bd. I: *Jonas Eriksson Steggos Lieder.* Uppsala/ Copenhagen (Schriften des Instituts für Mundarten und Volkskunde in Uppsala, Ser. C:2).

GRUNDSTRÖM, Harald & Sune Smedeby
1963   *Lappische Lieder, Texte und Melodien aus Schwedisch-Lappland,* Bd. II: *Lieder aus Arjeplog und Arvidsjaur.* Uppsala/Copenhagen (Schriften des Instituts für Mundarten und Volkskunde in Uppsala, Ser. C:2[II]).

GÜNTHER, Robert
1965   'Zur Musik der Lappen, Erläuterungen anhand neuer Feldaufnahmen'. *Kölner Ethnologische Mitteilungen* 4: 71-88.

HAEGER, Ellika
1955   'Om de första joikningsuppteckningarna i Sverige'. *Svensk Tidskrift för Musikforskning* 37: 146-55.

LAGERCRANTZ, Eliel
1966   *Lappische Volksdichtung VII: Sonagraphische Untersuchung lyrischer lappischer Volkslieder aus Karasjok und Enontekiö mit Noten und Erklärungen.* Helsinki (Mémoires de la Société Finno-Ougrienne, 141).
1968   *Lappische Volksdichtung IV: Seelappische Gesangsmotive des Varangergebietes.* Helsinki (Mémoires de la Société Finno-Ougrienne, 120).

LAUNIS, Armas
1908   *Lappische Juoigos-Melodien.* Helsinki (Mémoires de la Société Finno-Ougrienne, 26).

LÜDERWALDT, Andreas
1976 *Joiken aus Norwegen, Studien zur Charakteristik und gesell-schaftlichen Bedeutung des Lappischen Gesanges*. Bremen.

SAASTAMOINEN, Ilpo
1987 'Kolttasaamelainen leu'dd: Sattuman entropia vai saluttua järjestystä?' [The leu'dd song of the Skolts in Lappland: the entropy of chance or a hidden order?]. *Etnomusikologian Vuosikirja* 1986, Jyväskylä, pp. 66-95 (English summary).

STOCKMANN, Doris
1987 'Bericht über eine Informations- und Sammelreise zu den Samen'. *Kungl. Musikaliska Akademien Årsskrift 1986*. Stockholm, pp. 39-46.
1989 *En utgåva av samisk musik* (Samisk musik i förvandling, Caprice Records, CAP 1351). Sumlen, Årsbok för Vis- och Folkmusikforskning, Stockholm.
1990 'Formprinzipien samischer Joiken und ihre Zusammen-hänge mit der Gattungsfunktion'. *Probleme der Volksmusik-forschung*, ed. H. Braun (Bericht über die 10. Arbeitstagung der Study Group for Analysis and Systematization im ICTM, 1987 in Freiburg i. Br.). Bern, Frankfurt/M., New York, Paris, pp. 22-46.
1991 'Symbolism in Sami Music'. *Tradition and Its Future in Music*, Report of SIMS 1990, Osaka, pp. 263-73.
1992 *Repertoar-strukturen och kön i Samens musik* (Repertoire-struktur und Geschlechterrolle in der samischen Musik). Tromsø Museums skrifter, Tromsø.
1993 *Epische Züge und narrative Strukturen in samischen Joik.* Sumlen, Årsbok för Vis- och Folkmusikforskning, Stock-holm.

TIRÉN, Karl
1942 *Die lappische Volksmusik, Aufzeichnungen von Juoikos-Melodien bei den schwedischen Lappen.* Stockholm/Uppsala (Acta Lapponica, 3).

TRAVINA, Irina K.
1987 *Saamskije narodnye pesni.* Moscow.

ZEMP, Hugo
1987 *Head Voice, Chest Voice.* Geneva: CNRS Audiovisuel and Ateliers d'Ethnomusicologie. 16mm colour film.

The Eastern Roots of Ancient Yugoslav Music

Ankica Petrović

It is frequently held that, from geographical, historical and cultural points of view, the Balkans serve as a bridge between East and West. The Balkans are not unique in this respect; many other areas can also be considered cultural 'bridges' between East and West. With respect to the musical cultures of the central and western parts of the Balkan peninsula, however, we may come to regard the area more as a cultural barrier than as a cultural 'bridge'.

Dinaric and Western European Music: Differences

Archaic forms of village musical practice in the central mountain or Dinaric region of Yugoslavia are recognized as *starinsko pjevanje* ('ancient singing'). These forms are orally transmitted and belong to rural, cattle-breeding societies, which often live in isolated environments.

With respect to musical structure and aesthetic experience, these rural vocal musical traditions differ fundamentally from the folk and art music of Western Europe. It is difficult to connect the products of this archaic culture to Europe, where we do not meet with similar musical phenomena except in a few unique cases, as in the fifteenth-century description of the Lombard practice of 'howling in seconds' (Ferand 1939). These forms were often treated as lower cultural strata in comparison with the musical practices of urban environments. From the viewpoints of so-called culturally superior societies, applying standard European aesthetic values or Eastern cultural concepts to archaic forms of village musical practice, the cultural values represented by such forms do not merit careful investigation.

Only in the twentieth century did the kinds of musical expression that are found in isolated mountain regions of the central Balkans become the object of theoretical-musical discussion. They have not been mentioned in secondary sources such as the diaries and journals of travellers, except in sporadic accounts of vocal music. Although it is difficult to attempt to interpret the cultural ties embodied in musical structures, the archaic musical structures found in certain regions of Yugoslavia and the Balkans should not be seen merely as isolated phenomena.

The characteristic style and aesthetic values of musical traditions in the central Balkan region are manifested in certain structural elements, such as exceptionally limited tonal ranges of chants (mainly within the limits of tetrachords with flexible interval values which are frequently close to microintervals); a tendency for descending melodic motion; free rhythmic values (except in dance-related music); specific polyphonic structures (mainly dominated by an interval close to a major second which is experienced as a consonance); and emphatic use of ornamental tones which are an end in themselves or serve to stress the expressive factors, such as dynamics.

The limited tonal range of a fourth (perfect, diminished or augmented) is well suited to the medium register of the human voice. The tetrachord is also the basic unit of the ancient Greek tonal system. Just as the ancient Greek modes were presented in a descending direction, which probably corresponded to musical practice, the ancient melodies of the Dinaric cultural zone mainly move downwards. Within the limited tonal range, a melodic path based on 'narrow' intervals (the major and minor seconds, and the *limma*) develops. Chromatic genera are more frequent than are diatonic; successive semitones of different values are sometimes separated by a whole tone (as in the oldest forms of secular and religious chant in Istria, the Kvarner Islands, and northwestern Bosnia).

In specific localities of the Dinaric cultural region, different forms and modes contain narrow intervallic relationships, with diatonic or pronounced chromatic leading of the melodic line. These characteristics are found especially in Passion chants, called 'Madonna's Cry', from the Isle of Hvar, where they are considered to be the oldest musical relics (Petrović 1985). The style is different from all other existing forms of folk, secular and religious singing. Having the character of a lament, this form is a remnant of the Medieval liturgical dramas that were usually performed on the eve of Good Friday in Central Europe and in Catholic regions of the Mediterranean. It has survived on the Isle of Hvar in central Dalmatia as a particular style and aesthetic concept.

In the villages of Hvar, the 'Madonna's Cry' is always performed in unison by two experienced male singers, with a perfect harmony of tones, dynamics and vocal colours. This type of chant is a long musical piece, sequentially shaped. The text uses only one rhymed couplet of eight-syllable lines. The rhythm is freely formed, i.e., it depends exclusively on the melodic character that is emphasized. The expressiveness of this singing is attained through a graduated tension of melodic and dynamic growth. The extended melodic line has a relatively wide frame; the melody progresses with chromatic movement and frequent changes of mode. The intervallic relationships between tones do not correspond to the values of the tempered system.

Due to the emphasis on melismatic shaping and extension of the chant, this form is unique in comparison not only with other musical forms of Hvar, Dalmatia and Yugoslavia but with the forms of Passion chant in other Mediterranean areas of Europe. If the Passion chant of Hvar is not linked with European musical relics, future research must be oriented to the East. The Isle of Hvar was a Greek colony in ancient times and subsequently fell under the rule and cultural influence of Byzantium. The retention of these musical phenomena can be explained by the fact that at times Hvar has been exposed to foreign cultural influences yet it has remained an isolated locality.

In the villages of inland mountain regions of Yugoslavia, as well as further along the Balkan peninsula in Albania and Bulgaria, monodic and polyphonic musical forms have especially limited spans and narrow intervals that do not correspond in value with tempered intervals. Such rural songs differ among themselves according to locality and function. People distinguish between wedding songs, shepherd songs, male and female extended songs (namely the epics and the songs of a ballad type), ritual songs and work songs. Villagers also distinguish various sub-categories of these types.

In this region, tonal flexibility is one of the most significant stylistic features. It cannot be considered from a European point of view to constitute tonal uncertainty or 'pitch deviation' because the singers themselves have an established relationship with definite limits of tonal flexibility. Despite the absence of an established system of verbal explanation of these tonal values and contents, we find a subtle and developed relationship between the interpreters and this aspect of style. Here we cannot speak of tonal systems or modes of either the European or the Eastern classical types. (However, the Eastern *maqāms* are partly present in the chants of urban communities within the same territory, created under the influence of Turkish culture.) It is simply a question of understanding tonal content in another way: certain tonal concepts exist, but not in modal systems. Similar musical phenomena involving tonal content are also found in rural areas of Asia Minor and Central Asia, among some nomadic and semi-nomadic peoples who live under economic conditions and forms of social organization that resemble those of the village populations of the central Balkans (Belyayev 1933).

Dinaric and Asian Music: Similarities

Besides the tones that ethnomusicologists recognize as being basic to a melody, an entire spectrum of different ornamental tones is evident in the mountain regions of Yugoslavia — in the form of short ornamental pre-strikes, trills, mordents, and richly developed melismatic groups. Their significance in these environments is much greater than many experts have been prepared either to accept or to respect. Hence we find transcriptions and analyses of melodies in which ethnomusicologists have neglected or entirely omitted these ornamental elements of style. In the culture itself, however, these elements are signs of the genre and are salient local characteristics of chants. Their generic significance is determined by the type of ornamentation used and its position in the overall form (e.g., in certain parts of polyphonic forms).

Certain kinds of ornamental tones of cattle-breeding peoples in Yugoslavia, Albania and western Bulgaria, which are considered archaic within the culture, are also found in the musical traditions of some Asian peoples: in Kurdistan, Kazakhstan, Uzbekistan, the Pamir region and other parts of Central Asia. For example, one of the basic factors of polyphonic form in the polyphonic genre *ganga* (cultivated in Hercegovina, in part of Bosnia, and in Dalmatian Zagora in Croatia) is the compulsory presence of melismatic tones in the accompanying part before the progression of each principal tone (Petrović 1977). These short pre-strikes — single, or trilled in the manner of *gruppetti* — are performed falsetto in a certain intonation and called *jecanje* or *sjecanje* ('sobbing' or 'cutting') by the people of this region (see Example 1).

A similar kind of ornamental singing is used in the traditional music of

Example 1: *Jecanje* or *sjecanje* from the polyphonic genre *ganga*

Persia, where it is called *takīyah*. Caton has described *takīyah* as 'a falsetto or yodelling ornament' (1974:42), 'one of the most characteristic and essential aspects of vocal style in Persian music'. In this type of ornament, the 'intention is a "sobbing" on a note with the singer concentrating on the ornamental impact rather than on specific pitches in themselves'.

In the central and eastern mountain regions of Yugoslavia as well as in some areas of Albania and western Bulgaria, most of the traditional rural songs with different forms and functions must be performed polyphonically by small groups of two to five singers, mainly of the same sex. Important distinctions are made between voices during ensemble singing according to the arrangements and roles of the voices in different villages and regions. As mentioned above, major seconds are common vertical sonorities in the traditional rural polyphonic songs of this area; many ancient musical forms in Yugoslavia end on this interval.

The most frequent types of polyphony found in this region can be classified as *organum* in a narrow relationship of parallel seconds, *bourdon, ostinato* or *canonic imitative* techniques. The latter type of polyphony is most frequently encountered in certain older forms of ritual songs, such as the St. Lazarus songs of Serbia.

Even though these categories of polyphonic singing are products of systems devised to classify European music of the later Middle Ages, the same types are present in the archaic folk polyphony of the Balkan region and are known there as 'ancient singing'. Those forms survived in conditions of geographic and cultural isolation and have continued as a part of the ancient folk culture.

Once again, musical phenomena based on similar types of polyphony are encountered in various parts of the Caucasus and a wider region of Central Asia, as well as in cultures that are considered to be exclusively monophonic areas. Using recorded material, Gerson-Kiwi (1968) showed that musical forms of Yemenite Jews, Samaritans and members of the Jewish community on the Isle of Corfu should be taken into consideration by students of folk polyphony. Reminding us that it is entirely a matter of vocal liturgical music, where there could not have been imitation of instrumental techniques, Gerson-Kiwi concludes that the different forms of polyphony in these communities are very old.

The most common structural and aesthetic concept in Gerson-Kiwi's examples from the Yemenite Jewish, Corfu and Samaritan communities is that of the bourdon forms. The same polyphonic phenomenon is present in a wide area of the Balkans, applied in forms of Orthodox sacred music (mainly of responsorial character between precentor and chorus) and also in older forms of secular song and in instrumental music. The diffusion of bourdon forms covers almost the entire area of Byzantine cultural influence, extending along the southern shore of the Black Sea (Picken 1954) to Armenia and Georgia (Belyayev 1933).

Some experts on Yugoslav and Balkan polyphonic music have treated these forms as a very archaic, local and exclusively Balkan heritage dating back to the Illyrians and Thracians (Rihtman 1958). This thesis is supported by the fact that somewhat similar forms of polyphony occur in the traditional music of many Southern Slavic peoples — Serbs, Croats, Macedonians, Montenegrins, and Bulgarians — as well as in Albanian traditional music. They are rare in the music of other Slavic nations and are even rarer in Western European musical expressions except in a few limited instances — e.g. Sardinian polyphony (Collaer 1960:51) and Lombard diaphonic singing in seconds, as recorded in the fifteenth century (Ferand 1939).

Nonetheless, one cannot disregard the musical-stylistic similarities with the more or less distant cultures of Central Asia and the Middle East, with which cultural ties were established through migrations and wars when favourable conditions — geographic, socioeconomic, political or religious — existed. Whole musical forms may not have been transmitted, and they may not have been retained in unchanged forms. Clearly, however, some crucial elements of style remained, since in orally-transmitted forms a certain degree of change is unavoidable. The elements of musical culture which, in my view, moved from the East into the Balkan region found there favourable conditions for assimilating and remaining in the culture of the cattle-breeding peoples who were inclined to migrate. Mountain ranges provided suitable conditions in which to reject unfamiliar influences from the Occident, a rejection motivated by deeply-rooted conservatism. (Even today, this conservatism is still present to a certain degree, although socioeconomic conditions are rapidly changing.)

Considering all of the above-mentioned facts and comparing the essential elements of traditional musical culture with similar rural musical phenomena in other countries, it is possible to conclude that the central mountainous regions of Yugoslavia serve as a natural boundary for the diffusion of older layers of Eastern musical culture as well as constituting a barrier between the Eastern and Western cultural hemispheres.

References

BELYAYEV, Victor
  1933   'The Folk Music of Georgia'. *The Musical Quarterly* 19:417-33.
CATON, Margaret
  1974   'The Vocal Ornament *Takīyah* in Persian Music'. *Selected Reports in Ethnomusicology* 2/1:43-53.
COLLAER, Paul
  1960   *Atlas historique de la musique.* Paris: Elsevier.
FERAND, Ernest T.
  1939   'The "Howling in Seconds" of the Lombards'. *The Musical Quarterly* 25:313-24.
GERSON-KIWI, Edith
  1968   'Vocal Folk Polyphonies of the Western Orient in Jewish Tradition'. *Yuval* 1:169-93.
PETROVIĆ, Ankica
  1977   'Ganga: a Form of Traditional Rural Singing of Yugoslavia'. Ph.D. dissertation, The Queen's University of Belfast.
  1985   'Passion Chants from the Island of Hvar in Dalmatia: The Relations of Ritual and Music-Poetic Content'. *Musica Antiqua,* Folia Musica 3/2, Bydgoszcz.
PICKEN, Laurence E.R.
  1954   'Instrumental Polyphonic Folk Music in Asia Minor'. *Proceedings of the Royal Musical Association* 80:73-86.
RIHTMAN, Cvjetko
  1958   'O ilirskom porijeklu polifonih oblika narodne muzike Bosne i Hercegovine'. *Rad Kongresa Folklorista Jugoslavije,* Zagreb, 99-104.

Wedding Laments in
North Russian Villages[1]

Margarita Mazo

Lament, a rich and diverse genre of Russian traditional music, is a necessary symbolic component of village funerals, weddings and other rituals. Lament is also a conventional means by which a village woman expresses personal grief and sorrow on non-ritual occasions in everyday life. In north Russian villages, lament is a particularly common form of expressing a certain psychological and emotional state. It is a part of contemporary life even in villages where no other traditional genres have survived, although wedding laments are preserved mostly in the memory of the older generation.

Russian folklorists and ethnomusicologists have discussed laments performed at funerals, at weddings, and on the departure of young men recruited into the army.[2] Laments can also be sung when parting with friends or relatives who are leaving even for a short time. On all of these occasions, laments are 'performed' while non-performers listen attentively. There are also occasions when a woman laments alone.[3]

> Sometimes I sit alone at home, and I feel so hard. I would shut the door and the windows, and lament on my fate. I would cry hard, and I would speak out [*vyskazhu*] my distress to the end. I would feel better after that. (Vologda province, Nikol'sk district, 1969)

Terms Used to Describe Laments

Several words in the Russian language mark off the differences between verbal and non-verbal expressive means which do not have exact equivalents in English, words whose meanings can only be given indirectly. Used by Russian villagers as well as by folklorists and ethnomusicologists, these words refer to vocal gestures and sometimes to a category of traditional singing that, in varying proportions, combines singing, excited speech and exclamations with the natural sounds of weeping.

Plachi (pl.) and *prichitaniya* (pl.) are the general Russian terms for the category of laments. Each word implies a particular manner of expression and articulation. *Plachi* encompass many kinds of exclamatory utterings (*plach* means 'weeping'), whereas *prichitaniya* or *prichety* connote an uninterrupted complaint which is rhythmically monotonous, highly emotional, almost obsessive, bitter and sad.[4] Another important Russian word is *vopl'*, a loud, momentary vocal gesture made by someone who cries. It is usually spasmodic inhalation or exhalation which indicates the beginning or end of a breath cycle. Traditional laments in north Russian villages are often called *prichety,* while in central and western Russia *plachi* are more common.

The non-musical utterances *plach, prichet* and *vopl'* are sketched on a musical stave in Example 1. The sketches are intended only to convey general contours and are not meant as musical notations *per se. Plach* is usually accompanied by the enunciation of words or their fragments, as in *prichitanie* and by *vopl'*.

The degree of affinity of Russian laments with *plach, prichet* or *vopl'* depends not only on the performance or the performer but also on the local tradition. In addition to singing, the performances of laments include a variety of intonational devices, such as *vopl', plach,* vocalized breathing (particularly during inhalation), rests filled with *vskhlip* (sobbing) and other identifiable attributes of sobbing and wailing. Whether, when and how often they are used within a lament depends largely on local tradition. The two laments in Example 2 were recorded within a distance of fifty kilometres and illustrate the point that laments and their manner of intoning[5] could be used as one of the identifiers characteristic of a local style (Mazo 1978). The second is mostly general singing, and would probably not be recognized as a lament outside its context, while in the first, intoning includes *vskhlip* and vocalized breathing. Both are called *prichet* and cause a similar emotional reaction within their respective traditions.

In different regions a woman who performs laments is called *plakal'shchitsa* (she who cries), *voplenitsa* (she who wails), *vytnitsa* (she

Example 1

Example 2

who howls) or *prichitalka* (she who recites). These are local names for one function that the women carry out on a professional basis. The women are well-known in the area and are invited to lament by the family who pays for their services. In many local Vologda traditions, every woman is expected to be able to lament at her wedding (as well as at the funeral of a close relative), a practice she normally learns as a child.

Not knowing how to lament is as shameful as not knowing how to milk a cow.

Local Performance Practice

The emergence of laments in the Russian folk wedding has often been interpreted in the scholarly literature as a reflection of the *Domostroi,* an unwritten civil code formed during the Middle Ages, according to which the life of a married woman in rural Russia was miserable and hard (see, for example, Popova 1977:64). However, the wedding ritual as a whole should be considered within the larger framework of initiation rituals and rites of passage. Practised by many peoples, they enact the transition of initiates into a substantially different period of their lives. This transition is often understood, and supposed to be experienced, as a 'temporary death', a journey into another world and a sort of rebirth, or a return as different personalities. Within this framework, lament is a representation of funeral rites, a representation of death (Skvortsova 1974:244-51). Young persons cannot undergo a rebirth and become different persons without also undergoing a symbolic death of their former personalities. As Vladimir Propp suggested in his study of the wondertale, initiation rites were understood as 'a temporary death' and 'were bound to representations of death so tightly that it is impossible to discuss one without dealing with the other' (Propp 1946:72).

Every lament is created anew for the occasion. The improvisatory nature of laments has been highlighted in various studies (such as Chistov 1960). The lament is a poetic and melodic improvisation; it is both spontaneous and structured. Tradition controls the musical, poetic and behavioural patterns. For centuries the verbal images and poetic structures as well as the musical features of laments have been inseparable from the specific occasion on which the lament is performed. It is imbued with a profound meaning and retains a ritualistic value, which induces a special psychological state and conveys a deep communal experience. For the local people, the sound of a lament is a hallmark of the situation and an unconditional trigger of collective emotion. In this respect it resembles the sound of the church bell (*nabat*) which informs the people of fire, war or other disasters and thus causes anxiety. The lament is a symbol of funerals, just as wearing a black shawl is a sign that a woman is in mourning. The associations awakened by a lament, or even by the characteristic posture of a woman about to lament where she covers her eyes with one palm or a shawl as if detaching herself from the outside world, cause people to weep.

The response from those participating in the event is important. In discussing a particular lament, Vologda women always discuss whether or not everyone cried. They exchange words and detailed images used by the lamenter. They also speak at length about the lamenter's physical behaviour and gestures. In evaluating a performance, they consider the quality of the vocal sound, whether or not it sounds 'tearful', or 'pitiable',[6] and whether it makes them cry.

According to the performers, only those laments that are common to a given area are accepted by the local listeners and cause them to respond with the appropriate emotional reaction. In some villages I asked the singers to listen to recordings of laments from a neighbouring area. In that particular region they combined sobbing, gliding, vocalized breathing and rhythmical speech. The listeners insisted that 'they were not lamenting in our way'. Here is an approximate translation of one woman's remarks:

> Over here, when some woman is lamenting, then everyone cries; but with this one from another place we wouldn't even think of crying. To them, their laments are really better and sadder. One's own lament is always most pitiable, but if it's not one's own, then it doesn't touch one emotionally. (Tot'ma, 1971)

This statement was made in a conversation among old women in which they recalled details of past weddings, how lamenters interpreted traditional images and related the verbal text to the situation, and particular participants in the ritual. The similarities and differences between laments of different areas they seem to locate in the manner of singing and the voice quality. For example, one woman said:

> The tune [in this other area] seems fine, but the voice is different. We lament with a very thin,[7] very poor [bednen'kii] voice — not like theirs. We lament and cry together. They just sing as though not lamenting at all. (Tot'ma, 1971)

Such judgments clearly indicate that the singers draw a sharp dividing line between the tune and the quality of the voice. They distinguish two different types of intoning, which they refer to as 'singing' and 'lamenting'. 'Singing' is associated with a fixed and stable set of pitches and intervallic relationships, while 'lamenting' is characterized by a gliding pitch contour and by varying intervals within the same melodic gestures. These are often called *popevki* in Russian scholarship.[8]

A discussion of local performance practice of wedding laments must include one particular abrupt body gesture called *khlyostan'e* or *khryostan'e,* when a lamenter literally drops herself to the floor, then rises quickly and continues her lament. I was often told how such and such a woman hurt herself while lamenting, but usually this gesture is learned and practised in advance. The lamenter *khryostaetsya* ('makes *khryostan'e'*) from time to time, as though trying to accentuate certain points of the lament. She clearly structures this gesture, timing it between the end of one line and beginning of the next. Often the gesture is combined with an exclamation, such as 'O-oh, mamon'ka!' or 'O-oi, okh-kho khoi!' The practice of *khryostan'e* was described by nineteenth-century observers. In his preface to the 1894 volume, Istomin delineates an action reportedly called 'self distraction' or 'killing the bride':

> Accompanying her laments with sobbing, at certain places she articulates a wail, loud and futile 'i-akh!' and simultaneously she collapses to the floor or onto the table, beating herself with the whole weight of her body; not infrequently she repeats this procedure until the lower parts of her arms, from elbows to wrists, which take upon themselves the whole weight of her falls, became swollen and bruised. (Istomin and Dyutsh 1894: xviii)

This practice seems to be peculiar only to the local area and has not been studied in detail.[9]

Lament Pitch Structure

A lament usually progresses from one poetic line to the next, leading from singing to passionate wailing. Then, evading a musical conclusion, it breaks into crying and weeping.

Laments have a modal structure with an unstable scale, where the mode and the scale are disengaged.[10] However fluid and variable, the scale in solo laments reflects a definite pattern of melodic shapes and unequivocal modal relationships. In Example 3 this is seen, for instance, in a constant number of tones and in the relationships between the main melodic tone and the supporting or auxiliary tones. Example 4 shows these relationships schematically in various stanzas. This modal basis is apparent in many different manifestations of the scale, all of which are functionally the same within a given modal system and are freely combined, regardless of their actual pitches or the absolute values of the intervals.

Example 3

Modes with unstable scales can be classified in two categories: either the pitch of the main melodic tone is constant, or it rises — sometimes as high as the singer's voice permits (see Example 5). The rising, most probably a result of emotional build-up, occurs in some cases very slowly and is barely noticeable (as in Example 3), in other cases stepwise or even by leaps (see Example 5). Although the pitch of a tone is free to fluctuate in either direction, there is a tendency toward narrower intervals. Intervals between functionally identical tones of the modal structure can take on different absolute values, whereas intervals that are quantitatively equal can occur between functionally different tones. It would be improper to describe the ascent of the melody in terms of a transposition along a fixed scale. A better approach is one that suggests an awareness of the musical mode as a living and flexible structure which keeps its characteristic identity intact even as its components are capable of intervallic expansion and contraction.

Professional lamenters make a clear distinction between stability and instability of the scale, and they use this distinction consciously, cleverly, and for specific purposes. Whether a lament is performed in a stable or unstable style depends on the circumstances. When the recording process is no hindrance to the performer's natural behaviour, she will most likely sing a version with an unstable scale. Otherwise she will most likely choose a more formal interpretation based on a set of fixed pitches. In the latter case, the verbal text and the performer's external behaviour most often lose their improvisational properties and turn into a sequence of pre-established patterns.

Traditional Wedding Ritual and Polymelodic Forms

Generally, the local wedding ritual consists of a long and intricate series of contrasting episodes. Their sequence and duration, the number of main participants and the participants' behaviour strictly conform to the local tradition (see the outline of episodes in Mazo 1990:116-18). As a part of a ritual, these episodes, even if presented as highly tense and emotionally charged, are not intended to express the feelings of actual participants in the wedding: rather, they are impersonal responses to the requirements of a ritualized situation. This peculiar combination of emotional intensity and detachment is especially evident in the fact that a wedding lament can be performed not by the bride herself but by a proxy woman (*prichitalka, plakal'shchitsa, plakusha*) who knows the tradition and leads the whole ceremony.

The traditional wedding consists of two large parts. The first symbolizes the separation of the bride and groom from their previous lives; the second is the wedding feast, *Krasnyi stol,* a greeting and celebration of the new family with rituals that assure its proper future. The first part takes place in the bride's house and the second one usually at the

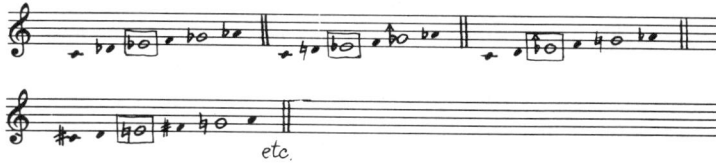

Example 4

Example 5

bridegroom's. The two parts are separated by the parents' blessing and by the church ceremony of the crowning, where the priest assumes the sacramental function and only a few people are present. Laments are a necessary aspect of the first part of the folk wedding, but they are not allowed to cross the wedding's main watershed into the feast episode, not unlike the funeral ritual.

The first part lasts up to four weeks. When the ritual is approached in its entirety, as a continuum where all activities of a ritual cast are taken into account, laments mark the key moments in the ritual among household activities — comings and goings, meetings, conversations, ritualistic speeches and exclamations. The first lament often concludes the matchmaking episode. During the following weeks the bride laments at every dawn and sunset, sometimes in place of the regular prayer. She can also lament in response to any action or activity which stands in some relation to her coming marriage (the lament in Example 3, for instance, was supposed to be sung as the bride's aunt walks into the bride's house), then during meetings with her girlfriends; she laments when her mother covers her with the tablecloth or shawl. She also laments handing over the symbol of virginity (*krasota,* beauty) to one of the girls (who is expected to be a bride in the near future), then when her braid is being undone, on her way to and from the sweat-house (*banya*) where the ritual bath takes place, and when bidding farewell to her parents, relatives and home.[11]

If her lamentation is not a solo, either another soloist (the mother, another female relative) or the girls' chorus can be added. Toward the end of the first part, as the ritual intensifies, they merge to form a continuous flow in which the three freely combine and alternate within a single, uninterrupted episode (see Example 6). Within this continuum two soloists lament within the same format and melodic/rhythmic pattern. (All females who lament during this part of the wedding are from the same area, and thus their laments are governed by the same local rules.) A solo lament may be combined with a choral song that sometimes does not belong to the category of wedding songs. The path of musical unfolding in which a lament is incorporated within such episodes is never known in advance.

A solo lament combined with a choral song creates a two-layered texture. Every aspect of this texture is dual, so that one may speak of a bi-timbre, bi-melody, bi-rhythm, bi-tempo and bi-structure. Mostly, this texture appears when the bride laments together with a choral *prichet,* a

Example 6

wedding ritual song (see Example 7).

This form combines two unrelated musical entities: the upper layer (bride's lament) is saturated with semi-naturalistic exclamations and sobs, and moves on in free time, whereas the lower layer (girls' song) sustains a rigid, strongly accentuated syllabication, and its melody flows like a song. The two layers move in different tempos, and their vertical alignment changes with each stanza. Both layers are improvised independently, each within its own framework and with no fixed idea as to note-to-note correspondence and coordination between them. Here, in contrast to familiar polyphonic forms, the temporal (vertical) alignment between two layers is not rigid. All phrases of the solo lament are similar melodically, but the variants are not equal in length, nor are the rests between the phrases equal. Even if two layers use the same text (as in Example 7), and this is not always the case, the words are given different shapes and verse structures.

Example 7

By no means do the two layers join or overlap mechanically. They comprise an organic unity which is a unique and transient phenomenon. This improvisatory nature demands fluid superimposition of parts, but the combined parts converge on a common stylistic ground. Thus, in the one local tradition, there is a common stock of *popevki:* in Example 7, melodic gestures in both layers are often confined within a third, where the lower tone functions as the melodic centre and the upper one as the supporting tone. Descending motion prevails, even when the melody includes short ascents within the third. Both layers develop under the same modal conditions but at different pitch levels.

A certain fluidity can be observed in the pitch level. The fluidity is almost imperceptible in the choral *prichet*, which remains on a stable pitch level throughout and uses a scale of stable intervallic structure. In the solo *prichet*, both the pitch level and the sizes of the intervals are subject to changes that cannot be precisely expressed in conventional musical notation. Yet, bearing in mind the limitations of the notation, I would still use it to portray the general pitch panorama in question. In the solo lament notated in Example 7 the pitch level gradually rises and the intervals of similar motives vary in size. Combined and coexisting with a stable pitch framework in the chorus, these features should be considered to be inherent elements of the lament tradition. (In funeral laments the degree of instability can be much greater.) We are left to assume that a modal pattern (called *lad* in Russian) can exist in polyphonic forms in states that correspond to two scales — stable and unstable, with the solo part floating above and restrained by the stable treatment of the scale in the chorus part. The fact that the scale fluctuates does not mean that particular melodic functions of the specific pitch-areas cease to exist.

Similar relationships between solo and chorus can be observed in their interpretation of the *prichet* text. Here, too, the soloist freely moves ahead or holds back, adds exclamations or truncates the ends of sentences, yet the choral stanzas serve as the frame of reference and synchronizing force. In Example 7 both layers share the same words, which are only rendered differently. With its 'tempo rubato' and abundance of rests, the text in the bride's lament corresponds approximately to two lines in the chorus. The stanzas in the chorus are connected chain-wise: ab, bc, cd, etc., whereas the single-line structure in the bride's lament includes only the new line introduced by the chorus: a, b, c, etc. Such is the picture in theoretical abstraction. In fact the two-line stanza in the chorus does not always coincide with the bride's one-line sentence. Sometimes its ending extends into the beginning of a new choral stanza; sometimes the bride starts a new line before the chorus ends.

On the surface, concrete musical rhythms in the solo and chorus laments are different (see Example 8, left side). However at a deeper level they are unmistakably related by the shared temporal proportions of syllables, which constitute the background structure of the temporal organization in Russian traditional music. Thus durations of corresponding syllables set to the melody (see Example 8, right side) coincide in both solo and choral parts. Example 8 visualizes this correlation. It is based on the second stanza from Example 7 and maps out the temporal relations between text and music. The frame shows the part of a text line that coincides in the solo and chorus lines, and cuts out three non-meaningful exclamatory syllables at the beginning and two final syllables of each line in the solo lament; it is characteristic of solo laments for the latter not to be pronounced at all, as though they are being swallowed in sobs (they are sung, though, in the choral lament). Example 8 also demonstrates an important feature of the relationship between text and music in Russian traditional songs: in singing, the stress and duration of syllables are independent. The local pattern of a syllabic nucleus consists of eight syllables, with two symmetrical stresses on the third syllable from the beginning and the third syllable from the end. The distribution of longer sung syllables is not constrained by the pattern of stresses in the text, however; non-stressed syllables can be prolonged as well.

Example 8

The term *prichet,* shared in the local tradition by both the solo lament and the chorus, reveals the inner similarity of the two musical forms. The solo and choral laments and their peculiar approaches to pronunciation of the text show different properties of lamenting. Connections with *plach* and *vopl'* are more prominent in the solo than in the chorus, where *prichitanie* is more conspicuous.

In the area studied, the same women who lament for brides during weddings are often invited to lament over the dead during funerals. Wedding and funeral laments share the same tune formula in the majority of local Vologda traditions. In the funeral ritual of the region studied laments mark every significant moment, starting with the announcement of death in the family and continuing up to the moment when the body is laid in the ground. The latter moment could be understood as the watershed of the ritual, the moment when the deceased relative becomes 'an ancestor'. At this moment laments must stop and the ritualistic feast begin, as in the wedding *Krasnyi stol.* Such an approach illustrates once again the fundamental role of laments in other rites of passage, such as weddings, where the ritual secures a proper transition of the initiate's psychological structure, self-image and attitude.

Notes

1   This study of Vologda wedding laments is based on field materials collected between 1969 and 1978 in villages of the North-European part of Russia, mostly in the eastern regions of Vologda province (according to contemporary administrative borders). I conducted fieldwork in this area as the director of interdisciplinary expeditions sponsored by the Leningrad Conservatory, in whose archives all collected material is now held. The expeditions took place in the districts of Nikol'sk, Babushkino, Tot'ma, Kich-Gorodok, Nyukse-nitsa, Tarnoga, Syamzha, Mezhdurech'e and Gryazovets. Several different local traditions exist in this territory. The present article (parts of which appeared in Mazo 1975, 1978, 1990) is based mostly on local traditions in the villages along the southeastern tributaries of the Northern Dvina. The English term 'lament' is too general, as applied to Russian village practice, and carries connotations that are alien to the phenomenon in question.

2   Studies of laments have customarily focussed on verbal texts, their imagery, social content and structure (Barsov 1872-82, Andreev and Vinogradov 1937, Azadovsky 1992, Chistov 1960, Worth 1987, 1988). From the late 1960s on, the lament became an object of ethno-musicological research. Previously, musical aspects of Russian laments were known only from sample recordings limited to a few initial lines (Pal'chikov 1888, Agreneva-Slavyanskaya 1887-89, Istomin and Dyutsh 1894, Istomin and Lyapunov 1899). Many twentieth-century anthologies contain transcriptions of one or several lines of a lament, which do not allow one to detect pecu-liarities of the musical whole. Full laments were published by

Mazo (1975) and Efimenkova (1980).

3　Razumovskaya recorded so-called laments 'with a cuckoo'. The verbal image cuckoo is a symbol of grief, loneliness and distress in Russian traditional arts. These laments are performed outside the village in a forest, swamp or field, where a person goes 'to lament and everything inside burns' (Razumovskaya 1984:160-79).

4　*Prichet* means to recite (*chitat'*, to read) enunciating the syllables (*schitat'*, to count). According to Dal' (1982), the stem points to a manner of expression that suggests enumeration (*prichislyat'*, to enumerate); the lament's text is often a recounting of all the performer's complaints.

5　By intoning I mean all aspects of the vocal utterance.

6　These terms were elicited in the field.

7　'Thin voice' is a local expression often used to define singing in the high register.

8　The term *popevki* (sing, *popevka*, from *pet'*, to sing) is used in Russian church musical theory to mean melodic gestures or formulas that make up each of the eight modes (*glas*); many are recognized by names and shapes in manuscripts and studies of Medieval music (see Brazhnikov 1972). Since the nineteenth century, the term *popevka* has also been used in studies of folk music, where it designates not only a specific contour but also the melodic function of each tone within a given modal structure (see, for example, Rubtsov 1964). This is the connotation of *popevka* as used in this paper. The term is polysemantic, and it is hard to define all of its implications; despite the absence of a single definition of the term, many Soviet scholars find it convenient and apply it widely in melodic analysis. For Asafiev's notion of *popevka* see Asafiev 1982:51.

9　According to my field interviews, this ritual was obligatory for weddings in the area until the 1930s. Since that time, weddings have rarely been celebrated in a traditional way. Istomin does not illustrate his description with a musical notation. My field observations and recordings of wedding ritual were made in the same general area where both of Istomin's expeditions worked.

10　I use the term *mode* here to designate a hierarchical system of correlation between various tones of melodies composed outside the Western system of harmony and tonality (see Powers 1980:377). In this connotation the term *mode* is equivalent to the Russian term *lad* (from *ladit'*, 'to be in concord with').

11 A detailed description of several local variants of the wedding ritual is presented in Balashov, Kalmykova and Marchenko 1985. Although my name is not mentioned, my students and I collected the over-whelming majority of the music recordings and a large part of the songs, texts and ethnographic materials published, according to a special questionnaire that I developed. The book was published after I left the Soviet Union, and the practice of suppressing the names of emigré authors was customary at the time. From 1969 to 1978 (but excluding 1976), I led annual field trips of the Leningrad Con-servatory. Before each trip, I conducted a special two-month seminar and workshop where all participants (including N. Kalmykova and Yu. Marchenko, two of the book's nominal authors) were trained in methods and techniques of interdisciplinary fieldwork. As a result of work undertaken in 1969-75, wedding songs and laments were seen as central in the traditional repertoire of older performers, and wedding ritual as one of the best preserved in their memory (Mazo 1975). It became clear to me that though music plays an especially important role in a ritual continuum of actions, the wedding ritual as a whole, with its richness of musical, ethnographic, poetic and verbal material, calls for an interdisciplinary representation in publication. In 1975 I invited Balashov, a folklorist and professional writer, to participate in the fieldwork and in preparation of the materials for publication. Balashov later conducted one additional field trip in order to clarify and verify the materials previously collected under my supervision. All the materials were combined for publication as a case study of local variants of the wedding ritual and their geo-graphical distribution.

References

AGRENEVA-SLAVYANSKAYA, Olga
    1887-89   *Opisanie russkoi krest'yanskoi svad'by s textom i pesnyami* [A Description of the Russian Peasant Wedding with Texts and Songs]. 3 vols. Moscow & Tver: A. Levinson & F. Muraviev.
ANDREEV, N. & VINOGRADOV, G.
    1937   *Russkie plachi (prichitaniya).* Leningrad: Sovetskii Pisatel'.
ASAFIEV, Boris
    1982   *A Book about Stravinsky,* trans. Richard F. French. Ann Arbor: UMI. First published in Russian as Igor Glebov, *Kniga o Stravinskom* (Leningrad, 1929).

AZADOVSKY, M.
1922   *Lenskie prichitaniya.* Chita.

BALASHOV, D., KALMYKOVA, N. & MARCHENKO, Yu.
1985   *Russkaya svad'ba* [The Russian Wedding], music edited by A. Mekhnetsov. Moscow: Sovremennik. [See Note 11.]

BARSOV, E.
1872-82   *Prichitaniya Severnogo kraya* [Laments of the Russian North]. 2 vols. Moscow.

BRAZHNIKOV, Maxim
1972   *Drevnerusskaya teoriya muzyki* [Old-Russian Theory of Music]. Leningrad: Muzyka.

CHISTOV, K.
1960   *Prichitaniya.* Leningrad: Sovetskii Pisatel'.

DAL', Vladimir
1982   *Tolkovyi slovar' zhivago Velikorusskago yazyka.* Moscow: Russkii Yazyk. Reprint of the 1882 edn.

EFIMENKOVA, B.
1980   *Severnorusskaya prichet'* [North Russian Laments]. Moscow: Sovetskii Kompozitor.

ISTOMIN, Feodor & DYUTSH, Georgii
1894   *Pesni Russkogo naroda sobrannye v Arkhangel'skoi i Olonetskoi guberniyakh v 1886 gody* [Songs of the Russian People Collected in Arkhangelsk and Olonets Provinces in 1886]. St. Petersburg: RGO.

ISTOMIN, Feodor & LYAPUNOV, Sergei
1899   *Pesni Russkogo naroda sobrannye v Vologodskoi, Vyatskoi i Kostromskoi guberniyakh v 1893* [Songs of the Russian People Collected in Vologda, Viatka and Kostroma Provinces in 1893]. St. Petersburg: RGO.

MAZO, Margarita
1975   *Pesni Nikol'skogo raiona* [Songs of Nikol'sk District]. Leningrad: Sovetskii Kompozitor.
1977   'Dinamika local'nogo pesennogo stilya v folklore' [The Dynamics of Local Song Style in Folklore]. *Sovetskaia Muzyka* (May).
1978   'Nikol'skie prichitaniya i ikh svyazi s drugimi ganrami mestnoi pesennosti' [Nikol'sk Laments and Their Relationships with Other Genres of the Local Tradition]. In *Muzykal'naya Folkloristika,* vol. 2, ed. Alexander Banin.

Moscow: Muzyka, pp. 213-36.

1990 'Stravinsky's *Les Noces* and Russian Folk Wedding Ritual'. *Journal of the American Musicological Society* 43: 99-143.

PAL'CHIKOV, Nikolai

1888 *Krest'yanskie pesni zapisannye v s. Nikolaevke, Menzelinskogo yezda, Ufimskoi gubernii* [Peasant Songs Transcribed in the Village Nikolaevka of Ufa Province]. St. Petersburg: A. Pal'chikov.

POPOVA, Tat'yana

1977 *Osnovy russkoi narodnoi muzyki* [Basics of Russian Folk Music]. Moscow: Muzyka.

POWERS, Harold S.

1980 'Mode'. In *The New Grove Dictionary of Music and Musicians,* ed. Stanley Sadie. London: Macmillan. Vol. 12, pp. 376-450.

PROPP, Vladimir

1946 *Istoricheskie korni volshebnoi skazki* [Historical Roots of the Wondertale]. Leningrad: Leningradskii Universitet.

RAZUMOVSKAYA, Elena

1984 'Plach "s kukushkoi." Traditsionnyi vopl' Russko-Belorusskogo ogranich'ya' [Lament with a Cuckoo: A Traditional Wail of the Russian-Byelorussian Border]. In *Slavyanskii folklor,* ed. N. Tolstoi et al. Moscow: Nauka.

RUBTSOV, Feodosii

1964 *Osnovy ladovogo stroeniya russkikh narodnykh pesen* [Principles of Modal Structures in Russian Folk Songs]. Leningrad: Sovetskii Kompozitor.

SKVORTSOVA, Zoia

1974 'O prichitaniyakh v svadebnom obryade' [About Laments in the Wedding Ritual]. In *Folklor i etnografiya,* ed. Boris Putilov. Leningrad: Nauka.

WORTH, Dean S.

1987 'Right Shifts in the Russian Funeral Lament'. *International Journal of Slavic Linguistics and Poetics* 35-36: 255-65.

1988 'Colon Breaks in the 13-Syllable Lament'. *Canadian American Slavic Studies* 22: 189-98.

Reflections of Continental and Mediterranean Traditions in Italian Folk Music

Marcello Sorce Keller

Introduction

Time and again Béla Bartók lamented in his articles and letters that nationalism or outright chauvinism often get in the way of objectivity in folk music research (Bartók 1977, 1969). That was, and still is, often the case. Scholars tend to describe the traditional music of their native land as comprising the widest variety of forms and styles imaginable and, at the same time, showing an underlying unity, and it is not hard to detect some patriotic fervour behind such statements. There are isolated cultures that develop considerable internal diversification, as for instance, among many tribal traditions across the globe, including some in Australia. In Europe, on the other hand, isolated cultures are rather rare because of a combination of historical and geographic factors. Best-known among them are probably those of Hungary and Sardinia. In general, however, states and nations seldom coincide with culture areas, and much of their internal diversity can be accounted for by contact with other cultures. This is particularly the case in Italy.

Scholarship accumulated over about a century shows very clearly that the Italian peninsula is not at all unified with respect to its folk culture. I shall argue below that much of its musical diversity is due to cultural contact with both the European mainland and the Mediterranean.

Diversity

One can gain a fairly accurate overview of the diversity of the Italian folk music scene by considering *song types, performance practices* and *compositional processes.*

Many song types can be found in Italy: ritual songs (for christenings, weddings, burials), calendrical songs (for Christmas, spring and carnival festivals), occupational songs (sung by such people as shepherds, soldiers and street vendors), recreational songs (such as dance songs), family songs (such as lullabies and children's songs), religious songs, cattle calls and others. In this article I shall focus on the ballad and lyric song repertoires.

Some Italian ballads are similar to British ballads in the canon established by Francis James Child, and some even have exact correspondents in that repertoire. Among them are: Ch. 12, 'Lord Randal' (*L'avvelenato*); Ch. 43, 'The Sleeping Potion' (*La bevanda sonnifera*); Ch. 53, 'Lord Thomas and Fair Annet' (*Danze e funerali*); and Ch. 4, 'Lady Isabel and the Elf Knight' (*L'eroina*). The small number of authors who have written on this topic includes Francello (1946) and Regnoni-Macera (1964). Others are broadsides, or in Italian, *fogli volanti.* Lyric songs (*canti lirico-monostrofici*) exist in great variety: *matinade, villotte, polesane, stornelli, strambotti, rispetti, stranot, canti alla boara, canti a vatoccu, canti alla stesa, canti alla longa, canti a pera.* Most of these are from central Italy. In Sardinia there are the *mutu* and the *mutettu* and in Sicily, among others, the *canzuna.*

There is considerable variety in the performance practice. In the vocal repertoire alone, there are straight monodic songs, diaphonic songs, choral polyphony, heterophony, antiphonal and responsorial singing. Performance practices often cut across genres. Ballads, for instance, can be performed solo or chorally, depending on the area (in the Alpine region choral singing is predominant) and on the availability of singers. So can lyric songs, although to a lesser degree than ballads and with a few exceptions: the *stornelli,* for instance, are typically solo songs, and the *canti a vatoccu* can only be performed by two or, at the most, three voices.

Equally, there is no lack of variety in the domain of compositional process. I shall briefly mention three dissimilar types: *modular, segmental* and *kaleidoscopic.*

The modular process is typical of the Sardinian *mutu* and *mutettu* (see Leydi 1973:22-3). As mentioned before, these are lyric songs of a sort.

They are modular in the sense that the whole song is developed, following precise rules, from elements or *modules* contained in the first stanza, called *isterria*. The *isterria* consists of a variable number of seven-syllable lines, from which derives an equal number of stanzas that make up the whole song. Through a subtle process of expansion, contraction and adaptation to the text, the initial lines of the *isterria* become the building blocks of the music that goes with the following stanzas.

The segmental compositional procedure is probably widespread. I studied it in Trentino, the region in northeastern Italy referred to by the Austrians as southern Tyrol (see Sorce Keller 1988). Some phrases in the folk song melodies of that area make up a small repertoire of what I call *segments*. Often as long as a four-bar phrase or a two-bar semi-phrase, segments may 'migrate' from song to song, sometimes with great frequency. The dynamics of their circulation are complex because, given their variable length, they may cause change at different structural levels in host songs. The development of songs in Trentino, therefore, is largely the result of the progressive circulation of segments.

The kaleidoscopic procedure was also verified in the circumscribed area of Montemarano, not far from Naples (Giuriati 1982). Tarantellas are often performed in Montemarano, and each time the music may be said to be the result of the kaleidoscopic permutations of elements coming from a large, but finite, repertoire. A new piece is actually just a rearrangement of elements that were present in previously performed pieces.

Culture Contact

Is this microcosm of musical styles and practices typically or uniquely Italian? The overall pattern of the mosaic is unquestionably Italian, and only Italian. That does not mean, however, that many of its constituents cannot be recognized in other traditions.

Canti lirico-monostrofici, for instance, are as Italian as the 'blues' is American. In central and southern Italy they are the dominant song-type. Still, philologists immediately recognize that some of those lyric songs owe their origin to another Romance culture: the very name *stornello* comes from the Provençal *estorn* (i.e. to challenge) and *strambotto* from the Provençal *estribar* (i.e. to lash). Another type of lyric song, the *canto a vatoccu,* is a form of diaphony that closely resembles the one found in Bulgaria, with its occasional intervals of a major or even a minor second (see Example 1).

Example 1 Vatoccu (Marche), transcr. U. Antonelli

Funeral lamentations, still practised in the southern part of the peninsula, clearly witness how southern Italy was an integral part of the Greek world (De Martino 1958). Indeed, in antiquity, southern Italy was in all respects part of Greece; long after the Roman conquest, Greek remained the everyday language.[1] That this was true in musical terms as well is confirmed by the fact that in southern Italy one still encounters a particular form of text fragmentation, in which lines or even words are left incomplete, to be repeated and completed in the next line:

> oi di sira ci
>   di sira ci passai
> oi di sira ci passai da ssa vinedda
>   da ssa vina   ia
>   ssira ci passai da ssa vinedda

This form of text fragmentation is still in use in the Greek islands of the eastern Mediterranean (Magrini 1985:30-34 and 1986).

These comments pertain to central and southern Italy. In the north, culture contact is still apparent in what I call the *Gallican Connection*. As early as the end of the nineteenth century, Costantino Nigra noticed that ballads (*canti epico-lirici*) are found mostly in the north, where Celtic languages were once spoken (Nigra 1957 [1888]). Lyric songs (*canti lirico-monostrofici*), on the other hand, are far more common below the Apennines, where Italic languages (Osco, Umbrian, Faliscan) and, later, Latin were once spoken. This dichotomy was detected by focussing solely on the narrative content of songs rather than their musical component. Although recent research has been unable to show exactly why such a correlation between linguistic background and song types exists, it has shown, nonetheless, that the dichotomy holds true not only in terms of the literary content of songs but in terms of their musical style as well (Sorce Keller 1991:140-47).

These new findings implicitly strengthen the thesis, also formulated by Nigra, that most Italian ballads (and balladry as a genre) came to northern Italy from the Francophone territories. Indeed, beginning in Piedmont and moving eastward across Lombardy, Veneto and all the way to Trentino and Friuli, one frequently encounters fanfare-like tunes showing a clear French flavour (see Example 2).

Example 2 Viva Condino (Trentino), transcr. M. Sorce Keller

Piedmont, a territory where local dialects still maintain a strong French colouration, would have functioned as a one-way bridge between France and the more eastern Italian regions north of the Apennines. Later, in the nineteenth century, in the wake of the Napoleonic army, the cultural ties between northern Italy and France were reinforced. This is evident in literary motifs still to be found in folklore and folksongs, such as the motif of France, 'the land where young people go never to return' (a reference to the military draft).

Curt Sachs once spoke of countries that 'sing, but their melodies are born from words and either merely convey poetry or else intensify it, and, beautiful as they may be, they are basically different from those melodies that follow purely vocal impulses.' He added that 'Europe, with the exception of the Mediterranean region, has been a typical non-singer's land' (Sachs 1943:307). This is indeed a good description of the two main areas that musically make up the Italian peninsula. In the north, especially in the Alpine area, choral singing of ballads is common. It is syllabic, the words are clearly intelligible, the tempo is *giusto,* and voices are full, blending and supported from the chest (see Example 3).

However, as soon as the Apennines are crossed to the south, the musical climate changes considerably, and even more so once Rome is left behind and the Neapolitan area is reached. Choral singing gradually disappears, the tempo becomes *tempo rubato,* and by the time Sicily is

Example 3 E picchia picchia l porticello (Trentino; fragment), transcr. A. Carlini

Example 4 Ninna nanna di Salemi (Sicily; skeletal tune), transcr. Favara

reached the embellished character of the melodies and the nasal quality of voice production are strongly reminiscent of Arabic music (see Example 4).

This is not surprising, since southern Italy was once ruled by Spain (which has had close contact with the Middle East), and Sicily, in particular, was once ruled by the Arabs (ninth and tenth centuries A.D.).

Conclusion

Italian folk song is remarkably diverse when compared with the art music, which has a unity of its own. For example, in the nineteenth century, the middle class from Piedmont to Sicily enjoyed opera, and such composers as Donizetti were equally popular in Milan and in Naples. At the rural level, on the other hand, where music was mostly circulated orally, Italy was and is by no means a unified country. In that sense, when the Austrian politician Metternich (1773-1859) said that Italy was nothing but a geographic expression, he was right and wrong at the same time.

The diverse pattern of folk song styles and practices to be found in the northern as opposed to the southern part of the Italian peninsula reflects the even sharper dichotomy between continental Europe and the Mediterranean area. Furthermore, this pattern shows that the peninsula is a bridge between the European mainland and the Middle East. It is a bridge along which may be seen an almost continuous transition from one tradition to another, through a series of links and a few sharp divides, until the last link is entirely different from the first.

Note
1 Parmenides, Zeno, Empedocles and Archimedes were all, geographically speaking, Italians but, culturally, entirely Greek.

References

BARTÓK, Béla
    1969   *Lettere scelte.* Milan: Mondadori.
    1977   *Scritta sulla musica popolare.* Turin: Boringhieri.
DE MARTINO, Ernesto
    1958   *Morte e pianto rituale.* Turin: Boringhieri.
FRANCELLO, Elvira
    1946   'An Italian Version of the "Maid Freed from the Gallows"'. *New York Folklore Quarterly* 2/1:139-40.
GIURIATI, Giovanni
    1982   'Un procedimento compositivo caleidoscopico: la tarantella di Montemarano'. *Culture musicali* 1/2:19-72.
LEYDI, Roberto
    1973   *I canti popolari italiani.* Milan: Mondadori.
MAGRINI, Tullia
    1985   *Forme della musica vocale e strumentale a Creta.* Milan: Ricordi.
    1986   'Dolce lo mio Drudo'. *Rivista Italiana di Musicologia* 21:215-35.
NIGRA, Costantino
    1957   *Canti popolari del Piemonte.* Turin: Einaudi. First published Turin, 1888.
REGNONI-MACERA, Clara
    1964   'The Song of May'. *Western Folklore* 23:23-6.

SACHS, Curt
   1943   *The Rise of Music in the Ancient World, East and West.* New York: Norton.
SORCE KELLER, Marcello
   1988   'Segmental Procedures in the Transmission of Folk Songs in Trentino'. *Sonus* 8/2:37-46.
   1991   *Tradizione orale e canto corale, ricerca musicologica in Trentino.* Bologna: Forni.

Political Implications of Croatian Opera in the Nineteenth Century

Zdravko Blažeković

The production of opera in nineteenth-century Croatia, though not as extensive as in some other European nations, showed similar character-istics to operatic productions in other parts of Europe. The common denominator in almost all operas was the choice of themes from national history for subject matter. Neither exceptional nor unusual in the European Romantic movement, historical subjects were used by many painters, poets and musicians. In the political circumstances in which Croatian opera developed in the nineteenth century, they were intensi-fied and given another dimension, stimulating national consciousness in periods of intensive Germanization and Magyarization, as audiences recognized analogies between historical and contemporary situations. Opera had a didactic intent, and psychological expression tended to predominate over lyrical elements (Seaman 1976:16); the same tendency is discernible in other vocal genres. This essay examines the political background that influenced the choice of subjects rather than the musical characteristics of nineteenth-century Croatian opera.

Lisinski and the Croatian National Revival

From 1527, when the Croatian nobility elected to be ruled by the Habsburg dynasty, the Kingdom of Croatia was a constituent part of the Austrian, and after 1867, the Austro-Hungarian Monarchy. Throughout this time Croatia retained its parliament and viceroy (*banus*), with autonomy in certain fields, including education, religious affairs and internal administration. However, Austria and Hungary repeatedly attempted to limit Croatian autonomy.

Opera has been performed regularly in Zagreb since 1799, and audiences were more or less well-informed about contemporary opera. In the early nineteenth century, Rossini was the most popular composer, followed by Boïeldieu (whose *La Dame blanche* was performed in 1828, three years after its French première), Hérold (*Zampa* was performed in 1833, two years after the French première), Auber, Mozart and Weber. Productions were usually presented by musicians and other artists from Zagreb and Italy.

Vatroslav Lisinski (1819-54) was one of the most talented Croatian composers of the first half of the century. His first opera, *Ljubav i zloba* [Love and Malice], completed in 1846, was also the first Croatian national opera. Appearing ten years after Glinka's *Zhizn' za tsarya* [A Life for the Tsar] and twenty years before Smetana's *Prodaná nevěsta,* it was a product of the Croatian National Revival (see Kuhač 1904 and Županović 1969).

Ideologically similar to other European national movements (especially the Czech, Polish and Italian), the Croatian National Revival of the period 1835 to 1848 signalled the birth of a patriotic awareness and a belief in the worth of one's own nation and the greatness of the Slavs. This was the ideological base on which Croats were preparing to fight Austrian and Hungarian domination. It affected all areas of cultural life, including music, which was seen as a powerful medium for stimulating and strengthening political awareness and for helping the Croats gain cultural recognition through the creation of an authentic or unique Croatian music (see further Vucinich 1975 and Andreis 1974).

In the 1830s and 1840s, the Zagreb press reported the appearance and success of Glinka's operas *Zhizn' za tsarya* and *Ruslan i Ludmila.* This provided the impetus for several leaders of the Croatian National Revival to start thinking about a Croatian national opera. They were inspired by the political idea that Croats should create their own authentic art in all areas, to stand alongside the arts of other European nations. Although Lisinski had not yet completed his music studies at that time, leaders of the National Revival suggested to him that he compose an opera; in two years he completed *Ljubav i zloba.* The first act was performed in Zagreb in February 1845 and the entire work in March 1846. The libretto, written by Dimitrija Demeter (1811-72) on the model of other Romantic opera plots, presents a naive love story placed in the Dalmatian region. The music was influenced both by the early nineteenth-century operas (of

Bellini, Auber and Boïeldieu) that had been performed in Zagreb, and by Croatian folk music. The enormous success of the opera stimulated efforts in other fields of national culture, as the Croats sought new ways of putting their ideas into operation. By mid-1846, the Croatian language was being taught at the Royal Academy in Zagreb, and in autumn of 1847 the Croatian parliament passed a law making Croatian the language of all public affairs.

During his studies with Bedřich Kittl in Prague (1847-50), Lisinski began work on a second opera, *Porin,* completed in 1851. The libretto, again by Demeter, made it easy for mid-nineteenth-century audiences to draw analogies with the contemporary situation, a post-revolutionary time in the Monarchy and the beginning of the decade of Habsburg absolutism. The main story — about the liberation of the Croats from Frankish rule in the ninth century — would have reminded listeners of their own desire for liberation. To make the opera more appealing, and in accord with audience tastes in the Romantic period, the main plot was connected to a love story. On the whole, Lisinski was judged to have succeeded in his attempt to emulate the European standards of his day in the music of *Porin.*

Ljubav i zloba and *Porin* are the only operas written in the national language of Croatia during the first half of the nineteenth century. They were preceded by a three-act opera with a German libretto, *Alexis,* composed in the 1820s by Juraj Karlo Wisner von Morgenstern (ca.1783-1855).

Zajc and Historical Themes

The central musical personality in Croatia during the second half of the nineteenth century was Ivan Zajc (1834-1914). Educated at the Milan Conservatory, he developed a taste for specifically Italian forms of stage music. He also assimilated the style of classical Viennese operetta during seven years of activity in Vienna (1863-70), where he belonged to the circle of Johannes Brahms, Franz von Suppé and Julius Epstein. Zajc composed nineteen operas in Italian, German and Croatian, and twenty-six operettas in German and Croatian.

The subject matter of these works changed in the different periods of Zajc's activity. During his years in Rijeka and Vienna (1855-70) he composed five operas: *La Tirolese* (1855), *Adelina* (1858), *Die Braut von Messina* (ca. 1860), *Amelia* (1864) and *Die Hexe von Boissy* (1866). At that time he was completely under the influence of Verdi and his 'trilogy', and he chose libretti with similar stories. After moving from Vienna to Zagreb in 1870, when he was named director of the Croatian Opera, Zajc turned to libretti based on historical events. He realized that he would gain greater popularity in Zagreb with subjects that appealed to Croatian pride over their long history. In *Mislav* (1870), the story was set in the original Croatian homeland, the so-called Great Croatia of the sixth century. The action of Zajc's next opera, *Ban Leget* [Viceroy Leget] (completed in 1872), took place in present-day Hercegovina, during the tenth century. His most outstanding opera, and the most popular Croatian opera up to the present, is *Nikola Šubić Zrinjski,* a musical tragedy in three acts completed in 1876. The libretto, by Hugo Badalić (1851-1900), based on the play *Niklas Graf von Zriny* by the German romantic poet Theodor Körner (1791-1813), depicts the battle between Croats and Turks at Siget in 1566, where the Croatian army refused to surrender Fort Siget despite overwhelming Turkish military superiority. Although the opera has undeniable musical value, the nineteenth-century audience was primarily attracted to its historical and political background. During the period of Magyarization, the heroic patriotism of the Croatian army at Fort Siget symbolized the struggle against Hungarian attempts to limit Croatian autonomy.[1]

Following these three operas, Zajc's interests changed once more, and in the 1880s and 1890s he concentrated on libretti based on stories having comical content or dealing with domestic folklore or fairy tales.[2] The late 1870s and 1880s were a relatively stable political period in Croatia. As manifestations of nationalism subsided, composers generally lost interest in historical topics. In Zajc's final period of creativity in the 1900s, when the labour movement was gaining strength in Europe, he wrote two operas that showed an understanding of workers' problems: *La dea della montana, ovvero I minatori, leggenda in tre atti* to a libretto by J. Fontana, commissioned by the Teatro alla Scala (1899), and *Prvi grijeh* [The First Sin], a musical allegory to a libretto by Silvije Strahimir Kranjčević (1907).

Other Composers of the Period

Zajc was not the only composer to take an interest in Körner's *Niklas Graf von Zriny.* Ten years before him, in 1866 (on the 300th anniversary of the battle at Fort Siget), August Abramović Adelburg (1830-73) had written an opera in the Croatian language based on the play. At the Austrian Imperial Library, Adelburg found the notation of a tune attributed to

Nikola Zrinjski, which he included in his opera along with some other Croatian tunes.[3]

The next composer to write an opera in Zagreb was Gjuro Eisenhuth (1841-91), who completed his only opera, *Sejslav ljuti* [Angry Sejslav], in 1878. Once again, the libretto was based on early Croatian history.

The administrative centre for the Dalmatian region in the nineteenth century was Zadar, which thus became the most important city in the territory of Croatia after Zagreb. Because of extremely strong influences from neighbouring Italy at the time, cultural life in Zadar (as well as in some other Dalmatian towns) was a combination of Croatian and Italian elements. Everything coming from Italy was fashionable: people were playing Italian music, reading Italian literature, and looking for Italian clothes. Italian *stagione* had been organized regularly since 1791, and the Italian language was used in everyday life by the middle class. In such circumstances, Croatian nationalists made efforts to promote Croatian culture, especially during the second half of the century.

The most prominent personality among the Zadar musicians was Nikola Strmić (1839-96), a graduate of the Milan Conservatory and a proficient violinist. During the 1860s and early 1870s he completed four operas, two of which have been lost. He took the subject of *Desiderio Duca d'Istria* (1860) from the history of Istria. The action of the second opera, *La madre slava* (1865), is placed in Montenegro and depicts a love story linked with a battle between Montenegrins and Turks.[4] The romantic story is set in a neighbouring Slavic nation. The 1860s was a time of development of the idea of unification of all the South Slavic nations, and a plot involving Montenegrins rather than Croats made no difference in the impression it made on the contemporary audience. People throughout Croatia supported efforts for liberation from Turkish rule and contemporary Croatian audiences recognized the Turks as their enemies. At the time Montenegro was regarded as the model of an independent Slavic country by other Slavic nations within the Monarchy; several Croatian artists and musicians were inspired by the Montenegrins.[5]

The example of Strmić allows us to recognize the main cultural characteristics in some Dalmatian towns of his day, and the conflict between intentions and results. Although the subjects of his two operas clearly show Strmić's intention to follow a Croatian political orientation, he was unable to speak or write Croatian, and his operas were written in Italian.[6] He intended to write in the style of Croatian national music and included some Croatian folk tunes in *La madre slava,* but he had been educated in Milan and was deeply influenced by Italian opera. On the whole, his operas were closer in style to those of Verdi than, for example, to those of Lisinski.

Neither of the two *opera buffe* of Salvatore Strino, the only composer who wrote operas during the last two decades of the century in Split, have subjects taken from national history.[7] Like Strmić, Strino set libretti written in Italian, but he did not join the political group of Croatian 'nationalists'. He composed fashionable music, without paying attention to social role or eventual political implications.

Conclusions

Croatian musical culture in the nineteenth century directly expressed or indirectly reflected the political situation. The Romantic movement and the National Revival of the 1830s and 1840s in Croatia were interrupted by the Revolution of 1848 and the subsequent decade of Habsburg absolutism. A pause occurred in the history of Croatian music, as the absolutism of the 1850s succeeded the Revolution of 1848, as part of a larger pattern in the music histories of other European nations involved in the 1848 revolutions (see Dahlhaus 1978). The October Diploma, issued in the fall of 1860, returned their constitutions to the nations of the Monarchy, and liberalization created the basis for the Croatian Parliament to declare the Zagreb Theatre a national institution headed by a board. Activities of the Zagreb *Musikverein* became more extensive, and numerous singing societies were founded. Another reason for a break in the continuity of development of Croatian musical culture in the 1850s was the death in 1854 of Lisinski, the most outstanding composer of the National Revival. By chance, the period of absolutism coincided with a time lacking a strong creative personality.

Music which grew out of the Croatian National Revival was a constituent part of the movement. Leaders of the movement were aware of the role which music can play in the propagation of ideas, and, before anything else, they ensured that vocal music was performed in public places in the national language. Thus all prominent composers of Croatian origin followed the ideas of the movement, tirelessly composing vocal music to awaken national consciousness. Numerous rousing song texts composed in the national language enjoyed wide popularity.[8] After the absolutist period, the situation changed but the music was still politically based. Opera and other music were no longer part of an organized cultural movement, but they were still a stimulus in a fight against foreign political domination.

The two operas created during the National Revival signified that the national language was suitable for opera and that the nation was able to produce complex works. *Ljubav i zloba* and *Porin* grew out of this atmosphere and stimulated new efforts in the field of national culture. The message for the audience had been built into both operas (though more clearly in *Porin* than in *Ljubav i zloba*). The librettist of *Porin* was not averse to employing the verse *'O dajte, dajte mi slobodu'* [Give me, o give me freedom].

Operas created in the second half of the century had different connotations. The national language was no longer an exception in the theatre, nor was the production of a domestic opera. However, subjects taken from the national history still held out an invitation to join the struggle against foreign domination; national feeling and allusive texts were an integral part of almost all operas. Productions of Zajc's *Mislav* or *Nikola Šubić Zrinjski* had the same impact on a Zagreb audience that Verdi's *Nabucco, I Lombardi* or *Attila* had on an Italian one (see Martin 1978). Fragments of texts in Croatian operas even parallel some of Verdi's.

The entire opera *Nikola Šubić Zrinjski* is dramatically and musically directed toward the final scene, where the Croats, in preparation for the battle, sing

> *U boj, u boj, mač iz toka braćo*
> *Nek dušman zna kako mremo mi.*

> [To battle, to battle, the sword appears from its sheath
> Let the enemy know how we die.]

This was the most popular piece in Croatia in the half-century after the opera was first performed, and this passage was sung regularly at concerts of most Croatian singing societies. In 1891 it was submitted as an entry in a competition to choose the Croatian national anthem. This chorus can be compared with Verdi's *'Guerra, Guerra'* in *I Lombardi,* in which the Italian audience cast itself as the Lombards, and the Austrians as the Saracens defiling the Holy Land. Similarly, the Croatian audience of *Nikola Šubić Zrinjski* saw the Turkish occupiers as Austrians or Hungarians.

Parallels can be found in other libretti. Just as the Italian patriots listening to *Nabucco* were touched by the words *'Oh, mia patria si bella e perduta!'* [Oh, my country so beautiful and lost!], the Croats were touched by the words of Zrinjski's romantic song as he left Fort Siget to enter the battle against the Turks:

Gle kako divno sjaji grad u Božjeg sunca traku.

[Look how beautifully the town glows in the rays of God's sun.]

When comparing Croatian operas with Verdi's, we should notice one difference. In both cases, historical actions sparked off patriotic feelings and were seen as paralleling the contemporary political situation. A number of Verdi's operas deal with the history of other nations (e.g. the Israelites' captivity in Babylon), but the action in almost all Croatian historical operas is taken from Croatian national history.

Croatian composers joined in a general trend of Slavic composers, taking subjects from their own folklore or historical past and paying great attention to verbal context. The historical setting is merely a pretext with no real interest in the historical background; history is a sort of mythological stage on which the contemporary situation and characters are placed. Although the nineteenth century was a time of Romanticism, here history was not the stage for stormy castles and their ghosts, but a framework for models of a political utopia, a celebration of past grandeur to oppose the miseries of national enslavement and foreign domination.[9]

Notes

1   When first performed in the early nineteenth century, Körner's play was a proclamation of defiance against the Napoleonic invasion of Europe. In other words, the social background was essentially the same as that of Zajc's opera in 1876. The play was first presented in Zagreb on the opening night of the new theatre, 4 October 1834.

2   *Lizinka* (1878), libretto by Josip Eugen Tomić after Pushkin; *Pan Tvardovski* (1880), libretto by J.E. Tomić; *Zlatka* (1885), libretto by August Harambašić; *Gospodje i husari* [Ladies and Hussars] (1886), libretto by Tomić after Alexander Fredro; *Kraljev hir* [The King's Whim] (1889), libretto by Harambašić and Stjepan Miletić. For detailed analyses of Zajc's operas of the 1870-89 period, see Pettan 1983.

3   Rejected by the Zagreb Opera, the work was first performed in Budapest on 23 June 1868, with the libretto translated into Hungarian and with the Croatian folk songs and dances replaced by Hungarian ones.

4   Luigi Fichert's play *La madre slava*, on which the libretto was based, was very popular in Croatian and Italian during the period 1857-79.

5   To mention just a few well-known works of art: in 1875, Ferdo Quiquerez (1845-93) painted a portrait of the Montenegrin military leader Novica Cerović; in 1878, the sculptor Ivan Rendić (1842-1932) exhibited his work 'The Montenegrin Heroes Duke Marko Miljanić and Novica Cerović' in Zagreb; and the Czech painter Jaroslav Čermak (1831-78) painted several scenes of Montenegrin life ('Kidnapping of the Montenegrin Woman', 'The Wounded Montenegrin', 'Montenegrin Women Returning to a Devastated Village'). In 1862, the Croatian composer Ferdo Livadić (1798-1878) wrote the song 'Crnogorski sin' [Son of Montenegro]; and in the mid-1870s, Ivan Zajc wrote three compositions for male chorus: 'Crnogorac' [Montenegrin], op. 331; 'Crnogorac Crnogorki' [The Montenegrin to the Montenegrin Woman]; and *Crnogorska kantata*, op. 337b, to a poem by Ljudevit Varjačić.

Two nineteenth-century French operas were set in Montenegro: *les Montenegrins*, completed in 1848 by Armand Marie Guillain Limnander de Niewehove (1814-92) to a libretto by Gérard de Nerval and premièred in the following year; and *La montagne noir* by Augusta Mary Ann Holmes, first performed in 1895. To the French composers, Montenegro was an exotic and fantastic region, almost the end of the world, whereas to artists in the Slav countries it was a symbol of liberation and independence.

6   In a letter of 1870, Strmić wrote that he was studying Croatian with a private teacher, but he never set a Croatian text to music (see Blažeković 1988).

7   *Le Sartine in carnavale* premièred in Split in September 1885; *Il Menestrello* premiered on 10 December 1892.

8   Other adherents to the Croatian National Revival's ideas in music were Franjo Ksaver Čacčković-Vrhovinski (1789-1865), Josip Juratović (1796-1872), Fortunat Pintarić (1798-1862), Ferdo Livadić (1798-1878), Ivan Padovec (1800-73), Pavao Stoos (1806-62) and Mijo Hajko (1820-48). Several of their contemporaries who did not follow the Revival's ideas were Juraj Karlo Wisner von Morgenstern

(ca.1783-1855), Aleksandar Kovačić (ca.1800-60), Antun Kirschhofer (1807-49), Karl Engelmann (active in Zagreb around 1835) and Valentin Ježek (d. 1835). Most of the latter were not native to Croatia but came from other regions in the monarchy and were not comfortable in the Croatian language. They were generally better educated and more skilled in music than the composers who followed the Revival's ideas. Many of their compositions were extensive orchestral scores, while those of the Revivalists were relatively simple choral compositions and songs. The domestic composers had a very clear idea of what they wished to achieve through their music, and they composed music based on these ideas. The other composers, whose music originated primarily from their artistic impulses, paid less attention to the role of their music in public life.

9   Umberto Eco's categorization of ten different kinds of 'Middle Ages' (1983) could also be applied to nineteenth-century opera subjects. Some of them are readily recognizable in the Croatian operatic output — Type 1, The Middle Ages as a Pretext; and Type 6, The Middle Ages as a National Identity. Others (e.g., Type 4, The Middle Ages as Romanticism) are less appropriate.

References

ANDREIS, Josip
   1974   *Music in Croatia*. Zagreb: Muzikološki Zavod Muzičke Akademije.
BLAŽEKOVIĆ, Zdravko
   1988   'Prilog biografiji Nikole Strmića' [A Contribution to the Biography of Nikola Strmić]. *Rad Jugoslavenske Akademije Znanosti i Umjetnosti* 409:285-313.
DAHLHAUS, Carl
   1978   'Über die musikgeschichtliche Bedeutung der Revolution von 1848'. *Melos/Neue Zeitschrift für Musik* 4/1:15-19.
ECO, Umberto
   1983   'The Return of the Middle Ages'. In Eco, *Travels in Hyperreality*. New York: Harcourt Brace Jovanovich, pp. 59-85.
KUHAČ, Franjo Ksaver
   1904   *Vatroslav Lisinski i njegovo doba* [Vatroslav Lisinski and His Time]. Zagreb: Matica Hrvatska.

MARTIN, Giuseppe
1978   'Verdi and the Risorgimento'. In *The Verdi Companion,* ed. William Weaver & Martin Chusid. New York: Norton, pp. 13-41.
PETTAN, Hubert
1983   *Hrvatska opera. Ivan Zajc, II* [Croatian Opera: Ivan Zajc, II]. Zagreb: Muzički Informativni Centar.
SEAMAN, Gerald
1976   'The Rise of Slavonic Opera'. *New Zealand Slavonic Journal* 2.
VUCINICH, Wayne S.
1975   'Croatian Illyrism: Its Background and Genesis'. In *Intellectual and Social Development in the Habsburg Empire from Maria Theresa to World War I,* ed. Stanley B. Winters & Joseph Held. Boulder: East European Quarterly, pp. 55-113.
ŽUPANOVIĆ, Lovro
1969   *Vatroslav Lisinski. Život-djelo-značenje* [Vatroslav Lisinski: Life-Work-Significance]. Zagreb: Jugoslavenska Akademija Znanosti i Umjetnosti.

Corpus Christi and its Octave in Andean Ecuador: Procession and Music, 'Castles' and 'Bulls'

John M. Schechter

The celebration of Corpus Christi and its Octave in the Andes mountains of Ecuador provides a multifaceted example of cultural contact through music. Dictates of the Roman Catholic liturgical calendar and of native Andean solstitial observances combine, in central highland Ecuador, to form a multi-day syncretic festival. The ritual juxtaposes European facets such as elaborate processional with native Andean aspects such as the harvest theme. With regard to performance practices, the harp, a European import, played a role in Ecuadorian and Peruvian Corpus rites through at least the nineteenth century. Pipe-and-tabor — strongly rooted in European practice as accompaniment to the dance — might well have merged with analogous native American performance practices in this hemisphere to create the modern custom of pipe-and-tabor accompanying indigenous dancers in Ecuadorian Corpus Christi. Outdoor theatre is another link in the chain that connects European with Andean Corpus festivities. Fifteenth-century European Corpus theatre focused on Biblical episodes, while twentieth-century Ecuadorian Corpus enactments both reflect the agricultural cycle — distribution of the harvest, and 'bulls' or 'oxen' that pull ploughs for 'planting' — and feature personages borrowed from either Caribbean or Bolivian 'devil' portrayals. I shall examine these syncretic characteristics as they contribute to the elaborate, festive and evocative ritual that is Corpus Christi and its Octave in Andean Ecuador.

Introduction

In fieldwork, both significant events and important insights are often unforeseen. Planning to investigate the contexts for Quechua song in Andean Ecuador, I found myself in a small sea of harpists in one region of Imbabura Province in the northern Sierra. Ultimately, I focused upon that instrument — including its role as accompaniment to vocal performance, notably in the child's wake. Seeking a comparative perspective for indigenous highland music-culture, I travelled during the second phase of research to Tungurahua Province in the central Sierra. One May day, a woman in a store in the provincial capital of Ambato remarked that the small village of Soga (pseudonym), about one hour's drive from the cantonal centre of Patate, was inhabited primarily by *indigenas* (indigenes) and that it had not been visited by foreigners. A preliminary visit with my wife, Janis, on 19 May 1980, resulted in some local interest in our establishing residence there. Four days later, we were interviewed in Soga by the village *cabildo* (chapter). After explaining our ethnomusicological purpose and showing photographs taken and canvases painted in Imbabura Province, and after declaring our hope to teach area children drawing and music-reading, we were invited to reside.

On the morning of 4 June, we arrived in Soga by pick-up truck and quickly moved into single-room lodgings near the plaza. By about 1.00 pm that day, costumed dancers, two men each playing vertical flute and bass drum, and a neighbouring band began to pass our house en route to the plaza.

'Corpus' in Soga, Ecuador

The next morning, Thursday 5 June, we spent some four hours in the plaza at the festivities of Corpus Christi proper. Despite our having just arrived, I was most fortunate to have received permission from Sr. Eleuterio Medina, the *teniente político* (the local authority), to photograph and make tape recordings. At midday, a wooden structure termed *castillo* (castle) was erected, using ropes, and two men ascended; they untied the foodstuffs (oranges, bananas, potatoes, peppers, gourds, breads) attached to the *castillo* and threw them down to the people below.

Corpus Christi, 5 June 1980. Tungurahua Province, Highland Ecuador. Photograph by John Schechter.

'Corpus' (Christi) *per se,* in Soga, was to be celebrated for some three days, followed by the Octave of Corpus, beginning 15 June, when two *castillos* would be raised. On both festive days, young people wearing regular clothes but with white cloths over their heads and cowhorns on top were referred to as *toros* (bulls). They constantly charged about making mischief — apparently their assigned role — grunting but not speaking. The *teniente* called the ensemble of *flauta* (cross-flute), *caja* (side-drum) and accompanying *bombo* (double-headed drum) the *orquesta de los toros.* Also present at Corpus were *vaca locas* — cane-fireworks shaped as cows. These were lit and exploded throughout the day, notably at the formal entrance (*entrada*) of the *danzantes,* or costumed dancers, into the plaza. To be selected as a *danzante* was a great honour, we were informed. It was evident that the two *danzantes* in Soga bore an enormous physical burden, dancing their back-and-forth stomp in heavy costume. Two other men were each responsible for one *danzante,* carrying his headdress when he was not wearing it and keeping him upright when he might have drunk too much. The *danzantes* and their two pipe-and-tabor (*pingullo*-and-*bombo*) musicians constantly travelled about — down to the lower plain where a new schoolhouse was being constructed, up again, and so forth. They performed with coloured handkerchiefs hanging over their hands; they would approach each other and hang these cloth-covered hands over each other's shoulders. The *pingullo* (duct-flute)-and-*bombo* players would 'greet' people — ourselves included — by approaching the person while they were playing and then dipping the *pingullo* down and up in a quick bow. One musician played *bombo* with the left hand and *pingullo* with the right, while the other musician reversed the instruments. The *pingullo* has two anterior holes near the bottom and a single posterior thumb-hole. Upper holes are played either with second and third, or with third and fourth fingers.

The Octave of Corpus

On the morning of 15 June — Sunday — I photographed *monos* (i.e. mimics — boys wearing hornless head-coverings and carrying rawhide whips) in front of our house. We were advised that on this day, the Octave of Corpus, performers would include *monos, toros,* and other actors, but not *danzantes*. The last-named were — by Soga tradition, at any rate — for the celebration of Corpus only.

Just before noon, the *orquesta de toros* was playing near the *tienda* (store) opposite the plaza. At Corpus, the ensemble had consisted of three musicians — *flauta-caja-bombo*. Here at the Octave, there were four — one more *flauta*. The grunting *toros* and the *orquesta de toros* always entered and departed the plaza together, and when in the plaza, they marched together. They (*orquesta* plus *toros*) were one of several pairs of individual or group performers that participated in the Octave. Again, the two *danzantes* with their pipe-and-tabor-musicians were absent. We were told that, in Soga, Corpus was the only day of the year that they were to be seen.

After the *toros*-cum-*orquesta* another 'pair' appeared in the plaza. A man with a green pot on his head and a black cloth over his face played a small two-headed drum while carrying a bottle of *trago* (cane alcohol). He was matched with the *mono,* a man with a cloth mask with tufts of varicoloured fabric. The *mono* was performing almost continuous pantomine with *his* partner, a small black doll termed *hijito* (dear son), or *churi mono* (mimic-son), which he beat with a rawhide whip or did somersaults alongside of. The *mono* and green pot-hat drummer appeared to be acting out a play, part of which entailed the *mono's* hitting the ground with the short part of a long whip, most of which was wrapped around his chest. He then lay prone on the ground, writhing and feigning injury.

At this point, we spied the only non-paired actor yet to appear — the *diablo*. His body was painted black. He wore a red and black mask, with a red scarf down the back of the head, and a white animal's-hair tail, gym shorts, white socks and jogging shoes. The *diablo* darted about unaccompanied — stopping and starting — now walking with long strides, now curled up on the church patio. One was reminded of other street-theatre devil-portrayals — to the north, in the Caribbean and Venezuela, and to the south in Bolivia. Black-satans have traditionally participated in Trinidadian Carnival (see, for example, the illustration of an 1888 Port-of-Spain Carnival procession, with prominent, prancing black-satan figure, in Myers 1980:148). A film by John Dickinson, *El Diablo de Cumaná* (1984), shows a 53-year-old Venezuelan, Luis del Valle Hurtado of Cumaná, near Trinidad, performing street theatre in which a 'devilist' uses Lucifer — black Satan — as a model for his performances at Carnival, New Year and religious holidays (see Schechter 1987). Ramón y Rivera (1969:111-12) and Béhague (1980:33) have elaborated upon the prominence of *el baile de diablos o diablicos,* or *diablos danzantes,* at Venezuelan Corpus Christi rites. In Oruro (highland Bolivia), multi-tiered devil personages are central to the celebration of Carnival. As Béhague writes for the Andean region:

> Numerous contemporary dances of the Andean highlands re-enact ancestral Indian myths in which reinterpreted fantastic figures or characters of native and Hispanic origins appear side by side or combined. The most conspicuous of these characters in the Andean area is related to the beliefs in and representations of the devil. The Catholic prince of the devils — Lucifer, Satanas — brought by the missionaries was soon syncretized with the equivalent devilish creature of the Indians of the Peruvian *sierra* and the Bolivian *altiplano, Supay* . . . The famous *danza de los diablos* or *diablada* of the Bolivian *altiplano* and the Peruvian Puno department exhibits some of the most spectacular masked dances of the South American continent. (1980:25)

Another mime-pair now entered the plaza, carrying a log for one of the two *castillos* to be constructed. One wore normal dress and came first, appearing as the 'servant'. Behind him came the 'master', dressed in a *blanco* (Caucasian) mask, wearing an old suit with a large hat. They dropped the log for the small *castillo*. Then, the 'master' pretended that his hobby-horse was bucking; the 'servant' came over, grabbed the 'reins', patted it on the 'head', and calmed it down. This mime-pair continued the bucking-calming routine for a short time, then left the plaza. One more pair appeared: a ram *(Pachito)* with four horns on his masked head, 'tied' by rope to his 'master'. They ran along, together, the 'master' constantly calling his ram: *'Pachito, Pachito'.*

At this point, the two *castillos* were under construction. The larger one was near the plaza-centre; the smaller one, built later, was near the church. *Castillo* logs were cut to their proper lengths with machetes. When greased and raised, both *castillos* would bear foodstuffs, handkerchiefs and cigarettes. The smaller *castillo* also bore live *cuis* (guinea pigs). Native to the Andes, *cuis* are raised in households, killed and broiled. In the plaza volleyball games were played nearly all afternoon amidst the fiesta, occasionally interrupted by one or another of the performing pairs.

At Corpus *per se* in Soga, some form of music was always being performed. However, at the Octave, once the *orquesta de toros* (accompanying its nine to ten *toros*) had departed the plaza, there was no music. The absence of the *danzantes* (with their bells), the *pingullo-bombo* pipe-and-tabor duo, and the neighbouring municipal band (which also performed at Corpus) made this Octave a relatively quiet celebration. The players did not even speak, miming only. At one point, a local band did arrive, with accordion, violin, thermos-güiro and small *caja*. They moved about the community, enticing people to come to the plaza for the fiesta.

After both *castillos* had been raised and secured in their holes with rocks, yokes of 'oxen' entered the plaza. One 'pulled' a (real) plough and was followed by the *orquesta de toros*. Behind the plough, a man was tossing out barley in powder, pretending to be planting seed. In the later June-July period, many Soga farmers were ploughing fields and planting maize and beans.

The Festival and Its Syncretic Aspects

Corpus Christi is a moveable feast in honour of the presence of the body of Jesus Christ in the Holy Eucharist. It is held on the Thursday (as in Soga), or in some countries the Sunday, after Trinity Sunday, which is the Sunday after Pentecost, or Whitsunday, the seventh Sunday after Easter.

In 1264, Pope Urban IV ordered that the entire Church observe the festival, that decree being confirmed by Pope Clement V in 1311-12. The celebration was established by the mid-fourteenth century in Europe, and it became a principal feast of the Church in the fifteenth century.

The Corpus Christi procession dates from 1279, in Cologne. From the beginning, the custom of wielding the Blessed Sacrament in that procession was a distinctive feature of the rite. The procession became the trademark of the festival, which was effectively transformed into a pageant in which members of the nobility, magistrates, guild-members, and/or religious orders took part. The procession was not confined to the church arena but moved through town, even into the open country.

In the fifteenth century, the procession was followed by guild members' performances of miracle and mystery plays. The frontispiece of Alan H. Nelson's book, *The Medieval English Stage: Corpus Christi Pageants and Plays* (1974), depicts a fifteenth-century Corpus Christi procession. The illustration appears to have been copied from a northern French or Flemish original. The left foreground has three minstrels, followed by a bishop bearing the Host, the Corpus Christi. One minstrel is playing pipe-and-tabor. Fifteenth-century English cities and towns celebrated Corpus Christi with enormous pageants and plays, frequently depicting episodes of Biblical history, from the Creation to the Last Judgment (Nelson 1974:1). As Nelson mentions, Corpus Christi and the summer solstice were linked:

> The prominence of Corpus Christi as the occasion of civic and guild ostentation was certainly related to its calendar day. Historians of medieval drama have long recognized that Corpus Christi was essentially a summer festival and that the activities of the day — processions, pageants, and plays — were more suited to summer weather than to the bitter days of Christmas . . . The movable feast of Corpus Christi . . . can fall on any date from May 23 to June 24. In about three years out of every four during the fifteenth century [due to calendrical discrepancies], Corpus Christi was closer to astronomical midsummer day than was the feast of Midsummer [Nativity of St. John the Baptist] itself . . . The long hours of sunlight on Corpus Christi and the relatively fine weather would . . . permit an elaborate spectacle. So the clergy marched with their colorful habits and with the Host; the civic officials marched with their scarlet robes and gold chains; and the

guildsmen marched in their livery, carrying banners and torches. (1974:13-14)

Fourteenth and fifteenth century English data illuminate, perhaps, the origin of the use of the term *castillos* in the twentieth-century Ecuadorian tradition. In Beverley, near York, 'The typical craft guild of the [late fourteenth and fifteenth] century . . . supported a castle . . . and a Corpus Christi pageant or play . . . town and guild records give . . . prominence to the crafts' "castles"'. The 'castles' were wooden structures covered with colourful cloth. They served as viewing stands for guild members at Corpus Christi processions, and at ecclesiastical processions on Rogation Monday, which is the first of the three minor Rogation days (the Major Rogation Day is April 25) prior to Ascension Day, forty days after Easter. The four Rogation days are associated with prayers for God's mercy and blessing, especially upon the fields, for the harvest (Nelson 1974:90-95; Pallen and Wynne 1929:832; *Columbia Encyclopedia* 1963).

Thus, in certain sites in fifteenth-century Europe, Corpus Christi, held near the time of the summer solstice, was prominently defined by processions of diverse persons, perhaps accompanied by pipe-and-tabor. It was observed by guildspeople in wooden 'castles' erected, as well, for propitiatory processions on Rogation Days, which had distinct associations with the harvest.

At about this time on the other side of the Atlantic, among the Incas, the southern winter solstice was celebrated annually in late June or early July. This festival was known as *Inti Raymi* (Quechua: Feast of the Sun). According to the chronicle of Pedro de Cieza de León, who lived in the Inca capital of Cuzco in 1550, barely eighteen years after the Conquest, thanks were offered during this Empire-wide festival to the Inca god of Creation, Ticiviracocha, and to the Sun, Moon, and other deities for a bountiful harvest (Schechter 1979:193).

In contemporary Spain, during the reign of Holy Roman Emperor Charles V (Charles I of Spain, r.1516-56), the Royal Chapel consisted of a *maestro de capilla,* a *maestro de órgano,* singers, and minstrels playing harps, shawms, flageolets, small bassoons and sackbuts (Soriano Fuertes 2, 1856:115). Given later data from Peru, harps may have been played during Corpus and Octave-of-Corpus processions during Charles V's reign. In 1545, Charles V ordered that his Royal Chapel include processions for these two occasions. Near the end of the long procession, which was specifically to include trumpets and drums, various priestly orders, including Augustinians, Dominicans and Franciscans, were represented. Then came the Cross of the Royal Chapel, after which came two lines of 'singers' and 'minstrels', following the priestly orders and parish priests (*ibid.*:117, note 1). My research on the Latin American harp (1992) points to its having been utilized in processional contexts in the eighteenth century in the Ecuadorian-Peruvian Marañón español region, in nineteenth-century Ecuador and Peru, and in twentieth-century Peru. It is possible that this performance practice might have been introduced by the evangelistic orders that arrived in the Western hemisphere during the sixteenth and seventeenth centuries, having observed harps similarly employed in sixteenth-century Spain.

In fact, the practice of Corpus in Spain dates back to 1280, when Toledo became the first Spanish city to incorporate the celebration, followed by Sevilla in 1282 and Barcelona in 1319 (Carreras y Candi 3, 1933:556). Exceedingly elaborate processions took place in early seventeenth-century Madrid and nineteenth-century Valencia (*ibid.*:558-62), including various ambassadors, along with variegated clergy, in the former, and sundry guilds, in the latter. The description for nineteenth-century Valencia includes an account of two children leading four blind musicians in the procession, the musicians playing zither, harp and other string instruments (*ibid.*:562).

The elaborate European Corpus Christi processions were sustained by the clergy who evangelized the hinterlands of South America in the sixteenth, seventeenth and eighteenth centuries. The Jesuits were very successful in their conversion efforts in South America: in a little over 250 years, they extended their domination over native enclaves of the Upper Amazon, eastern Bolivia, the Chaco, Paraguay, the Pampas and, in Brazil, the lower Amazon and Atlantic coast. The assiduous Jesuit accounts of these conversions are represented by P. José Chantre y Herrera's detailed description of missions in the Marañón River zone of the Peruvian-Ecuadorian Oriente region. This was written between 1770, when the Marañón-area Jesuits left the South American continent for Italy after the 1767 expulsion of the Jesuits from all Spanish dominions by Charles III (r.1759-88) of Spain, and 1801, the date of the author's death. The document details missionary labours over the period 1637-1767. Patron saints' days and Corpus Christi were included in the Jesuit festivals celebrated in the Spanish Marañón in the eighteenth century.

An unusually early Mass was held at Corpus to allow the procession to be held in the cool of the morning. No-one was excused from the procession and all behaved with great composure. Part of the procession consisted of male indigenes, in one or two groups, playing *claríns* (probably a valveless straight trumpet, possibly side-blown), drums, fifes and *cabos* (probably a cow's horn, called *bocina* in Ecuador). Clearly indigenous instruments were permitted in the Corpus procession.

Earlier that morning, before Mass, *castillos* had been erected in different spots along the procession route. They bore live animals, fish, fruit and other foods. The same term used in fifteenth-century England was employed (in Spanish) to denote (probably) wooden structures placed at different points along the Corpus procession route. The probable role of the structure was to display the fruits of the harvest rather than to provide viewing stands for the procession. Yet, as noted earlier, in fifteenth-century England processions-viewed-from-'castles' were held also on Rogation Monday, when a harvest theme was in evidence. Moreover, as I observed in Soga in June 1980, intrepid Ecuadorians climb the 30-to-40-foot-high (9–12 metres) *castillos* at Corpus today, obtaining an excellent view of the festive proceedings below.

In addition to the periodic *castillos,* palms were placed around the streets during the eighteenth-century Marañón español Corpus. Sacristans constructed chapels and altars for the stops that the procession would make where the Blessed Sacrament was set down. Singers with instrumental accompaniment would sing a hymn or devotional song, and the priest would give a benediction. In addition to the ensemble of mostly indigenous winds and drums was an ensemble of specially-trained musicians which accompanied the priest during the procession.

> The singers and instrumentalists closely accompanied the Señor and they sang throughout the procession, either the *Pange lingua* [hymn for Corpus Christi, *Pange lingua gloriosi corporis mysterium* − 'Sing, my tongue, the mystery of the glorious body' − by Thomas Aquinas, d.1274; *Liber Usualis,* pp. 950-2, or 957-9] or the *Sacris Solemniis* [Corpus procession-hymn, *Liber Usualis,* pp. 952-952B]. Six or eight steps away from the priest went ahead the standard or banner, carried by one of the principals (he who customarily was named every year as steward of the fiesta), and two companions picking up the tufts and strands on both sides. Near the banner a crowd of *danzantes* performed, who, well-rehearsed beforehand, danced with elegance and grace to the

sound of a flute and small drum played by an Indian. The priest, at each of the small chapels, placed down the Most Holy, giving way to the performance of something on harp and violin and to the singing of some devotional verses; the Sacrament having been said, he gave the benediction with the monstrance. (Chantre y Herrera 1901:661-2)

As this account indicates, there were dance performances by costumed and masked *danzantes,* who danced 'to the sound of a flute and small drum played by *an Indian'* (my emphasis). The suggestion that there was a single musician implies pipe-and-tabor playing, which is probably a European import. This is despite the pre-Conquest existence of aerophone-cum-membranophone, or aerophone-cum-idiophone, performance in the Western hemisphere, as pointed out by Boilès (1966). (See Carreras y Candi 3, 1933: 1st plate after p. 558; also Baines 1984:118, and Blades 1984:208-10 and plates 93 [16th-century England], 95 [15th-century Scotland], 96 [13th-century England] and 97 [15th-century Scotland].) Particularly to be noted, in this regard, is the vigour of the pipe-and-tabor combination in Spain, where this processional performance practice continues today (Baines 1984:118). Also, concomitant with the European practice is the accompaniment for the dance: 'Dance music was always the pipe and tabor's principal function, as is shown by many old miniatures' *(ibid.).* The pipe-and-tabor was popular in sixteenth- and seventeenth-century Europe as a one-person dance band *(ibid.)* in this period of Spanish colonization and Roman Catholic evangelization in South America, including highland Ecuador.

The account also suggests that the harp was used in the Corpus processional context, something we have already observed in nineteenth-century Valencia, in Spain, a tradition which may date back to the sixteenth century. A *mayordomo,* or steward, still bears the financial burden for the festivities of Corpus and its Octave.

The Peruvian side of the Marañón River unquestionably sustained the harp-in-Corpus-procession performance practice in the nineteenth century. The Lima watercolorist, Pancho Fierro (1803-79), portrayed the harp in several paintings. One of them, *Danza de Pallas* — 'Dance of Quichua noblewomen' (1820), shows a *castillo* and other vertical adornments in the background and a half-hidden harp being carried on the shoulder of a masked processioner (Palma 1935:38). In Fierro's *Los diablos (Procesión de Corpus de San Marcelo. San Pedro, en Chorrillos)* —

'The Devils (Corpus Procession in San Marcelo. St. Peter, in Chorrillos [environs of Lima])' (n.d.), one of the three figures present is a masked harpist, carrying his harp on his shoulder (Holzmann 1966:8).

This brings us full circle to the twentieth century. Many other matters remain to be discussed. One is the history and modern dispersion of masked dances at Ecuadorian Andean Corpus Christi celebrations, including the character and range of variation in *danzantes'* garb in distinct regions: these subjects have been addressed by Moreno Andrade 1972, Béhague 1980, Carvalho-Neto 1964, Muratorio 1981 and Coba Andrade 1985. Another is the various types of *castillos* found in certain Andean highland locations at Christmas, San Juan, and San Pedro celebrations, as well as at Corpus and its Octave. The *multiple castillos* of the Octave in Pujilí, Cotopaxi Province — each constructed by an ethnic group from a distinct ecological niche, with foodstuff-types reflecting that particular niche — might well be a kind of echo of the individual guild-castles of Europe. Another topic is the comparative study of *pingullo* melodies for Corpus *danzantes* in different Ecuadorian Andean provinces, data for which appear in Moreno Andrade 1972. In this regard, the transcriptions of Corpus *danzante* melodies all the way from northern Carchi down to southern Cañar and Azuay Provinces suggest significant uniformities of melodic style — many heavily tetratonic ($\hat{5}$-$\hat{4}$-$\hat{3}$-$\hat{1}$--$\downarrow\hat{5}$), some extending the tonal gamut to upper $\hat{7}$, creating pentatony, and others using the arpeggio of the minor dominant.

Rather than focussing on these intra-Ecuadorian ethnographical and ethnomusicological issues, though, this discussion has stressed elements of Andean Ecuadorian Corpus festivities suggestive of intercultural contact, notably between European and native Andean traditions: castles/*castillos;* solstitial observance; harvest and processional; pipe-and-tabor and harp performance practices; elaborate costume and dance; and outdoor theatre, including the devil figure. The diachronic and synchronic canvas of Corpus is vast. I hope to have accurately reflected its festive character in a single Ecuadorian Andean parish and to have suggested other fruitful avenues of research.

References

BAINES, Anthony C.
>   1984   'Pipe and Tabor'. In *The New Grove Dictionary of Musical Instruments,* ed. S. Sadie. London: Macmillan; New York: Grove's Dictionaries. Vol. 3: 117-19.

BÉHAGUE, Gérard
>   1980   'South American Masked Dances: An Overview'. *The World of Music* 22/1: 23-38.

BLADES, James
>   1984   *Percussion Instruments and Their History,* rev. edn. London: Faber and Faber.

BOILÈS, Charles L.
>   1966   'The Pipe and Tabor in Mesoamerica'. *Inter-American Institute for Musical Research Yearbook* 2: 43-74.

CARRERAS Y CANDI, F., dir.
>   1931-33   *Folklore y Costumbres de España.* 3 vols. Barcelona: Casa Editorial Alberto Martín.

CARVALHO-NETO, Paulo de
>   1964   *Diccionario del Folklore Ecuatoriano.* Tratado del Folklore Ecuatoriano: 1. Quito: Editorial Casa de la Cultura Ecuatoriana.

CHANTRE Y HERRERA, P. José
>   1901   *Historia de la misión de los indios Mainas y de otras muchas naciones situadas en el Marañón español y en otros varios ríos que desembocan en él. . .* Madrid: Imprenta de A. Avrial.

COBA ANDRADE, Carlos Alberto
>   1985   'Danzas y Bailes en el Ecuador'. *Revista de Música Latinoamericana/Latin American Music Review* 6/2: 166-200.

The Columbia Encyclopedia, 3rd edn.
>   1963   'Rogation Days', p. 1821. New York: Columbia University Press.

HOLZMANN, Rodolfo, comp.
>   1966   *Panorama de la Música Tradicional del Perú'.* Lima: Casa Mozart.

MORENO ANDRADE, Segundo Luis
>   1972   *Historia de la Música en el Ecuador — Volumen Primero: Prehistoria.* Quito: Editorial Casa de la Cultura Ecuatoriana.

MURATORIO, Ricardo
1981 'Corpus Christi Dance Costumes of Ecuador'. *American Craft* 41/1: 8-13.
MYERS, Helen
1980 'Trinidad and Tobago'. In *The New Grove Dictionary of Music and Musicians,* ed. S. Sadie. London: Macmillan. Vol.19: 147-50.
NELSON, Alan H.
1974 *The Medieval English Stage: Corpus Christi Pageants and Plays.* Chicago: The University of Chicago Press.
PALLEN, Conde B., & John J. Wynne, comps. & eds.
1929 *The New Catholic Dictionary.* New York: The Universal Knowledge Foundation.
PALMA, Angélica
1935 *Pancho Fierro: Acuarelista Limeño.* Lima: Sanmarti y Cia., S.A.
RAMÓN Y RIVERA, Luis Felipe
1969 *La Música Folklórica de Venezuela.* Caracas: Monte Avila Editores.
SCHECHTER, John M.
1979 'The Inca *cantar histórico*: A Lexico-Historical Elaboration on Two Cultural Themes'. *Ethnomusicology* 23: 191-204.
1987 Film review. *El Diablo de Cumaná* [1984], one of three films in a series, 'Inhabitants of the Land of Grace', by John Dickinson. *American Anthropologist* 89: 529-30.
1992 *The Indispensable Harp: Historical Development, Modern Roles, Configurations, and Performance Practices in Ecuador and Latin America.* Kent, Ohio, and London: Kent State University Press.
SORIANO FUERTES, Mariano
1855-59 *Historia de la Música Española desde la Venida de los Fenicios Hasta el Año de 1850.* 4 vols. Madrid: Vol. 1, 1855; Vol. 2, 1856; Vol. 3, 1856; Vol. 4, 1859.

Discography

1986 *John Schechter/Ecuador-Quechua Collection.* Library of Congress, Archive of Folk Culture, no. AFS 24,124-24,203.

Cultural Interaction through Music in Tamilnadu

S. Venkatraman

The three most important musical systems of Tamilnadu are Karnatic, folk and popular music, which includes film music and other styles of light music such as devotional music and non-film pop music.

Karnatic music is one of the two major branches of Indian classical music, the other being Hindustani music. Karnatic music has long been associated with the Brahmins, who were the traditional educated priestly class (Béteille 1965; Srinivas 1985).[1] Traditionally, Karnatic music has been associated with the temples, the *bhakti* cult (the tradition of mystical devotion to God) and the royal courts.

Folk music, including tribal music, has a hoary tradition, deeply rooted in the ancient culture and civilization of the people of the South. Karnatic music has traditionally drawn many of its elements from folk music. Generally speaking, non-Brahmins who live in the rural areas of Tamilnadu practise or enjoy folk music.

While Karnatic music has borrowed many of its raw materials from folk music, there has been little borrowing in the opposite direction. Karnatic music slowly began to detach itself from folk music during the latter half of the nineteenth century. This process can be attributed mainly to certain drastic social changes which took place at that time. As Brahmins lost their strong positions in the social hierarchy and migrated to urban centres, the gap between these two musical systems increased (Béteille 1965; Singer 1959).

Such was the situation in the 1930s, when the musical world in

Tamilnadu saw the coming of what is now called film music. Film music in the present discussion mainly includes the songs, not the background score. Almost all Indian films have songs and dance sequences, which are very popular with audiences. Film music draws from Western classical and pop music as well as Indian classical and folk music.

Interaction between Popular Music Systems and Sociocultural Fields

The present-day music scenario of Tamilnadu presents a complex mosaic of these three musical systems. Popular music has the advantage of appealing to both urban and rural audiences, and film music has added a third dimension to the traditional interaction between Karnatic and folk music. This kind of interaction, which is currently taking place, can be diagrammed as follows (Figure 1):

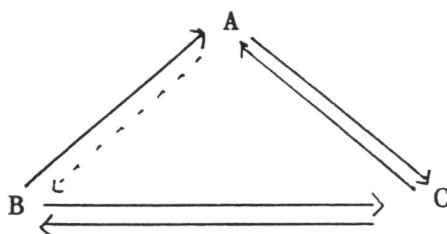

Figure 1: Interaction between the Musics of Tamilnadu
A represents Karnatic music, B represents folk music, and C represents popular music. The extent to which these interactions take place varies.

Interaction Between Classical and Folk Forms: the Classical System Borrowing from the Folk System

The Karnatic style of music has developed into its present form through centuries of refinement. Great masters, like Tyagaraja (1767-1847), Muthuswami Dikshitar (1775-1835) and Shyama Sastri (1762-1827), endowed it with fame and glory. From the time of the ancient Tamil literary work *Tholkappiyam*[2] onwards, classical music borrowed many of its raw materials from folk music. For instance, many of the Karnatic ragas owe their origins to folk music, the links being shown in the table on the adjacent page:

Karnatic ragas	Folk melodies
1. Nadanamakkriya	Ananda Kalippu
2. Ananda Bhairavi	Ananda Kalippu
3. Punnagavarali	Odam
4. Cenjuritti	Temmangu, Cindu
5. Kurunji	Gowri Kalyanam
6. Nilambari	Thalattu

Table 1: Karnatic ragas derived from Folk Melodies

Kavadicindu is another folk form which has been freely drawn upon by Karnatic musicians. It is one of several forms of the *cindu* type of folk music; others include *nondi cindu* and *vazhi nadai cindu*.

Modern Tamil Theatre and Classical Music

Modern Tamil theatre gave considerable prominence to music. Only those who could sing well were selected and trained as actors. With the disappearance of temple and royal patronage of the traditional theatre, modern theatre formed *sabhas* and *boys' companies* to support it. There were several such sabhas, among them Suganavilasa Sabha, which trained and created a cadre of professionals. Two such legendary personalities are S.G. Kitappa and K.B. Sundarambal. Tamil theatre also provided the base for recruitment of artistes for Tamil cinema.

Tamil Cinema and Classical Music

The first Tamil talkie, *Kalidas,* was released in 1931. It had a tremendous reception and with it the roots of the Tamil film industry were firmly established. Many leading classical musicians, such as G.N. Balasubramaniam, V.V. Sadagopan, M.S. Subbulakshmi, Papanasam Sivan, Dandapani Desikar and Musiri Subramania Iyer, were attracted to cinema. Several cinema studios sprang up in Madras. Film production proved to be a gold mine for those who ventured into it. As in Tamil theatre, cinema recruited only those artistes who sang in classical Karnatic style.

Musical scores of films produced during this period had a strong classical flavour. Most of the popular ragas of Karnatic music were successfully employed in these early film compositions, and all proved to be popular hits. Musical hits like *Nandanar*[3] (late 1930s) and *Haridass* (1944) became household names in Tamilnadu. *Haridass,* embellished with the music of veteran M.K. Tyagaraja Bhagavatar, ran for an all-time record of 133 weeks! Songs from this film were hummed through the length and breadth of Tamilnadu due to his golden voice and versatile singing. Many leading Karnatic musicians still participate in film-making as playback singers, music directors, actors, playback instrumentalists, etc. (see Table 2).

Performer	*Active as*
1. Balamuralikrishna	Actor, playback singer, composer
2. Late Sirkazhi Govindaraj	Actor, playback singer
3. Kunnakudi Vaidyanathan	Actor, composer, film producer
4. T.N. Seshagopalan	Actor, playback singer
5. T.V. Gopalakrishnan	Playback instrumentalist
6. Sulamangalam sisters	Composers, playback singers

Table 2: Musicians Active in Film-Making

Influence of Radio

In the late 1940s, the Radio of Sri Lanka (then known as Radio Ceylon) became very popular in Tamilnadu, allotting increased time for Tamil film music. Radio Ceylon started its commercial broadcasts with Tamil film songs, which began the popularization of these songs, now reaching almost every corner of Tamilnadu. All India Radio followed suit and later even outdid Radio Ceylon with its own commercial broadcasting.

Folk Music and Film Music

Even when classical music dominated the Tamil cinema, such artists as N.S. Krishnan attempted with some success to introduce folk music into Tamil cinema music. N.S. Krishnan was a very popular comedian, and it is to his credit that the folk art form *villuppattu* (bow songs)[4] was successfully introduced into film music and spread far and wide. Even Karnatic musicians engaged in film acting, such as Dandapani Desikar, sang some of the folk tunes in their films. Some of the *villuppattu*-based songs in the film *Nallathambi* were great hits, and ensured that folk music had come to stay in Tamil film music.

Borrowing from the Classical Form by the Folk Form

I have remarked that classical musicians always borrowed from folk music but not vice versa. However, after the advent of cinema and its increased use of music, there have been instances where folk musicians have borrowed from classical forms. For example, in the *villuppattu* performance of Subbu Arumugam and Kodandaraman, Karnatic ragas are introduced. One of Subbu Arumugam's compositions on the theme of agricultural development uses the raga *Nattai*. Tyagaraja's Pancharatna kriti 'Jagadananda' was set to music in this raga. And Kodandaraman, a *villuppattu* musician from the Kanyakumari district of Tamilnadu, uses such ragas as *Hindolam, Mohanam* and *Kalyani* in his compositions.

Film Music and Other Popular Music of Tamilnadu

Film music

While Karnatic ragas became popular in film music, folk music made a slow but sure entry. Over the years, film music became lighter in character, freely borrowing from Hindustani, Western and other styles. At present there is a resurgence of Karnatic ragas in film music. Through films, not only the ragas but several famous compositions of Karnatic music have become popular (for example, several of Tyagaraja's compositions have been used in films). There has also been a film devoted exclusively to the life and compositions of Tyagaraja. Another recent film hit, *Sankarabharanam,* includes several of Tyagaraja's compositions, even though the film is set against a modern background.

The secret of the popularity of film music seems to be its predilection for simplicity. It is light and flexible enough to absorb all other forms, be they classical, Western, folk or Hindustani.

Innovations in Film Music

Ilaiyaraja, the most popular contemporary composer of film music, is one of the few music directors to use Western classical music forms in Tamil film music. He is also attempting to fuse the various systems of music into a new synthesis which he has termed 'Music of Ilaiyaraja'.

Film music has become so popular in Tamilnadu that it is heard in places that do not yet have roads. According to a recent survey conducted by the Centre for Social Research in Madras, about 77% of all film viewers went to the movies only to listen to the musical scores, while 65% of the phonorecords sold in India in 1985 were of film music. The statistics relating to Tamilnadu are not available, but they are likely to favour film music. Tamilnadu now makes the largest number of movies per year, as illustrated in Table 3.

Year	Total Output	Tamil	Hindi
1951	219	26	100
1961	303	49	109
1971	433	73	120
1981	737	137	153
1984	833	148	165
1985	912	190	187

Table 3: Output of Feature Films in India from 1951 to 1985 (Source: *Mass Media in India,* 1986:184-5)

Borrowing from Film Music by Karnatic Music

Some of the film songs based on Karnatic raga styles have proved so popular that musicians commonly sing these songs during their classical concerts. For example, some of the songs of the modern Tamil poet Bharathiyar are invariably sung in Karnatic music concerts by popular demand. 'Chinnanchiru Kiliye Kanamma' is an illustration of this point. Most of these songs were originally sung in films by such famous Karnatic musicians as D.K. Pattammal and M.L. Vasanthakumari.

Another Karnatic musician who has drawn on film music is Kunnakkudi Vaidyanathan, who includes certain film songs in his classical music concerts. (He himself composed the scores of those films.)

Another aspect of Karnatic music's borrowing from the film music world is the use of interlude music between stanzas, which is the basic structure for film music compositions. Balamuralikrishna, the famous Karnatic musician, has used this technique in his rendering of compositions by Bhadrachala Ramadas, which are set to classical tunes using interlude music between stanzas.

Light Devotional Popular Music

New light devotional music recently began to borrow from classical as well as folk music through the medium of film music. Popular Karnatic musicians, film playback singers and non-professional singers flood the market with light devotional songs on records and pre-recorded cassettes. They have almost replaced the traditional rendering of temple music, such as the singing of *Tevaram* by Oduvars.[5] Light devotional recordings are played in urban temples such as in Madras, Madurai and Tiruchy. Famous singers include Sirkazhi Govindarajan, a classically trained musician who has also sung in films as a playback singer; the playback singer P.B. Srinivas; eminent classical exponent Balamurali-krishna; film playback singer T.M. Soundararajan; a non-professional singer, Veeramani; and film playback singer trained in Karnatic music, K.J. Jesudoss. Besides Hindu devotionals, these singers render Christian and Muslim devotional music using the same popular, film-music based format.

Conclusion

In Tamilnadu a threefold interaction is taking place between Karnatic, folk and popular music. The intensity of interaction between these systems is not uniform, however. Popular music has an edge over the other two forms, thanks to its film base and its consequent wider reach. In bringing about certain widespread changes in behaviour, it demon-strates its power and potential. It has conveyed Karnatic music to the remotest corners of Tamilnadu and has brought folk music to urban audiences. Film-based popular music has acted as a bridge between different systems of music and their different adherents within the state. It has made the classical form of music accessible to a wider section of the population – music which until recently was the exclusive preserve of the Brahmin community, especially those living in the urban centres.

Notes

1   The concept of *varna*, by which Hindu society was traditionally divided, had four orders: Brahmana (Brahmin, traditionally priest and scholar), Kshatriya (ruler and soldier), Vaishya (merchant) and Shudra (peasant, labourer and servant). The first three castes are

'twice-born', as the men from them are entitled to don the sacred thread at the Vedic rite of *Upanayana* while the Shudras are not. Tamil Brahmins are divided into Smarthas and Sri Vaishnavas, the former being followers of Shiva and the latter followers of Vishnu.

2   *Tholkappiyam*, by Tholkappiyar, is one of the oldest extant Tamil literary pieces.

3   The film *Nandanar* is based on the story of one of the Nayanmar saints. A nineteenth-century composer of Karnatic music, Gopala-krishna Bharathiar, used to perform *Harikatha*, a distinctive technique of storytelling using songs and dramatic exposition with musical accompaniment. He was the first to tell the story of Nandanar through this form by composing songs. A few of his compositions are used in the film, along with others written for it by the composer and singer Papanasam Sivam. The role of Nandanar is played in the film by another Karnatic musician, M.M. Dandapani Desikar.

4   The bow song or *villuppattu* tradition has its origin in two districts of Tamilnadu: Kanyakumari and Tirunelveli. This form derives its name from *vil*, the bow that is played by the lead singer. This bow is set up in front of the performing group, which consists of five to ten persons. Other important instruments used are the *udukkai* (hourglass drum) and the harmonium. In Tirunelveli district there is no harmonium, but musicians use a pair of small wooden blocks called *kattai* and a small cymbals called *jalra*. Nowadays some *villuppattu* musicians add instruments such as *kanjira* and *tabla*. *Villuppattu* is considered to be one of the oldest existing folk arts of Tamilnadu.

5   Oduvars are temple singers. They are Shaivaites (followers of Shiva) and sing the traditional Shaivaite hymns, the *Tevaram*.

References

ALAVANDAR, R.
  1981   *Tamizhar Thor Karuvigal.* Madras: International Institute of Tamil Studies.
BÉTEILLE, André
  1965   *Caste, Class and Power.* Berkeley & Los Angeles: University of California Press.
BLACKBURN, Stuart
  1987   'Performance of Paradigm: A Rhythm in a Tamil Oral Tradition'. In Peter J. Claus & Jawaharlal Hondso (eds), *Indian*

Folklore, Vol. 1, pp. 157-209. Mysore: Central Institute of Indian Languages.

BLACKBURN, Stuart & RAMANUJAM, A.K. (eds)
   1986   *Another Harmony: New Essays on the Folklore of India.* New Delhi: Oxford University Press.

DEIVAPICCHAI, S.
   1986   Tamil Cinemavil pattu *Ini,* 25-28. Madras.

DORSON, Richard M. (ed)
   1972   *Folklore and Folklife: An Introduction.* Chicago & London: University of Chicago Press.

GOMATHINAYAKAM, Ti Ci
   1979   *Tamil Villuppattukal.* Madras: Tamil Pathippagam.

JAGANNATHAN, Ki Va
   1958   *Malaiyaruvi.* Saraswathi Mahan Library Series No. 77. Tanjore: Saraswathi Mahal Library.

LAKSHMANA CHETTIAR, S.M.L.
   1980   *Folklore of Tamilnadu.* New Delhi: National.

LOURDU, S.D.
   1981   *Naattaar Valakkarriyal Aivukal.* Tirunelveli: Paryvel Pathippagam.

MUTHUSWAMY, N.
   1982   *Andru Puttiya Vandi.* Sivagangai: Annam Pvt. Ltd.

PERUMAL, A.N.
   1984   *Tamizhar Isai.* Madras: International Institute of Tamil Studies.

PERIYASAMI THOORAN, ma, pa (ed)
   1974   *Pan Araichiyum Adan Mudivugalin Thoguppum.* Madras: Tamil Isai Sangam.

RAMANATHAN, S.
   1969   'Ragas derived from Folk Music'. *Shanmukha* 9/3: 42-3. Bombay: Sri Shanmukhananda Fine Arts and Sangeetha Sabha.
   1969   *Divya Prapandha Pan Isai.* Madras: Kalaimagal Isai Katturi.
   1970   *Tevarappan Isai.* Madras: Isai Katturi.
   1972   *Gopalakrishna Bharathiyar Iyattriya Nandana Caritra Kirtanai.* Vol II: Madurai. Published by the author.

SAMBAMOORTHY, P.
   1970   *Great Composers: II Tyagaraja.* Madras: Indian Music Publishing House.

1980   *South Indian Music, Books I-IV.* Madras: Indian Music
        Publishing House.
1982   *History of Indian Music.* Madras: Indian Music Publishing
        House.
1985   *Great Composers, Book I.* Madras: Indian Music Publishing
        House.

SARASWATHI, V.
1982   *Nattuppura Padalgal: Samūga Oppaiyvu.* Madurai: Madurai
        Kamraj University.

SINGER, Milton
1959   'The Great Tradition in a Metropolitan Centre: Madras'. In
        Milton Singer (ed), *Traditional India: Structure and Change.*
        Philadelphia: American Folklore Society, pp. 141-82.

SRINIVAS, M.N.
1972   *Social Change in Modern India.* New Delhi: Orient
        Longmann.
1985   *Castes In Modern India and Other Essays.* Bombay: Media
        Promoters and Publishers Pvt. Ltd.

SUBBU, Arumugam
1979   *Nellin Kathai: Villuppattu.* Madras: Pooravi Pathippagam.

THURSTON, Edgar
1909   *Castes and Tribes of South India.* Government Press.

VANAMAMALAI, Na (ed)
1971   *Kăthavarăyan Kathai Pādal.* Madurai: Madurai Palkalai-
        kazhagam.
1980   *Pazhankadaiglum Pazhamozhigalum.* Madras: New Century
        Book House.

Discography

Dr. M. Balamuralikrishna

    n.d.   *Sree Bhadrachala Ramadas Keerthanams* (vocal). EMI-HMV HTCS 03B-11170.

    n.d.   *Sri Vinayakar Thuthiyamudu.* SANGEETHA, 4 ECDB-7217.

Illaiyaraja

    n.d.   *How To Name It?* ECHO E-MCR-5017.

M.S. Subbulakshmi (vocal)

    n.d.   *Popular Melodies of M.S. Subbulakshmi.* EALP 1374.

Kunnakkudi Vaidhyanathan (violin)

    1974   Columbia-EMI 8/33 ESX 6085.

M.L. Vasanthakumari

    1972   *Thiruppavai* (vocal). Columbia-EMI 33 ESX 6053/6054.

    1983   *Just for You.* EMI ECSD 40512.

Religion, Media and Shows:
The Effect of Intercultural Contacts on
Papua New Guinean Musicians

Don Niles

Intercultural contact is not a new phenomenon in Papua New Guinea or other parts of the Pacific. Internal contact occurred through social, economic and political activities, and especially through trade with specific trading partners and neighbouring and quite distant groups.

Following European colonization in the late nineteenth century, PNG groups were exposed to music and dance very far removed from these traditional realms of interaction. New contacts took place with more distant PNG societies, other Pacific Islanders, and Western societies. This paper focusses not on traditional relationships but on contacts following colonization.

Three main forces — religion, media, and cultural shows — have been responsible for introducing new music, dance and performance contexts (see Webb and Niles 1987 for a chronology of many important events discussed here). Another early motivator of contact was plantation work. Papua New Guineans from many different areas were brought together for about two years' contract work. Many returned to their villages to introduce new songs and dances they had learned. As possibilities of employment increased, plantation labour became less attractive, and contact through music and dance greatly diminished in importance.

Religion

From 1872 missionaries worked vigorously to convert the population to Christianity. The London Missionary Society (now the United Church), Methodists, Catholics, Lutherans and Anglicans all began work in PNG before the end of the nineteenth century. The first hymn books with texts in local languages sung to European melodies appeared during this time. Such hymns are still the main Christian music in many areas. Catholics also introduced the singing of Gregorian chant in Latin and, after Vatican II, in local languages and Tok Pisin (New Guinea Pidgin). Recent fundamentalist missions have emphasized the importance of singing their hymns in English, and thus numerous groups performing in a barbershop quartet or country-and-western style have become popular.

Missions responded in different ways to the traditional music and dance they found. The London Missionary Society (LMS) reacted harshly along the coast of present-day Central Province, prohibiting traditional music and dance there. Instead, a Polynesian form now known as *peroveta anedia* (Motu, 'prophet songs') was introduced. *Peroveta* originated in the *himene* singing style introduced by LMS missionaries in Tahiti and the Cook Islands in the mid-nineteenth century. Oral tradition credits its introduction to Ruatoka (b. 1846), an LMS missionary from Rarotonga who, arriving with the first wave of missionaries, worked in Central Province from 1872 until his death in 1903 (see Crocombe 1982). *Peroveta* texts are based on Biblical themes and events. Some are still sung in Rarotongan and other Polynesian languages; others have been composed in PNG languages. Musically this style is distinctive because of the use of two polyphonic parts (one for men, one for women), moving in Western harmony. 'Malokihi Neganai' is one such song. It is an adaptation of an event in Acts (16:25-28), where Paul and Silas are praying and singing in prison and an earthquake opens the prison doors and unfastens their chains.[1]

Songs with secular texts in the same musical style are called *ute,* a familiar Eastern Polynesian word for song. In contrast to *peroveta, ute* employ secular texts and are often accompanied by guitars and ukuleles. *Ute* and *peroveta* continue to be important contemporary forms of expression in parts of Central, Gulf, and Milne Bay Provinces.

Polyphonic singing based on Western concepts of harmony also proved to be important in the development of Central Province string-bands – groups consisting of singers accompanied by guitars, ukuleles and, occasionally, drums. Many Central stringband song texts refer to the aftermath of a failed relationship; usually the singer laments the loss of a lover. But he can also offer freedom to his ex-girlfriend.[2]

In contrast to the practice of introducing new music to accompany new religious concepts, Lutherans and Anglicans often set Christian texts to traditional melodies. Lutheran hymn books contain these texts and the name of the traditional songs to which they should be sung (mostly deriving from the areas of initial proselytisation); for examples see *Gedaged* (Anon. 1975), *Kate* (Anon. 1973), and *Yabim* (Anon. 1969). Thus coastal languages and music with Christian texts were introduced to the Highlands, regardless of the fact that the languages and musical styles in the two areas were unrelated. These processes began as a way of making Christian principles more meaningful through integration into traditional forms. However the translations of song texts could not keep up with the zeal to spread Christianity.

Now that some missions have been established for many years, some progress has been made in adapting traditional songs as hymns. This practice is often dependent upon the efforts of the individual missionary involved; it does not represent the doctrine of any specific church. Catholics have also begun this practice, as in the following example from Mendi in Southern Highlands Province. Here the monophonic melody and vocal timbre are derived from traditional music, while the text reflects Christian principles:

> *Ake loa Yekin Anda ipuluma?*
> *Minamina Yeki anga lakata.*
> *Yeki nere nina ap.*
> *Jisas nere nina ame.*
> *Jisas nere nina an.*
> *Maria nere nina ama.*
> *Ake loa Yekin anda ipuluma?*
> *Minamina Yeki anga Lakata.*

(Mendi congregation)[3]

In missions which follow this practice, Papua New Guineans themselves have been encouraged to compose such hymns. This is the driving force behind work by ethnomusicologists at the Summer Institute of Linguistics, a group devoted to learning local languages for the purpose of translating the Bible. They attempt to analyze traditional music with the goal of producing music primers so that people from the areas concerned can learn to read and write traditional music in staff notation (e.g. Chenoweth 1980 and 1984).

Media

The first radio broadcast in PNG took place in 1953 (see Mackay 1976). It took a few decades for radio to develop and spread, but it is now the primary means by which Papua New Guineans are exposed to music from different areas of the country, the Pacific and the West. Besides radio broadcasts of traditional PNG music, primary interest focusses on programs presenting old Viking recordings of Pacific Islands pop and Western popular music. Muzak, country-and-western, rock and reggae are all prominent on radio in PNG today. All of the Western popular music is in English, with most bands originating from the USA, Australia or England. Besides the Polynesian hymns introduced by missionaries, these are the most important influences on the development of PNG popular music.

The first known recordings of PNG stringbands date from the early 1950s (Webb and Niles 1987:55), although Tok Pisin songs were being composed before World War I (Laycock 1977), and it is likely that there were some stringbands before 1945. What is certain is that the guitars and ukuleles introduced by servicemen during World War II proliferated after this time.

Early stringband songs followed simple Western models and used three basic chords — tonic, dominant and subdominant — which still predominate in stringband music. The music is played at a village level, often serving as a young people's substitute for the traditional music that would normally accompany small social functions.

Following the legalization of drinking for Papua New Guineans in 1962, power bands or electric bands (i.e. bands using electrified instruments) became popular in urban, outdoor drinking areas in hotels. Consisting initially of mixed-race males who performed imitations of overseas bands (cover versions), this music was called 'kopikat'. Later, as more Papua New Guineans could afford the equipment and such bands became more popular, original songs were composed in local languages and were sometimes influenced by overseas hits. For example, the melody of the song 'Vero' by Gaba Kaluks is similar to a popular Elvis Presley song, 'You Were Always on My Mind' (NBC B 226, B4).

While many bands today are heavily influenced by overseas rock, some have imitated popular Samoan, Tahitian or Fijian performers such as the Five Stars, Mariterangi or Sakiusa. Others have sought ideas from traditional PNG music. Although employing electric guitars and a drum set, the following example by the Double Vision Band resembles traditional Tolai music in melodic contour and energy level of the performance, with a text about an affair a man had with a married woman and the angry relatives waiting to attack him after the affair was discovered.

1. *Mur mur tinorom tara wawina Wairiki*
    Joe pa uga nuknuk likun
2. *Uga mur ra taulai*
    na wawina Wairiki
    Joe uga mur ram vinirua

Chorus:
    Matuagu tara marum
    tu tu tur para lime
    ra tarai
    tanomo ian a taulai
3. *Uga virua marmarum*
    kan ra wawina Wairiki
    Joe uga ti lia ra niruva

('Joe', Double Vision, Pacific Gold PAC-71, B1)[4]

Although radio played an important part in the dissemination of recordings of PNG popular music, a large cassette industry developed in PNG following independence in 1975. The government-run National Broadcasting Commission has been responsible for issuing many PNG popular music cassettes since 1977. In the past eight years a number of independent commercial studios have begun successfully to compete with NBC.

Today the market is dominated by two long-established Chinese families who formed independent commercial companies. Chin-H-Meen has been issuing recordings since 1980, while Pacific Gold began in 1983. The former was established by a Chinese businessman who played in a band in the 1970s. Pacific Gold is run by another Chinese musician who has trained in sound engineering overseas so as to raise the standards of commercial recordings in the country. Competitiveness between the two companies increased in 1987 when Chin-H-Meen opened a studio in Rabaul, where Pacific Gold's 24-track studio is located. Chin-H-Meen maintains this studio as well as its original studio in Port Moresby. Smaller studios also exist. Well over 1200 cassettes of PNG music have been issued by local companies in the last ten years.

Shows

Cultural shows for foreign audiences are mainly given on such occasions as Festivals of Pacific Arts, where groups perform from throughout the Pacific. The largest intercultural event ever mounted in PNG was the Third South Pacific Festival of Arts in 1980. Groups from every province in PNG as well as from overseas were represented. While many Papua New Guineans were particularly fond of the Cook Islands and Tahiti performers, a common impression in evaluating the different groups was a reaffirmation of PNG cultural superiority. PNG music and dance traditions appeared to be intact compared to many of the other performances heard from Polynesia in particular, but also from Micronesia and parts of Melanesia. While there was a certain familiarity with the vocal music performed by many of the Polynesian contingents, it was readily recognized as being appropriate music for church, but not for a performance stressing ancestral traditions. Within PNG, groups from many different parts of the country have performed at regional shows since the 1950s, when the first Highlands Show was mounted.

Conclusions

Religion, media, and shows have been dominant forces in cultural interaction within PNG. They do not, however, account for all the newly-introduced forms in contemporary PNG music. There are also marching bands associated with the police, bagpipes and drums associated with the army and corrective institution services, and some Western orchestral and choir performances. These forms are restricted to small, specific groups and are not living forms to the extent that Papua New Guineans are contributing much to the repertoire.

Performances of traditional music and dance commonly accompany the opening of new churches, roads, schools and hospitals. For example, I recently documented a Tolai dance being performed in Port Moresby in honour of a softball team that won its regional division championship. However, traditional music has always been used to celebrate events or places of special social importance.

One of the difficulties facing PNG as a nation is finding a way to enable the great diversity of cultural activities to continue while developing a sense of national unity. It is unlikely that traditional music will provide such an avenue as it is tightly bound to the groups that produce it. However, it binds disparate groups together simply by continuing ancestral traditions. Perhaps stringband music has the greatest potential to become the national music, but few groups attain nationwide popularity or explore the possibilities of the most widely-understood language, Tok Pisin. At present, then, music plays a minor role in developing a national feeling of unity.

Notes

1   The text of the song is as follows:
   Malokini neganai Paulo mai Sila e etere era e
   Ie ie ae
   Malokini neganai Paulo mai Sila e etere era e
   E au e ae he
   Vada e gurigurimu ane e abimu e Dirava e hanamolaia e
        ikoudia taudia e kamonai
   Tanobada e laga dagu dibura ruma badina vada e
   heudeheude iduaradia idoidiai vada e kehoa haraga

   Mitia mitia te Paulo vada e lolomu
   Mai e gaobadana e ini e gwau toma
   'Oi sibomu asio hadikamu madi be'.

   ['But about midnight Paul and Silas were praying and singing hymns of praise to God, and the prisoners were listening to them; and suddenly there came a great earthquake, so that the foundations of the prison house were shaken; and immediately all the doors were opened, and everyone's chains were unfastened. And when the jailer had been roused out of sleep and had seen the prison doors opened, he drew his sword and was about to kill himself, supposing that the prisoners had escaped. But Paul cried out with a loud voice, saying, "Do yourself no harm, for we are all here!"']

   ('Malokihi Neganai', Kilakila United Church, NBC B8, A1)
2   For example:
   Ena be mai emu lau gabuna una na madi namo
   Kekeni e una na madi namo

Bema oi mai lalohadai dibamu be do boma loumai
Kekeni e una na madi namo

Emu nihi ai basio lalogu badina vada atai manuna
Kekeni e una na madi namo.

('Madi namo', Bamogu Union Band from Babaga village, NBC KS 2, B2)

3 'Why do we come to God's house?
To talk to God.
Jesus, you are my brother
   [man speaking to someone of same sex]
Jesus, you are my brother
   [woman speaking to someone of opposite sex]
Mary, you are my mother.
Why do we come to God's house?
To talk to God.'

4 1. You made friends with
         the woman from Wairiki
         Joe, you didn't think first
   2. You made friends with
         the married woman from Wairiki
         Joe, you made trouble for yourself
       Chorus:
         They are waiting at night
         to fight my uncle,
         the relatives of this married woman.
   3. You made trouble for yourself at night
         When you became friends with this Wairiki woman
         Joe, you made trouble for yourself.

References

ANONYMOUS
    1969   *Leng Ngagoling.* Madang: Kristen Pres.
    1973   *Lutheran Gae Buk.* Madang: Kristen Pres.
    1975   *Kanam Buk.* Madang: Kristen Pres.
CHENOWETH, Vida
    1980   *Music for the Eastern Highlands: A Written Theory for an Oral Tradition.* Ukarumpa: Summer Institute of Linguistics.

1984   *A Music Primer for the North Solomons Province.* Ukarumpa: Summer Institute of Linguistics.

CROCOMBE, Marjorie Tuainekore

1982   'Ruatoka: A Cook Islander in Papuan History'. In *Polynesian Missions in Melanesia,* pp. 55-78. Suva: Institute of Pacific Studies.

LAYCOCK, Donald C.

1977   'Creative Writing in New Guinea Pidgin'. In Stephen A. Wurm, ed., *New Guinea Area Languages and Language Study,* Vol. 3: Language, Culture, Society, and the Modern World, pp. 609-38. Pacific Linguistics, C40. Canberra: Australian National University.

MACKAY, Ian K.

1976   *Broadcasting in Papua New Guinea.* Melbourne: Melbourne University Press.

WEBB, Michael & Don Niles

1987   'Periods in Papua New Guinea Music History'. *Bikmaus* 7/1 (March): 50-62.

Discography

National Broadcasting Commission

B 8   *Peroveta Anedia.* 1978. Kilakila United Church. One cassette.

B 226   *Gaba Kaluks.* [1985]. Gaba Kaluks. One cassette.

KS 2   *Soldier Boy.* [1984]. Bamogu Union. One cassette. Pacific Gold

Pacific Gold

PAC-71   *Eye Giris.* [1985]. Double Vision. One cassette. South Pacific Commission

South Pacific Commission

PR 1874   *Native Songs.* [1956?]. Sogeri School Choir. One 25 cm, 78 rpm disc.

See also:

NILES, Don

1987   *Commercial Recordings of Papua New Guinea Music: 1986 Supplement.* Boroko: Institute of Papua New Guinea Studies.

WEBB, Michael & Don Niles

1986   *Riwain! Papua New Guinea Pop Songs.* IPNGS 007. With 2 cassettes. Goroka and Boroko: Goroka Teachers College and Institute of Papua New Guinea Studies.

Urban Fijian Musical Attitudes and Ideals: Has Intercultural Contact Through Music and Dance Changed them?

Chris Saumaiwai

Audiences at the 1988 South Pacific Festival of Arts in Townsville had the opportunity to see performances by the many divergent cultures which co-exist in Fiji. Indigenous Fijians come within the boundaries of both Melanesia and Polynesia. Some areas are more Melanesian (as in Western Viti Levu), others more Polynesian (as in the Lau group in the eastern part of Fiji). Non-indigenous groups include Indians, Chinese, Rotumans, Europeans (Caucasians), Banabans, Tongans, Solomon Islanders and other Pacific Islanders. This paper covers musical events of the last three decades and how they have influenced urban ethnic Fijian musical attitudes and ideals.

The 1960s

Outlets for traditional music in the urban areas were basically the Hibiscus Festival, held annually in Suva, and the Methodist Church Conference. In this period the performances at these events included *mekes* (dances) such as *seasea,* a women's standing dance; *meke moto,* a men's spear dance; *meke wau,* a men's club (war) dance; and *vakamalolo,* a sitting dance — some *vakamalolo* are performed by men and some by women.

The main religions were Methodist (about 80% of Fijians) and Catholic. In the Methodist church, choirs participated enthusiastically in competitions both at circuit level and annual national conference level. It was the goal of many choir directors to learn tonic sol-fa: the majority of the anthems written in tonic sol-fa came from England. At this time only a few Fijians were able to write music in tonic sol-fa and even fewer could read staff notation. Because of its immediate results in its application to choral music, tonic sol-fa became the popular form of written music. However, few entire choirs could read this notation. In addition to Methodist hymns and anthems, two genres evolved; *same* (psalm) and *taro* (catechism). *Same* is based on a Biblical theme, story or idea and is structured similarly to traditional chants. The first voice (*laga*) is joined midway through the first line by the second voice (*tagi*). The voices proceed in counterpoint and are joined by the drone (*druku*), which is sung by the rest of the group. *Taro* is similar to the *same* except that the question is spoken and is answered by the *druku*. In the Catholic church, Gregorian chant was used, but to the best of my knowledge such genres as *same* and *taro* did not evolve.

In this period schools catered basically to single ethnic groups. In Fijian schools children sang songs with themes such as 'My school' or 'Fiji, my land'. Because traditional *mekes* are regarded as the property of specific composers, this was a difficult and expensive avenue to pursue in schools. Therefore teachers often composed their own *mekes,* employing the traditional structure of the *meke* but using Western harmonies. One school did bring in a traditional composer to teach a *meke,* but the attempt ended in failure as the composer declared that the students were not capable of singing the traditional harmony and could not grasp the essential dance movements. Several *meke* groups catering for the tourist industry during this period modelled themselves after the Fijian group then performing at the Polynesian Cultural Center in Hawaii and presented *mekes* with 'Hollywood' smiles.

The transistor radio became popular in this period. With only one radio station, the musical materials presented by Broadcasting House were bound to shape musical attitudes. Jim Reeves and guitarist Peter Posa were popular. Young people liked the Beatles, and parents of toddlers encouraged them to 'do the twist'. 'String bands', consisting of several acoustic guitars and ukuleles and occasionally a mandolin, sprang up, entertaining at dances as well as at informal gatherings of young men around the *tanoa* (the kava bowl) who gathered to sing love songs and songs about getting drunk. In this decade there was very little interaction between ethnic groups in urban areas and scant cultural exchange — save for an occasional mixed concert.

The 1970s

Fiji gained independence in October 1970. During the decade major changes took place, with the government urging moves toward a multi-racial society, for example by urging school rolls to be made multi-racial. Government and mission schools soon had students of different races on their rolls, although committee-run schools were slower to change. Population densities and distribution in urban areas ensured that change occurred more quickly in urban than in rural areas.

In 1972 the first South Pacific Festival of Arts was held in Suva. This was a cultural extravaganza of a dimension never before seen in the Pacific. Performances took place in theatres, auditoriums, schools, sports grounds, parks and city streets. People brought songs, dances, drama, arts and crafts from more than fifteen Pacific nations. Although the emphasis was on traditional performance and skills, the Festival also presented the modern and avant-garde. Fijian audiences enjoyed Fijian and Tongan presentations and admired Australian Aboriginal performances, and the performance by the Cook Islands contingent was also very popular. The final report of the 1972 SPFA records about 2000 Fijian performers with 1000 of them coming from the outer islands. Nearly all provinces in Fiji were represented. Most types of *meke* were represented, as well as *lali* (large slit gong) beats, games, lullabies, and a rare demonstration of the Fijian nose-flute (*dulali*).

Following the first SPFA, Manoa Rasigatale was trained in theatre production in Australia and subsequently established the Dance Theatre of Fiji. The performances presented by this group married with drama traditional materials which were thoroughly researched; permission was sought for the use of *meke* materials. The Director reduced long *mekes* to short lively vignettes while retaining their flavour. Men of the troupe grasped the essence of traditional dance movements but the women found some difficulty in understanding the subtleties of measured (but not rigid) movements. The Fiji Visitors' Bureau has frequently used the Dance Theatre of Fiji to present a brief overview of a number of Fijian musical genres and a fast-moving piece of theatre to attract holiday-makers to Fiji.

In 1972-73 the Education Department introduced an in-training course for music teachers at junior secondary level. Tutors gave instruction in music pedagogy, Fijian music, Indian music and Western music fundamentals. This was the first time such a course had been available in Fiji. While some Fijian teachers were receptive to learning about Indian music, others were not. There was an equally mixed reaction by Indian teachers to Fijian music. Because of logistics and economic restraints, subsequent music courses became part of a broader scheme to train teachers to specialise in a combined music, art and physical education course.

In 1973 the Pacific Conference of Churches organised a Pacific Musicians' Practicum. Thirty participants from eighteen Pacific nations gathered for the intensive eighteen-day programme which offered a free choice of training in staff notation, tonic sol-fa or church music. Each participant either composed or learned to transcribe one or more musical works which were then taught to the rest of the group and performed.

The second South Pacific Festival of Arts was held in Rotorua, New Zealand, in 1976. In contrast to the 1972 SPFA many Fijian presentations were newly composed and carried the theme 'We are very happy that our group was chosen to participate in the SPFA in Rotorua'. When I sought permission to attend rehearsals of an older *meke,* a senior Fijian member of the organising committee said: 'What do you want to attend that for? It's only an old *meke'.* The 1970s saw a major choral workshop where choir directors learned about choral dynamics and added new dimensions to choral skills. In this decade, the Fiji Composers and Performers Association was formed to look after the rights and interests of Fijian musicians, including composers' copyright. This helped composers to understand their own rights and those of the composers whose songs they translated. The Hibiscus Festival continued to be held annually, but not always with the enthusiasm of previous years. Many other urban centres held similar events on a smaller scale. A highlight of the school year was the annual Secondary Schools Music Festival. Made up of a massed choir and items from individual schools, it was held in conjunction with the Secondary Schools Drama Competition.

The 1980s

By the 1980s the young generation of Fijians had grown up without knowledge and experience gained under the more traditional lines of Fijian administration, and this has had a major effect on all aspects of society. The whole system of traditional authority and influence has gone through major changes in the last two decades which have affected village and musical activities that were organised through traditional systems. This has also led to a further weakening of the system in urban areas.

In 1982-83, there were several signs of a cultural renaissance. The visit of Queen Elizabeth II to the chiefly island of Bau in October 1982 provided an occasion for the performance of some of the highest ceremonies and the presentation of some of the most outstanding *mekes* in the nation. Chiefs from all over Fiji were present wearing ceremonial dress of a standard never seen before. In the morning, ceremonies of welcome included the *meke ni yaqona* — the highest form of the *yaqona* or kava ceremony, performed by men of Bau *tikina* (district). After lunch the Queen visited the church and heard a large choir sing a work by Handel, after which four *mekes* were performed — a *Vakara* (war dance) from Nakorotubu, Ra Province; *Lakalaka* (Tongan dance) from Lakeba, Lau; a *Meke Wesi* (spear dance) from Vaturova, Cakaudrove; and a *Meke Wesi* from Navatu, Cakaudrove.

In 1983 the University of the South Pacific's Extension Services sponsored a workshop on Fijian costumes in Suva. Women from Suva and selected students were invited to attend, and resource leaders came from Cakaudrove and Lau provinces. The workshop concluded with a display of chiefly costumes from these areas. Six weeks later, the people of Cakaudrove Province held the Tagimoucia Festival in Suva. One of the festival's aims, apart from fundraising, was a revival of *mekes* in the province. Each district had a stall at the two-day festival and presented a collection of funds and a *meke*. A new *seasea* (women's dance) was presented, composed by a woman from Cakaudrove living in Suva; it was unusual in that the movements were partly those of a men's war dance. The large majority of the *mekes* presented were *vakamalolos* (sitting dances). A number of *meke* genres for which the province is noted were absent.

Broadcasting has had a great deal to do with the musical tastes of the nation. The largest proportion of broadcasting time goes to pop music, country and western, and reggae. The Fiji Broadcasting Commission is a statutory body which broadcasts nationwide; its three main streams of programmes are in English, Fijian and Hindi. Most listeners to this station in urban areas are over the age of thirty. Ethnic groups tend to listen to programmes in their first language. However, request programmes in English attract a good response from Fijians and part-

Europeans in particular and command a large percentage of air time. Traditional Fijian music can be heard from time to time as a part of other programmes.

In 1985 a second radio station came on the air. Privately-owned FM 96 served the Suva area initially and later expanded to cover Lautoka (Fiji's second-largest city) and hotels on the western side of Viti Levu. Popular with listeners under the age of thirty, it carries predominantly pop music. Top 40 broadcasts from the USA stimulate a great deal of interest and discussion. Request programmes get responses mostly from Fijian and part-European listeners and a few Indian listeners. Fijian and Hindi popular music is also broadcast on this single stream station. Listeners tend not to switch off the radio when music of another ethnic group is played.

For the last few years, the national radio station has organised a 'talent quest' type of programme attracting contestants aged between 8 and 60, with the majority in the 15-22 age bracket. Weekly heats are run over a period of several months each year, with six to nine contestants in each heat. Audiences are enthusiastic, both in the theatre and at home. Materials most frequently chosen are by the contestant's favourite artist in the area of pop, reggae, or country and western. Artists most frequently imitated are Whitney Houston, Jennifer Rush, Miami Sound Machine, UB40, Lionel Ritchie, Billy Ocean and Michael Jackson.

Bands using electronic equipment increased in number in the 1970s. Although the interest continues, the number of bands has declined in recent years because of lack of opportunity and financial constraints. Another deterrent has been the foreign pirating of local cassette tapes. In the 1980s a number of youth groups — particularly Chinese, Rotuman, and, to a lesser extent, Indian — formed performance groups.

The growing interest in Fijian costumes in the 1980s was not paralleled in traditional Fijian musical performance. In urban areas *mekes* are still performed, but despite impressive costuming, they often lack the finer details of traditional *meke* movements, and most modern *meke* texts tend to lack the depth of meaning found in earlier *mekes*.

Many traditional musical genres play no part in urban life, and many Fijian children have never heard Fijian lullabies or played Fijian games. Exposure to traditional Fijian music is certainly less available to the urban Fijian than is exposure to materials presented by the media. Although other ethnic groups have not significantly influenced Fijian music, the 1972 South Pacific Festival of Arts and a steady diet of Western culture through the media have markedly influenced urban Fijian musical attitudes and ideals in the period from 1960 to the present.

References

SAUMAIWAI, Chris Thompson
1980   'Melanesia: 2. Fiji'. In *The New Grove Dictionary of Music and Musicians,* ed. Stanley Sadie. London: Macmillan. Vol. 12: 82-5.

SOUTH PACIFIC FESTIVAL OF ARTS
1972   *Final Report of the Organising Committee,* South Pacific Festival of Arts, 6-20 May 1972. Suva: Ministry of Labour.

THOMPSON, Chris
1971   'Fijian Music and Dance'. *Transactions and Proceedings of the Fiji Society for the Years 1966 and 1967* 11: 14-21. Suva.

Cultural Contact with the West: The Development of Theories of Javanese Gamelan by Indonesian Theorists[1]

Sumarsam

Introduction and Historical Background

People's perspectives are shaped by the intellectual, sociopolitical and technological circumstances of a particular place and time. When cultural conditions change, people's world-views may change as well. A gamelan theory is written by an individual from his or her distinctive perspective. In order to understand fully such a theoretical text, one should view it in the social and institutional contexts in which it was written. Starting from this premise, I wish to examine gamelan theories that have been written by Indonesian theorists since about 1900.

Throughout much of its history, Indonesia has had contact with foreign civilizations. Such contact, with both religious and secular elements, has stimulated the development of Indonesian culture. But the presence of the Dutch in the archipelago brought about a different phase of Indonesian history. In the late seventeenth century, the Dutch began to intervene in the sociopolitical affairs of Indonesian states. By the middle of the nineteenth century these interventions had accumulated to such an extent that Indonesia was fully under the control of the Dutch colonial rulers whose land base was Java. By then, Central Java's traditional rulers had become puppets of the Dutch, so much so that almost all aspects of court life were under the supervision of the Dutch authority.

It was in the midst of this political crisis in the nineteenth century that a particular intellectual atmosphere was created. This intellectual climate arose as a consequence of the desire of a handful of Dutch people to know more about Indonesian people and their cultures. Dutch civil servants and intellectuals began to study Javanese arts and culture. The presence of a number of Dutch scholars, artists and art connoisseurs and their interactions with Javanese court poets (*pujangga*) and leading artists characterized the intellectual climate at the time. It was this atmosphere, I believe, that triggered and fostered the development of the writing of gamelan treatises.[2]

By the second half of the nineteenth century, Dutch scholars and art connoisseurs had intimate relationships with their Javanese colleagues. Javanese scholars and artists were paid for revealing their knowledge. For example, as part of his income, the last and supreme Surakarta court poet, Ronggawarsita, may have received cash regularly from his Dutch colleagues (Day 1980:184-6).

In the performing arts, tradition alludes to the important role of the European as patron of the arts. For instance, it is said that the rise of *Langendriyan* (a Javanese opera, a specialty of the Mangkunegaran court) was the result of direct involvement by Tuwan Godlieb (Soetrisno, p.c. 1979; Moergiyanto, p.c. 1987) or Godlieb Kiliaan (Partohudoyo 1921-40:4), either with regard to artistic conception or financial support, or both.[3] An early written source also indicates that Tuwan Kiliaan was known for his interest and expertise in Javanese dance (Djakoeb & Wignyaroemeksa 1913:106).

Kusumadilaga, in his *Serat Sastramiruda* (written in the mid-nineteenth century), also states that Europeans had this kind of direct involvement in Javanese performing arts. In particular he mentions a European woman (*sawijining nyonyah bongsa Eropah*) who in the early nineteenth century created masked dance drama presenting stories of the *wayang purwa* (Kusumadilaga 1981:106).

Clearly, by the end of the nineteenth century Javanese court intellectuals had become good friends with their European colleagues. Both sides had ample opportunity to exchange ideas and to familiarize themselves with each other's works, interests and modes of thought.

Serat Gulang Yarya:
A Nineteenth-Century Gamelan Treatise

The earliest known text devoted specifically to gamelan is a treatise entitled *Gulang Yarya* [Joy of Learning], written in 1870 by Raden Harya Tondhakusuma of the Mangkunegaran, a son-in-law of Mangkunegara IV (r.1853-81) and the creator of *Langendriyan,* mentioned earlier.[4] One part of the treatise, *Dhandhang Gula,* is written in *macapat* poetic metres and is in the form of a dialogue between a servant, Setu, and his master, Kyai Gulang Yarya. In one of the passages on gamelan theory the master says: 'Setu, I would like to ask, how many tones (*wilahan*) are there in *slendro,* and what are their names?' Setu replies:

Setu matur saléndro Kiyai
wijinipun wilahan
  mung gangsal
satunggal enam namané
tegesipun pangumpul
myang panata kajengirèki
panatanirèng laras
kumpul embatipun
kaliyé nama geng asal
tegesipun geng ageng
  = asal wiwinih
dados pikajengira
lamun arsa adamel wiwinih
sorog ageng saking
  wilah gengsal
punika wau yektiné
déné katiganipun
wilah tengah labet nengahi
sakawan wilah jongga
dumunung nèng gulu
wilahan barung gangsalnya
tegesipun barung bareng
  angrangkepi
nimbangi wilah gengsal.

(Tondhakusuma 1870:2)

['Master, in *salendro* the principle (*wiji*) of the key (*wilahan*) consists of five tones.

The first, *enam,* means *pangumpul* (one whose function is to assemble) and *panata* (arranger).

This means that *enam* has the function of arranging *laras,* causing the tuning temperament (*embat*) to be in accord.

Second, *geng asal. Geng* means *ageng* ("large"), *asal* means *wiwinih* (one that inseminates).

Thus, it means that if one is going to create the kernel, the low tone (*sorog ageng*) should be tone *gengsal.*

That is a fact.

The third is tone *tengah* (middle) because of its middle position.

The fourth is tone *jongga* (neck), located on the "neck".

Tone *barung* is the fifth, meaning "in accord" or "replication" — to balance out tone *gengsal'.*]

Tondhakusuma explains the meaning of the names of these pitches by way of *jarwa dhosok* (etymologizing or imposed interpretation). The names of three pitches are altered in order to fit his interpretation: *enem > enam, gangsal > gengsal,* and *barang > barung. Jarwa dhosok* is an indigenous explanatory strategy which aims to reveal the intrinsic meaning of words (Becker 1980:236).[5] From this passage we learn the importance of pitch *nem* as a kind of 'standard' pitch, the status of pitch *gangsal* as a significant pitch in the lower register, and the position of pitch *barang* as the *kempyung* (an interval separated by two keys, approximately a 'fifth') of pitch *gangsal*.

It is uncertain what motivated Tondhakusuma to make such an explication. It is possible that the need to give the meanings of the names of the pitches and other such interpretations[6] was directly or indirectly born of Tondhakusuma's discussions with his European colleagues (perhaps C.F. Winter, Tuwan Godlieb and others). In fact, in the same treatise (1870:19) he refers to the work of Karel Pedrik Winter on *tembang* (Javanese sung poetry).

The Influence of Western Intellectuals on Gamelan Theoretical Writings

Western-type education provided by the colonial government strengthened the exposure of Javanese court intellectuals to European modes of thought. This was especially apparent when the *ethische politiek* (ethical policy) was adopted by the Dutch colonial government, whose purpose was '"to uplift" the Indonesian people through education and closer cultural association with the Netherlands (van der Veur 1969:3). Extending from elementary to high school levels, such education was provided for the children of the aristocracy and the wealthy (*ibid.*:1-3).

Besides education, two other elements strengthened the intellectual atmosphere: the accessibility of publishing about the performing arts, and the activity of the Dutch learned society, the Java Instituut. These elements increased interaction between Javanese and Dutch scholars, both informally and formally, and in person as well as in writing. Collaborative works by Javanese and Dutch authors dealt with vocal music or gamelan. For example, *Serat Rarya Saraya* [Book of the Child's Companion], concerning the meaning and notation of children's songs, was written by K.P.H. Kusumadingrat (Koesoemadingrat) and D. van Hinloopen Labberton in 1913. Djakoeb and Wignyaroemeksa[7] wrote two volumes of gamelan instruction, on the making of the instruments (1913) and the notation of *gendhing* (1919). For the chapter entitled 'Maskerspelen in de Vorstenlande' in *Javaanse Volksvertoningen* [Javanese Performing Arts], Pigeaud relied heavily on the works of Javanese court intellectuals and artists (1938:39-90).

These collaborative works prove the existence of intimate relationships between Dutch and Javanese intellectuals, for example in the monthly journals *Djåwå* and *Poesåkå Djawi,* which often published essays or lectures on Javanese performing arts or Javanese culture in general. A few institutions, such as Widyapoestaka, presented special monographs on gamelan and dance. It was in this special series of publications that Djakoeb and Wignyaroemeksa's books and R.B. Soelardi's *Serat Pradongga* [The Book of Gamelan] (1918) appeared. These books attempted to explain some basic aspects of gamelan, including history (Soelardi), how to make and tune the instruments (Djakoeb & Wignyaroemeksa) and the relationship between gamelan and *wayang* or dance. They were intended as manuals for teaching. For this reason, a guide to the use of notation and the notation of *gendhing* were included. The books use cipher notation and contain basic drumming notation. Unlike today's notation, these authors did not employ spaces to separate basic metrical units (*gatra*). *Kenong* and *gong* strokes are the only important markers of the musical phrases included (see Figure 1). This practice parallels the earlier notation system employed by Ki Gondapangrawit in the late nineteenth century.[8]

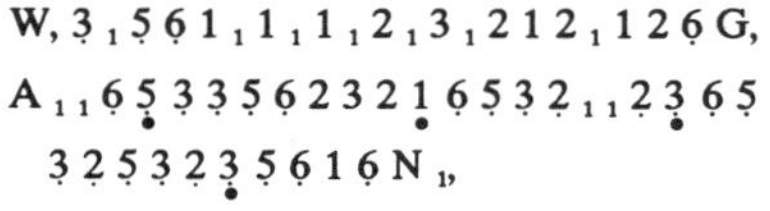

W, 3 ₁5 6 1 ₁1 ₁1 ₁2 ₁3 ₁2 1 2 ₁1 2 6 G,

A ₁₁6 5 3 3 5 6 2 3 2 1 6 5 3 2 ₁₁2 3 6 5

3 2 5 3 2 3 5 6 1 6 N ₁,

Figure 1: Excerpt from Gendhing *Damar Kèli* (Djakoeb & Wignyaroemeksa 1919:164)

Note:
W = *Wiwit* (introduction)   G = *Gong*
A = *Awit (begin)*   N = *Kenong*
• = *Kethuk*   ₁ = rest

These authors assigned numbers to the gamelan tones in a different way from that used today (see Figure 2). Djakoeb and Wignyaroemeksa used the same order of numbers as in today's Kepatihan notation system, except that in *slendro* they assigned number 7 for the upper register of pitch *barang*. Thus, the order of *slendro* is 1 2 3 5 6 7, instead of 1 2 3 5 6 1̇. On the other hand, Soelardi used a quite different set of numbers. He assigned number 1 for pitch *nem*, 5 for *barang*, 4 for *gulu*, 3 for *tengah*, 2 for *lima*, 1 for *nem alit*, and 5 for *barang alit*.

Names of tones:	Nem	Barang	Gulu	Tengah	Lima	Nem	Barang
Today's system	6̣	1	2	3	5	6	1
Djakoeb/Wignya		1	2	3	5	6	7
Soelardi	1̲	5	4	3	2	1	5
Daminatila	1	5	4	3	2	1	5̣

Figure 2

The Java Instituut, whose members consisted of both Dutch and Javanese intellectuals, maintained and fostered the intellectual climate. Its activities included conferences and the sponsoring of cultural events. Conference topics might include Javanese performing arts, and music and dance performances. Program notes of the performances were printed and distributed.

Pertinent to this discussion is a competition sponsored by the Java Instituut, where Javanese were invited to write monographs on Javanese music. As reported by Brandts Buys (1923), seven monographs were submitted. The jury consisted of Dutch and Javanese scholars: J.S. Brandts Buys, R. Ad. Ar. Danoesugonda, J. Kats, J. Kunst and R.M. Ng. Soedjanapoera. The first prize, worth 300 gulden, was awarded to M. Ng. Lebdapradongga (*mantri-niyaga* of the Kepatihan of Surakarta) in collaboration with M.P. Djatiswara (the 2nd Lieutenant *Kapelmeester* [music director] of the European string ensemble of the Surakarta court).

The second prize of 175 gulden was awarded to R.T. Djajadipoera in collaboration with Mevrouw Hofland, whose pseudonym was Linda Bandara (note the collaboration between the Dutch and Javanese authors here), and R. Ng. Soetasoekarya (rank/status: *mantri-tjarik kaboepaten*) with the help of M. Ng. Mlajadimedja (*mantri-niyaga* of the court of Surakarta). In addition, four honourable-mention prizes were awarded to R. Soelardi Hardjasoedjana of Surakarta, R. Loerah Dajengoetara of Jogjakarta, R.M. Ad. Ar. Tjakrahadikoesoema of Temanggung, and R. Tirtanata of Temanggung.

The competition affected subsequent writing about gamelan; for example, it stimulated attempts to compare gamelan and Western musical practice more closely. Such an attempt can be seen in the work of the Committee of Gamelan Instruction [*Komisi Pasinaon Nabuh Gamelan*] of the museum of Radyapoestaka of Surakarta. It was not coincidental, perhaps, that two of the committee members (M. Ng. Lebdapradongga and M.P. Djatiswara) received first prize in the competition. The other members were Mas Ngabehi Sutasukarya (court rank *Mantri Garap Bumi Gedhe*) and Mas Ngabehi Atmamardawa (court rank *Mantri Ordenas Kamisepuhing Niyaga Panakawan*). This committee was assigned the writing of a book for gamelan teaching (Komisi 1924), containing an introductory explanation of gamelan and notation of *gendhing* in Western solfege.

Despite the inclusion of gamelan musicians on the committee and the committee's acknowledgement of their adoption of an earlier notation system invented by Wreksadiningrat,[9] the book follows a Western approach to notating and teaching gamelan, including the exclusive use of Western musical terminology in Dutch, and the use of bar lines (see Figure 3). Certainly this is a departure from the earlier notation system employed by Ki Gondapangrawit and Djakoeb and Wignyaroemeksa in the late nineteenth century. These authors employ neither bar lines nor spaces to separate basic metrical units (*gatra*). *Kenong* and *gong* strokes are the only important markers of musical phrases.

The attempt to analyze gamelan music as Western scholars have analyzed Western music continued into the middle of the present century. Perhaps this was the result of increased exposure to Western music through schools, private lessons and film music, especially among Javanese students and intellectuals in the cities. Ki Hadjar Dewantara, for example,[10] explains gamelan modal practice (*pathet*) in *Sari Swara* (1930) by using the analogy of the Western concept of the changing of

Irama I.

W | ɬo6̣ | 7̣235 | 3653 | 2o7̣o | 6̣o2o | 3o2o |

                      G

               langzr ....

| 7̣o2o | 3o2o | 7̣o2o | 3o5o | 3o5 | 2o7̣o | 6̣o2o |
N   N   N   G

Irama II.

| C ‖ : 3o2o | 7̣o2o | 3o2o | 7̣o2o | 3o5o | 3o5o | 2o7̣o |
         N   N   N

Figure 3: Excerpt from Ladrang *Manis* pélog pathet barang (Komisi 1924: 29)

Pathet Nem			Pathet Sanga			Pathet Manyura		
1.	ji	= gulu	1.	ji	= lima	1.	ji	= nem
2.	ro	= dhadha	2.	ro	= nem	2.	ro	= barang
3.	lu	= lima	3.	lu	= barang	3.	lu	= gulu
4.	pat	= nem	4.	pat	= gulu	4.	pat	= dhadha
5.	ma	= barang	5.	ma	= dhadha	5.	ma	= lima

Figure 4

keys (or the concept of movable *do*). He designates a cipher *ji* (1) as tonic (*dhasar*). As illustrated in Figure 4, pitch *gulu* (2) functions in pathet Nem as the *dhasar,* in pathet Sanga *lima* (5) functions as *dhasar,* and in pathet Manyura *nem* (6) functions as *dhasar* (Dewantara 1930:10).

Furthermore, Dewantara regarded *wirama* as the Western concept of metre. He employed 4/4 metre and illustrated his explanation with the hand gestures and fractional duration of the notes appropriate to this metre (Dewantara 1930:12-18). Using 4/4 metre and the Western concept of the changing of keys, he notated 31 songs from different genres of vocal music (*ibid.*:23-124; Figure 5).

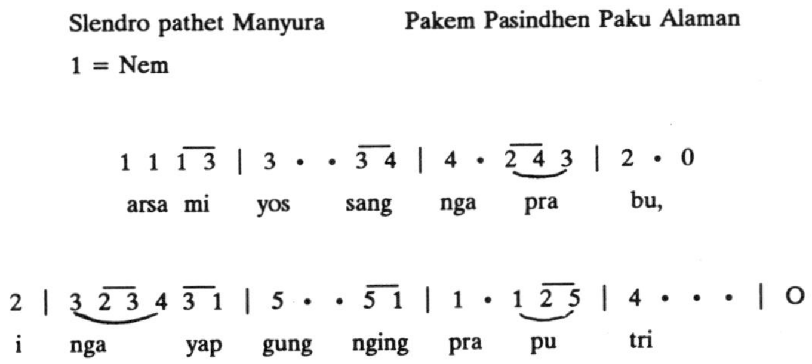

Slendro pathet Manyura   Pakem Pasindhen Paku Alaman

1 = Nem

1 1 1̅ 3̅ | 3 · · 3̅ 4̅ | 4 · 2̅ 4̅ 3̅ | 2 · 0
arsa mi   yos   sang   nga   pra   bu,

2 | 3̅ 2̅ 3̅ 4 3̅ 1̅ | 5 · · 5̅ 1̅ | 1 · 1̅ 2̅ 5̅ | 4 · · · | O
i   nga   yap   gung   nging   pra   pu   tri

Figure 5: Excerpt from *Puspa Warna* (Dewantara 1930: 85).
Sekar gendhing lampah Kinanthi, Prabu Bumiloka.

At this time Javanese intellectuals increasingly emphasized the view
that gamelan was as valuable as Western music.[11] As Ki Hadjar
Dewantara aptly stated (1936:41):

> Pasinaon gendhing *punika boten namung prelu kanggé* ngudi
> kawruh saha kasagedan gendhing *kémawon, nanging wigatos ugi
> kanggé* tuwuhing gesang kabatosan, *awit tansah nenuntun dhateng*
> raos kawiraman *(rhythmisch gevoel)* . . . raos kasusilan *(aesthetisch
> gevoel)* . . . raos kasusilan *(ethisch gevoel)* . . . *(Kasebut ing wewarah*
> Sultan Agungan, *tuwin piwulanging* para sarjana kilènan.)
> (emphasis in original)

> [*Instruction in gendhing* does not only have importance for
> searching out the *knowledge of and the ability to play gendhing*, but
> is also essential for the *growth of inner life.* This is because
> gendhing always guides *rhythmic feeling* . . . enlivens *aesthetic
> feeling* . . . strengthens and clears *ethic feeling* . . . as stated in the
> instruction of *Sultan Agungan* and *Western scholars.*]

Dewantara also pointed out the compatibility of gamelan and Western church music in imparting spiritual power (*ibid:* 41-2):

> 2. Ing tanah Jawi kacariyos para *pandhita lan wali* sami ang-
> gatosaken dhateng kagunan gendhing, malah kathah ingkang
> sami tumut ambangun wewangunan gendhing tuwin kidung,
> (Sunan Kali Jaga, Sunan Giri, Sri Sultan Agung). Makaten ugi ing
> tanah kilènan para *manggalaning agama tuwin gréja* (para paus lan
> pandhita) sami ngecakaken daya prabawaning gendhing, min-
> angka *pambikaking raos kabatosan* (religieus gevoel), punapa
> déné minangka *pangasahing budi* (karakter vorming) ingkang
> adhedhasar landheping cipta, alusing rasa tuwin kiyating karsa.

> [2. In the land of Java the *Javanese priests and saints* have paid
> attention to the art of gendhing. Moreover, there were many of
> them who took part in composing gendhing and sung poetry (e.g.
> Sunan Kali Jaga, Sunan Giri, Sri Sultan Agung, among others).
> This is also the case in the West, where the *religious and church
> leaders* have applied the power of music, with the aim of imparting
> *religious feeling* as well as *forming character,* all of which are based
> on the sharpness of creative force (*cipta*), refinement of feeling
> (*rasa*) and strength of mind (*karsa*).][12]

Until this time the content of most of the gamelan texts remained at an
introductory level, and the theoretical concepts embodied in the writing
were rudimentary. Many of the writings were done by authors — often
court intellectuals — who were not necessarily active practitioners of
music. Input from musicians on the subtlety and complexity of gamelan
practice was lacking. Djakoeb and Wignyaroemeksa (1913:6) stated that,
in order to know many *gendhing,* authors had to observe *niyaga* playing
the gamelan, thus suggesting that they were not themselves musicians.
In the case of the Radyapoestaka's Committee of Gamelan Instruction,
Djatiswara (music director of the European string ensemble of the court
of Surakarta) may have been involved in the work of the committee,
writing the book of gamelan instruction. He was a European ensemble
musician but not a gamelan player. Soelardi was an intellectual of
the court of Mangkunegaran whose interests were Javanese language,
Javanese culture and painting (Mellema 1933). Other court intellectuals
writing on gamelan theory were Sumanagara, Purbacaraka and Pur-
banegara.

The Involvement of Musicians in the Formation of Gamelan Theories

Among these gamelan intellectuals, Ki Sindusawarno is an exception. First, he was not a high-ranking court intellectual. His interest in Javanese art and culture led him to become a member of the advisory committee of *Taman Siswa* school and a good friend of its creator Ki Hadjar Dewantara (Becker 1988:440-41). He then pursued his education in the field of engineering, though he did not complete his course of study. For a time he was a mathematics teacher in a high school in Solo. His interest in music had allowed him to discuss gamelan with and to read the works of both Javanese and Dutch intellectuals. When the gamelan conservatory (Konservatori Karawitan Indonesia or Kokar) was founded in 1950, he, as one of the founders, was active in gamelan research and education, working with members of the 'staff'[13] and teachers of the school, who were mostly court musicians. He also acted as the head of the research department and teacher of *Ilmu Karawitan* [Knowledge of gamelan music].[14] He had ample opportunity to communicate with players/singers of Javanese music. Moreover, he discussed his research with Balinese and Sundanese musicians who were in residence at the school.[15]

Sindusawarno's career took an exceptional turn compared to other theorists. Writing about and teaching gamelan theory became his profession. The success of his independent study of Indonesian music earned him the title *Ki,* an honorific bestowed on a highly esteemed person because of expertise in a particular field. His most important work was intended as a textbook for his students at the gamelan conservatory: *Ilmu Karawitan* [Knowledge of Gamelan Music], volume 1 (1955). Although largely dealing with Javanese gamelan, the book also includes a comparative discussion of Balinese and Sundanese gamelan. In this work Sindusawarno shed much new light on gamelan performance practice, especially in regard to the concept of *irama* ('tempo and density level') and melody. I believe that he gained his deep knowledge from his interaction with gamelan players in the 'staff' division at the gamelan conservatory when he was the head of the school's research division.

Like his contemporaries, Sindusawarno discusses almost all aspects of gamelan practice in his book. His treatment of melody, though brief, sheds light on gamelan practice. He is aware of the importance of examining all aspects of melody: *laras* (tuning system), *pathet* (modal practice), *jenis-lagu* (gendhing forms), *padhang-ulihan* (question-answer melodic phrases), *wirama* (tempo and density levels), *cengkok* (melodic pattern), *luk* (vocal ornament) and *wilet* (ornamentation) (Sindusawarno 1955:46). Although he does not discuss in detail these elements, their relationships and musical examples, he leads us to new ways of understanding some of these aspects of gamelan melody.

Sindusawarno is the first theorist clearly to elucidate *irama.* He explains that *irama* embodies two elements: tempo (*waktu*) and density (*isi*) (1955:35). 'The element of tempo expresses fast and slow' as well as 'moderate'. 'The element of density determines the levels of *wirama'* (35-6). The levels are differentiated by the number of pulses of certain instruments in their ratios with the basic pulses of the *gendhing,* that is, the change of *irama* should be identified in terms of the changing of tempo, as it is accompanied by the rise or fall of density levels. This is an advance on the old notions of *wirama* that ignored density as an important element.

In some of his discussions Sindusawarno reflects on the atmosphere of Western gamelan scholarship at that time. He was familiar with the work of the Dutch scholars Kunst and Brandt Buys, among others (Sindusawarno 1955:58), and of an American ethnomusicologist, Mantle Hood (Hood 1988:14-15). His discussion of *laras* and *pathet* conforms with the atmosphere of gamelan scholarship provided by Western scholars such as Kunst and Hood. In his unpublished *Ilmu Karawitan,* volume II, he discusses the *teori kempyung tiup* (blown fifth theory) of Hornbostel, a theory of the derivation of *slendro* and *pelog.* He also discusses (n.d.:7-9) a Chinese *teori kempyung-kawat* (tone-system produced by series of division of monochord) and the theory of his colleague, Hardjosubroto, comparing the Western diatonic and the *slendro/pelog* systems. Figure 6 (overleaf) is a chart based on the series of fifths as a way to generate tone-systems (n.d.:8).

Sindusawarno, like Kunst and Hood, discusses *pathet* (n.d.:36) in terms of its scalar aspects, identifying each *pathet* from the functional degrees of the tones. Such degrees are determined by the *kempyung* intervals. He neatly presents the *kempyung* theory as a derivation of *laras* and discusses the importance of the *kempyung* in *pathet.* Figure 7 contains Sindusawarno's diagram of *pathet* in *slendro* (n.d.:11). It is the kind of diagram that can be found in Kunst's discussion of *pathet,* as initiated by Dewantara (Kunst 1973:83-4) (overleaf).

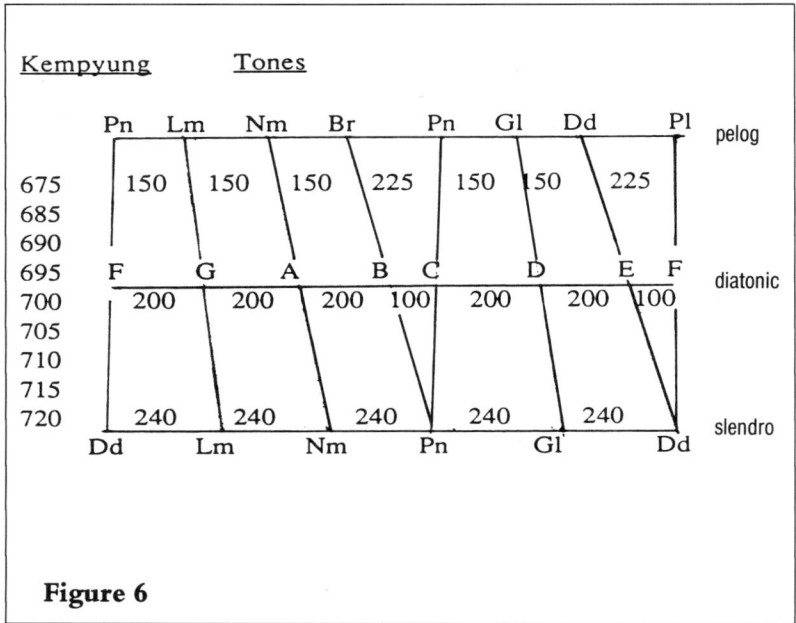

Figure 6

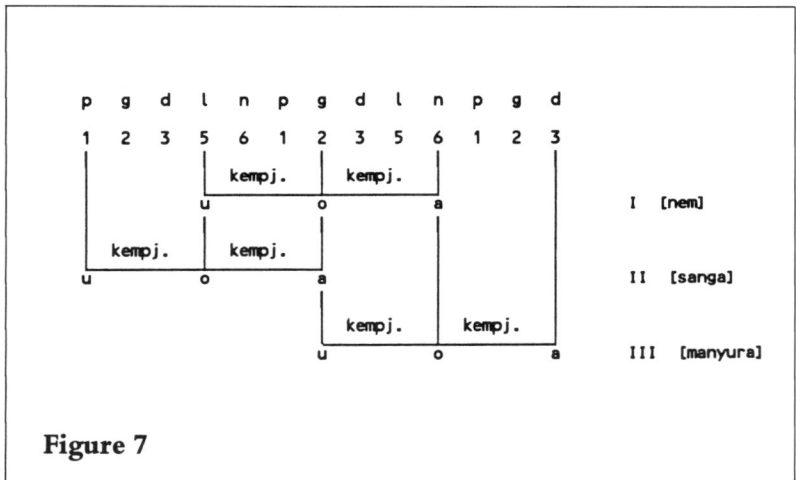

Figure 7

In short, Sindusawarno became a specialist in the study of gamelan. His interaction with European and American scholars and his familiarity with gamelan scholarship (both indigenous and non-indigenous) gave him a wide perspective. His relationships with Balinese and Sundanese musicians in the gamelan conservatory allowed him to relate his discussion of Javanese gamelan to these two other gamelan traditions. As research department head, his interaction with members of the 'staff' division at the gamelan conservatory helped him shed light on gamelan performance practice.

In the 1960s a talented and intelligent musician/composer, R.L. Martopangrawit, became directly involved in scholarship. Like Sindusawarno, Martopangrawit was not an élite intellectual. He was born and grew up in the circle of the family of a court musician. Because of lack of funds, his education in the Dutch school ended when he was thirteen years old (Hatch 1979:14).[16] Subsequently, Martopangrawit was promoted as a musician in the court. When the gamelan conservatory was founded in 1950, he was appointed a member of the 'staff' division of the school, where he worked together with Ki Sindusawarno and other members. It was his relationship with Ki Sindusawarno that subsequently encouraged him to write on gamelan theory and practice.[17] His first monograph, *Tetembangan: Vocaal Jang Berhubungan Dengan Karawitan* [Singing: Vocals which Relate to Gamelan], was published in 1967, two years after he was appointed as *docent* of the gamelan academy (ASKI). In the following decade he wrote a number of books and monographs. His most important theoretical works are contained in his two-volume *Catatan-Catatan Pengetahuan Karawitan* [Notes on Knowledge of Gamelan Music] (1969, 1972).

Martopangrawit attempted to present a thorough and substantive elucidation of gamelan practice, acknowledging at the outset (1972:5) that his work is based on *praktek* (musical practice). Some of the introductory material, however, shares similar definitions with those of Sindusawarno's works. For example, they both explain the function of instruments in the gamelan in terms of two basic ingredients: *irama* and *lagu* (Sindusawarno 1955:2; Martopangrawit 1972:5-8). They both recognize the difference between *laya* and *irama*. As I mentioned earlier, when they worked together in the research division of the conservatory, they influenced each other's works.

What is especially useful about Martopangrawit's work is his discussion of *cengkok,* and in particular his illustration of the *cengkok* in the playing of *gender* (1972:65-81). He also discusses *pathet* at length (2-17), going beyond scalar aspects of this modal practice and pointing to the melodic aspects, such as the role of *cengkok* (melodic pattern), *gender* (2-17) and 'modus' (scale degrees) performed on the *rebab* (11-31). His advanced gamelan theory is based on the musician's point of view. Indeed, the interdependence of music theory and musical practice is essential in the discipline of musicology. This means that theorizing and music-making must go hand in hand, remaining in equilibrium. Martopangrawit and the generation of Indonesian musicologists after him have kept the spirit of this particular approach.

Conclusion

The late nineteenth century marks the beginning of the writing of gamelan theory. A certain intellectual climate, marked by ample interactions between a handful of Dutch scholars/art connoisseurs and Javanese court poets and leading artists, probed the possibility of writing gamelan treatises. Searching for rational explanations of gamelan, which are important in Western scholarship, Tondhakusuma based his written gamelan theory on the Javanese scholarly tool available to him: etymological interpretations of gamelan terms.

In the middle of this century musicians became more involved in the formation of gamelan theory, and a substantive knowledge of gamelan practice began to enrich the gamelan literature. There is a continuum in the perspective of these gamelan writings: to a certain extent Sindusawarno's perspective entered Martopangrawit's work.

Direct and indirect Javanese contact with European or Western modes of thought has consistently fostered the development of gamelan theory written by Javanese. Social contacts with gamelan musicians determined the musical content of the theory.

Notes

1   I would like to thank William Austin, Martin Hatch, Marc Perlman and Otto Steinmeyer for their invaluable comments and suggestions after reading an early draft of this paper, and Philip Yampolsky for discussions we had during my residency at Cornell in the summer and fall of 1987. Thanks also to Mas Poedijono and Mas Djoko Waluyo for many lengthy discussions during my stay in Melbourne. Finally, thanks to Judith Becker, Jennifer Lindsay and R. Anderson

Sutton for their responses, comments and questions during the presentation of this paper.

2   Such gamelan writing has precedents. The *Serat Centhini,* written at the beginning of the nineteenth century, contains sections on gamelan music. My point here is that interactions between Dutch and Javanese intellectuals fostered the early writing of gamelan treatises. And treatises devoted only to performing arts did not appear before the late nineteenth century. On the interactions between Dutch and Javanese court intellectuals, especially with regard to the adoption of notation systems for gamelan, see the perceptive discussion in Becker 1980:12-19.

3   It is told that Tuwan Godlieb was the owner of a batik-making company. Perhaps in honour of his service to the community, a suburb where he used to live was named after him — Godliban. Among the stories of the rise of *Langendriyan,* Partohudoyo's acccount is the most inclusive. He says that when Tondhakusuma was ready to stage his new creation (i.e. *Langendriyan*), he asked R.G. Kiliaan (Tuwan Godlieb), a patron of Javanese performing arts, to finance its production. Mangkunegara IV saw *Langendriyan* when it was performed in the residence of K.P.H. Gondhasiswara. Only then did the prince ask that the dance drama become the prerogative of the Mangkunegaran.

4   Kusumadilaga's *Serat Sastramiruda,* which was written earlier than *Serat Gulang Yarya,* also explains gamelan, although only sporadically; it is mostly about *wayang.*

5   See also Becker 1980:237-8 for the use of *jarwa dhosok* by *dhalang* in the *wayang kulit* performance.

6   Interpreting the meaning of the names of the pitches of gamelan has continued to fascinate later theorists (see Sindusawarno 1960 and Sastrapustaka 1984). Other etymological interpretations in the *Gulang Yarya* include: *mirong,* the alteration of the word *rimong* ('to cover') — a section that should be uncovered or continued in another form; *ayak-ayakan,* derived from *ayak,* which means 'kira' (to approximate) — *kira-kiranen* means to be approximated by the musicians; *salebegan,* derived from *angglabeg seseg wradin* ('tough, fast and even').

7   Unfortunately I have no information about Djakoeb and Wignyaroemeksa. Djoko Waluyo, gamelan instructor at the Institut Seni Indonesia in Jogyakarta, told me that according to his uncle, the late

Sri Handoyokusuma (who was an expert on *tembang*), Djakoeb was an Arab of Surakarta. But according to R.T. Wasitodipuro (p.c., 1989) he was an employee of the museum of Radyapustaka in Surakarta.

8   There is no information on when Ki Gondapangrawit wrote his book of *gendhing* notation. The manuscript mentions him (or perhaps the copyist) as a *rebab* specialist (*miji pangrebab kiwa*); accccording to R.L. Martopangrawit he held that position under Paku Buwana IX (r.1861-93) (Florida: Cornell University SMP catalogue, SMP 645, p.2).

9   Unfortunately I have not yet found examples of Wreksadiningrat's use of notation, but it is commonly held that he is the inventor of today's Kepatihan notation system (Sindusawarno 1960; Warsodiningrat 1979:97-8). I do not know if he originally used spaces or bar lines to separate basic metrical units (*gatra*) of the *gendhing*.

10   Ki Hadjar Dewantara was the grandson of Paku Alam III (r.1858-64). He was well-known as leader of an 'indigenous' system of Indonesian education called *Taman Siswa* [Garden of Pupils]. His philosophy of education was influenced by the ideas of Montessori and Frobel in Europe, the Dalton school system in the USA, and Rabindranath Tagore in India (McVey 1967:133). He emphasized the necessity of including Javanese music and dance in the *Taman Siswa* curriculum.

11   The term *adi luhung* (exalted beauty or art par excellence) was commonly used to characterize Javanese performing arts. And Javanese elites and intellectuals equated the 'adiluhung' quality of the gamelan with the 'classic' quality of Western music.

12   For another *adi luhung* image of gamelan from Dewantara's contemporary, the following passages are quoted from Sumanagara 1935:1-2.

Kang ing ngaran krawitan winarni / tatabuhan gongsa lawan tembang / katriné winastan jogèd / kumpuling telu iku / karawitan dipun wastani / tegesé kaalusan / alus trusing kalbu / dadi tetengering bongsa / ing sadhéngah bongsa masthi andarbèni / lalangen karawitan. Marma parlu kudu pinarsudi / amamardi sambada lebdaa / dadi ana pratandhané / lamun ana wong ngaku / bongsa Jawa nanging tan ngerti / maring rèh karawitan / yekti nistha saru / béda lan bongsa Eropah / wiwit bacah padha didinau bangkit / ngertiya karawitan. Lah kacèka apa bongsa Jawi / iya darbé langen karawitan / malah ngluwihi alusé / gathuk kalawan kawruh / nawung rasa tekèng rahswa di / éman tan mangertiya . . .

13 The 'staff' was a division of the school whose members consisted mostly of musicians of the Surakarta court. Besides serving as resources for research, the 'staff' included among their activities the giving of performances for both the public and the students of Kokar. Some 'staff' members were also teachers. The 'staff' section existed when I was a student there in the early 1960s. Perhaps because of lack of funds, it was discontinued sometime in the late 1960s.

14 I would like to thank Pak Minarno, presently a gamelan teacher at the Indonesian Embassy in Washington DC, for sharing information about Sindusawarno's career in the gamelan conservatory. Pak Minarno has been a faculty member of the gamelan conservatory since 1957 and is thus familiar with Sindusawarno's work at the school.

15 Although the emphasis is on the teaching of theory and practice of Central Javanese music (especially Solonese style), Sundanese and Balinese music are also part of the curriculum.

16 See also a short biography of Martopangrawit written by Sri Hastanto in Becker 1988:431-3.

17 Thanks to Pak Minarno for confirming this point (p.c., 1988).

Glossary

barang: lit. 'thing'; in *slendro,* name of first degree of the gamelan tones; in *kepatihan* notation, tone barang = 1; in *pelog,* the name of the seventh degree. In *kepatihan,* tone barang = 7.

cengkok: melodic pattern, melodic style.

dhadha: lit. 'chest'; name of third degree of gamelan tones; in *kepatihan* notation, *slendro* or *pelog,* tone dhadha = 3 (see *tengah*).

dhasar: lit. 'base'; term used by some gamelan theorists referring to the tone having the most important function in the melody. It is often thought comparable with 'tonic' in Western music.

gamelan: generic term for musical ensemble in Java and Bali, usually an ensemble consisting predominantly of metallophone and gong-type instruments.

gangsal: lit. 'five' (in formal language); in *pelog,* name of fifth degree of the gamelan tones; in *slendro,* the name of the fourth degree; in *kepatihan* notation, *slendro* or *pelog,* tone gangsal = 5.

gatra: lit. 'embryo'; metrical unit of *gendhing,* usually consisting of four beats.

gender: instrument with bronze keys, each suspended with rope over tube resonator.

gendhing: generic term for any gamelan composition.

gong: generic term for medium or large hanging gong.

gulu: lit. 'neck' (colloquial language); name of second degree of gamelan tones; in *kepatihan* notation, *slendro* or *pelog,* tone gulu = 2.

irama: 1. tempo (see also *laya*). 2. process of expansion or contraction of *gendhing* structure, causing the expansion and contraction of the melodic content of the *gendhing* and doubling or halving number of strokes on certain instruments.

jongga: lit. 'neck' (in formal language). See *gulu.*

karawitan: gamelan and associated singing.

kempyung: interval separated by two intervening keys.

kenong: instrument consisting of set of large, horizontally-suspended gongs.

lagu: melody, song.

langendriyan: dance-opera. Specialty of the court of Mangkunegaran.

laras: tuning system.

laya: tempo; term borrowed by Sindusawarno from Indian musical terminology.

lima: lit. 'five' (colloquial language). See *gangsal.*

luk: vocal ornament.

macapat: sung poetry.

manyura: one of the *pathet* (modal systems) in Javanese gamelan.

nem: (from *enem,* lit. 'six') one of the gamelan tones; in *slendro* it is the fifth degree; in *pelog* the sixth degree; in *kepatihan* notation, *slendro* or *pelog,* tone nem = 6.

niyaga: gamelan player.

pathet: modal classification system in gamelan.

pelog: tuning system in which the octave is divided into seven non-equidistant intervals.

rebab: two-stringed bowed instrument.

salendro: tuning system in which the octave is divided into five non-equidistant intervals (although the intervallic differences are not as great as in *pelog).*

sanga: lit. 'nine'; one of the *pathet* systems.

slendro: see *salendro.*

tembang: generic term for unaccompanied or minimally accompanied song.

tengah: lit. 'middle'. See *dhadha.*

wayang: generic term for any traditional dramatic performance.

wayang purwa: shadow-puppet performance in which the stories are based on Mahabharata and Ramayana epics.

wilahan: keys of metallophone-type instruments; gamelan pitches.

wilet: melodic ornaments.

wirama: literary variant of *irama.*

References

BECKER, Alton
    1979   'Text-Building, Epistemology, and Aesthetics in Javanese Shadow Theater'. In A.L. Becker & A.A. Yengoyan, eds., *The Imagination of Reality: Essays in Southeast Asian Coherence Systems.* Norwood, N.J.: Ablex Publishing Corporation, pp. 197-210.

BECKER, Judith
    1980   *Traditional Music in Modern Java.* Honolulu: The University Press of Hawaii.

BECKER, Judith & Feinstein, Alan (eds.)
    1988   *Karawitan: Source Readings in Javanese Gamelan and Vocal Music.* Vol. 3. Ann Arbor: Center for South and Southeast Asian Studies, University of Michigan.

BUYS, Brandt
    1923   'Uitslag van de Prijsvraag inzake een Javaansch muziek-schrift'. *Djawa* 4 (December): 1-17.

DAY, Anthony
    1980   'The Meaning of Change in the Poetry of Nineteenth-Century Java'. Ph.D. dissertation. Cornell University.

DEWANTARA, Ki Hadjar
    1930   *Sari Swara.* Groningen-Den Haag-Weltevreden.
    1936   *Kawruh Gending Djawa.* Solo: Sadu Budi.

DJAKOEB & WIGNYAROEMEKSA
    1913   *Layang Anyumurupake Pratikele Bab Sinau Nabuh Sarta Panggawene Gamelan.* Batavia: Drukkerij Eertijd H.M. vn Dorp & Co.
    1919   *Serat Enut Gendhing Slendro.* Batavia: Drukkerij Eertijd H.M. vn Dorp & Co.

GONDAPANGRAWIT, Ki
Late 19th century
Buk Gendhing Slendro, Buk Gendhing Pelog. Manuscript (inscribed in Surakarta), Reksopustaka Mangkunegaran (RP/MN) Cat. #645; Cornell University Surakarta Microfilm Project (SMP), Reel 85/3 #180/186.

HATCH, Martin
1979 'Theory and Notation in an Oral Tradition: Some Notes on ASKI, Surakarta'. In Gloria Davis, ed., *What is Modern Indonesian Culture?* Athens, OH: Ohio University Center for International Studies Southeast Asia Program.

HOOD, Mantle
1988 *The Evolution of Javanese Gamelan,* Book III: *Paragon of the Roaring Sea.* Wilhelmshaven: Florian Noetzel Verlag.

KOESOEMADINGRAT, K.P.H. & D. VAN HINLOOPEN LABBERTON
1913 *Serat Rarya Saraya.* Buitenzorg: Widya-Poestaka.

Komisi Pasinaon Nabuh Gamelan ing Paheman Radyapustaka Surakarta
1924 *Buku Piwulang Nabuh Gamelan.* Surakarta: Swastika.

KUNST, Jaap
1973 *Music in Java: Its History, Its Theory and Its Technique.* 3rd edn., ed. E.L. Heins. The Hague: Martinus Nijhoff.

KUSUMADILAGA, Kangjeng Pangeran Harya
1981 *Serat Sastramiruda. Jakarta:* Depdikbud, Proyek Penerbitan Buku Sastra Indonesian dan Daerah.

MARTOPANGRAWIT, R.L.
1967 *Tetembangan: Vocaal Jang Berhubungan Dengan Karawitan.* Surakarta: Dewan Mahasiswa ASKI.
1969 *Pengetahuan Karawitan,* vols. 1a & 1b. Surakarta: Dewan Mahasiswa, ASKI.
1972 *Pengetahuan Karawitan,* vol. 2. Surakarta: ASKI.

MCVEY, Ruth
1967 'Taman Siswa and the Indonesian Awakening'. *Indonesia* 4.

MELLEMA, R.L. (ed.)
1933 *Serat Gancaran Warni-warni ing Jaman Sapunika.* Groningen-Den Haag-Batavia: J.B. Wolters U.M.

PARTOHUDOYO, Raden Ngabehi
1921-40 Manuscript (inscribed in Surakarta). In 'Aanteekeningen Betreffende den Javaansche Dans (en Muziek)'. Reksopustaka Mangkunegaran (RP/MN) Cat. #649 B; Cornell

University Surakarta Microfilm Project, Reel 205 #7:4.

PIGEAUD, T.

1938   *Javaanse Volksvertoningen.* Batavia: Volksletuur.

SASTRAPUSTAKA, B.Y.H.

1984   'Wedha Pradangga Kawedhar'. In Becker & Feinstein 1988: 305-34.

SINDUSAWARNO, Ki

1955   *Ilmu Karawitan,* vol. 1. Surakarta: Konservatori Karawitan Indonesia.

[n.d.]   *Ilmu Karawitan,* vol. 2. Unpublished monograph. Surakarta: Konservatori Karawitan Indonesia.

1960   'Radyapustaka dan Noot-Angka'. In *Nawawindu Radya-pustaka.* Surakarta: Paheman Radyapustaka, pp. 61-3.

SOELARDI, Raden Bagus

1918   *Serat Pradongga.* Weltevreden: Widya-Poestaka nr. 2.

SUMANAGARA, K.R.M.T.

1935   *Serat Karawitan.* Sragen: [n.p.].

TONDHAKUSUMA, Raden Mas Harya

1870   *Serat Gulang Yarya.* Manuscript (inscribed in Surakarta). Reksopustaka Mangkunegaran (RP/MN) Cat. #A 21; Cornell University Surakarta Microfilm Project #618, Reel #80.

VAN DER VEUR, Paul W.

1969   *Education and Social Change in Colonial Indonesia.* Athens, OH: Ohio University Center for International Studies Southeast Asia Program.

WARSODININGRAT, R.T.

1979   *Serat Wedha Pradangga.* Surakarta: Sekolah Menengah Karawitan Indonesia [1972].

Reinterpreting Indian Music:
Albert Roussel and
Maurice Delage

Jann Pasler

> It seems to be the case that we cannot hear music that is
> foreign to us except according to our own concepts and
> the categories of our Western music. For the listener of
> primitive or Oriental monody, there is the essential
> problem of knowing whether what one is hearing is
> what one should be hearing.
>
> Gisèle Brelet (1946:71)

The concern for grasping what one is supposed to hear in the music of
foreign cultures evolved considerably in this century. Previously those
interested in foreign music had essentially non-ethnographic motivations. In France, the imperialist government of the Third Republic (1871-
1940) saw music as an opportunity to expand its cultural horizons while
asserting its cultural superiority. It supported research trips by folklorists
in the 1880s and 1890s, and musicians and dancers were brought from as
far away as Java and Vietnam for the Universal Expositions of 1889 and
1900. The rebirth of interest in modality and composers' use of scales
other than the major and minor parallels the colonial curiosity and
acquisitiveness of the late nineteenth century.

This essay is concerned with other reasons that led French composers to non-Western cultures at the turn of this century. Hunger for escape was so widespread that novels about exotic subjects were sometimes published in serial form in the local newspapers: Rudyard Kipling's *Kim*, for example, based on the author's travels in India, appeared in the Parisian paper *Le Matin* throughout the spring of 1902. Like these novels, music setting exotic stories aroused visions of a different world. (The term 'exotic' at the time was used to refer to almost anything beyond French, German, Italian and English culture.) As throughout the nineteenth century, composers used unusual scales or rhythmic patterns to function as local colour, a signal to dream, an opportunity to escape the culturally-prescribed boundaries of their imaginations. Those at the Schola Cantorum considered folk tunes in particular as good, healthy nourishment for their listeners, capable of inspiring moral renewal in the world. But, fearing an increasing 'abuse of the picturesque', they felt that exoticism should be handled with caution, for it could become synonymous with facility, impressionism, and a lack of solid construction.

Efforts to understand reality in new ways and to redefine the nature of mental constructs also thrust the French beyond their own culture. Eastern thought offered alternative models to Western theories of causality and determinism. By 1914 the critic Louis Laloy pointed out that the Eastern 'process of thought' — with direct statement and juxtaposition replacing the Western genesis of ideas — had begun to influence composers like Stravinsky more than any 'local colour' or other superficial exoticism (Laloy 1928: 220). Eastern music itself helped early modernist composers to reevaluate the importance of timbre and gave them a way of validating their belief in the primacy of sound over syntax. Those who looked to and borrowed from Eastern sources had the possibility of addressing universal issues, both musical and cultural.

Few French composers actually travelled to the East to hear this music in its natural setting. Maurice Ravel once intended to go and, in August and September 1905, wrote to his friend and composition student Maurice Delage that he was asking the Minister of Fine Arts to sponsor an expedition to the Orient (Chalup 1956:46,49). But this never materialized. Only Albert Roussel (1869-1936) and Delage (1879-1961) made the trip, the former in the fall of 1909, the latter in the winter of 1912. Although Roussel continued on to Indochina and Delage visited Japan, both spent the bulk of their time in India.

What attracted these composers specifically to India is not clear. Parisians had little contact with Indian music, although they were familiar with its influence on Délibes' *Lakmé* and Massenet's *Roi de Lahore*. Fétis himself, in his major study of the subject in *Histoire générale de la musique* (1869-76), bemoans the little he had been able to learn. In *L'Inde sans les anglais* (1904), Pierre Loti described the Indian classical music he heard at a maharajah's court in 1899-1900, and in his *Le son dans la nature* (1900) the mystic Edmond Bailly published a short explanation of Hindu musical philosophy. But at the conclusion of his essay on Indian music, Julien Tiersot (1905) writes, 'In spite of so many written pages [on the subject], this art remains for us, in large measure, a dead relic [lettre morte]'. There is little record of Indian musicians in Paris before 1910.[1] To have any direct knowledge of the music itself, a composer almost had to go there or, like Debussy, have travelling friends like P.-J. Toulet and Victor Segalen who could bring back personal experiences to feed his or her enthusiasm.

With the documentary sources I have located after more than a decade of research — Roussel's musical sketchbook, recordings Delage purchased in India, the text of his radio program on Indian music, and various letters — together with the recent publication of Roussel's trip diary and Delage's letters to Stravinsky, we can begin to examine the relation between what these composers heard in India and what they did with what they heard, the relation of Self and Other as represented in their music. Given that Roussel and Delage visited many of the same places, it is astonishing to find such variance in the musical experiences they describe and in the influences of Indian music and culture on their compositions. Such differences reflect the composers' contrasting backgrounds, of course, but they also derive from the nature of each man's interest in India. I suggest that the meaning Roussel and Delage derived from their Indian experiences was a function of their own essentially Western preoccupations and that the self-criticism of modernist aesthetics predisposed composers to foreign cultures in their own terms more profoundly than did the more conservative aesthetics of the Schola Cantorum.

*   *   *

Albert Roussel, then a professor at the Schola Cantorum, left with his new wife for India on 22 September 1909 to tour the country whose shores he had often visited as a naval officer years before. After disembarking at Bombay, the newly-weds crossed the country from west to east, visiting the caves of Ellora, then Udaipur, the Tchitor ruins,

Jaipur, Delhi, Agra, Benares and Darjeeling, before turning south to Madras, Madura and Ceylon. In a letter written to Henry Woollett while at the Great Eastern Hotel in Calcutta on 29 October 1909, the composer described his impressions of the country's music:

> I just travelled through Hindustan from Bombay to Calcutta and everything I saw impressed me profoundly. From the musical point of view, however, I haven't heard anything up until this moment that is really curious. The Hindu music that I have heard, stripped of harmony and very different from Javanese or Japanese music, consisted uniquely of several popular songs in our ordinary tonalities. Maybe there is something else that I haven't yet encountered? (Roussel 1987:35)

The diary and musical sketchbook[2] Roussel kept during the trip reinforce this statement and suggest an answer to both his own question — was he exposed to the full gamut of Indian music? — and Gisèle Brelet's — did he hear what he should have heard? The notebook (21½ cm x 13½ cm) consists of 45 pages, filled, particularly in its first third, with monophonic tunes that are occasionally harmonized. Of the 79 musical ideas, 60% are short melodies without text, written predominantly in the middle range. The absence of complex melodic and rhythmic structures in these sketches, of ornaments (*gamaka*), and of microtones (*śrutis*) — otherwise characterizing the ragas and talas of Indian classical music — suggests that the composer may have sought out 'simple' music, or not have gained access to the courts and temples where classical music was regularly performed, or that his musical experiences, perhaps by choice, were limited principally, if not exclusively, to what in Europe would have appeared to him as folk music.[3] The intense interest in folksong among his colleagues at the Schola Cantorum — they taught an annual course on the topic and organized related conferences and publications — might also have inclined him toward seeking out folk music. Although indigenous Indian tunes differ from region to region, they are generally characterized by short, repetitive figures, simple talas (most commonly duple metre), and limited ranges.[4] Many of the melodies that Roussel notated have these features.

The first musical idea in this sketchbook, a 'chant de nègres hissant un fardeau' [song of negroes hoisting a load] heard in Bombay, exemplifies the most prevalent kind of folk music in India, the song of a leader followed by a chorus that responds with similar musical material (Example 1a). This work song is a diatonic litany alternating between F and G in an implied 4/4 metre. Its modal quality is also present in the other melody on that page, a 'Hymne du Maharana' (Example 1b). Roussel heard this tune performed in unison when the Maharana was leaving his palace in Udaipur. Notated in 6/8 and consisting uniquely of intervals of a second and a third, it has an antecedent and a consequent phrase, each two measures long and sharing an identical rhythmic structure. These features make it the most Western-like of the melodies in the manuscript.

On the following page Roussel sketched three melodies, marked 'danseuse', 'chant' and 'danse' (Example 1c). He heard them played in Benares by four musicians, two with string instruments resembling viols and the others with tambourines and rattles. The group surrounded and accompanied a 'balaydère' (*devadasi* or female dancer). This little concert — apparently the only one Roussel heard — was organized by his tour guide and is described in his diary:

> At first, there's a dance, accompanied by string instruments playing in unison and accentuated by the others. The movements are slow, movements of the arms and hands especially. The rhythm accelerates little by little, following the gestures of the dancer . . . Then there are songs in which, for each couplet — 'couplets divided into two very distinct parts' — the dancer successively addresses each of us . . . Other songs follow the first, always in the same form and in unison. Occasionally, however, one of the string instruments separates itself from the melody to ornament it with excessively rapid scale embroideries. Leaning toward the dancer, the musicians seem to follow her every move, and the player of the tambourines (they are really very small, fixed-pitch timpani) accompanies and reflects the mime. (Roussel 1987:193)

The sketches again capture the two-part structure and the duple metre characteristic of much folk dance music in India, and they reveal how 'song' melodies may differ from 'dance' tunes. Here the dance tunes in 2/4 emphasize the notes of the triad G, B, D, G′, span an octave and use leaps of a fourth, whereas the song has more rhythmic variation, a more restricted range (a sixth) and principally conjunct motion. The sketches

a. Bombay: 'Chant de nègres hissant un fardeau'

b. Udaipur: 'Hymne du Maharana'

c. Benares: Danseuse, Chant, Danse

d. Fakir au bord du Ganges

Example 1: Roussel's Musical Sketchbook

do not reflect the rhythmic acceleration and excessively rapid ornamentation that Roussel describes in his diary. The F sharps in the key signatures of two melodies suggest that Roussel heard them in G major, one of the 'ordinary tonalities' of which he wrote to Woollett, even though he consistently uses F sharp or C sharp in ascending lines and F natural or C natural in descending ones, which might imply the presence of ragas.

The last sketch on that page, an unmetred tune again with a key signature of F sharp (Example 1d), is Roussel's version of the litany he heard a 'fakir[5] au bord du Ganges' sing, without stopping, surrounded by the red of the setting sun. The vision of this half-naked young man who seemed to be addressing the gods and stars greatly impressed the composer even though his words were incomprehensible to the tour guide. Except for one accented C — a dotted quarter note leapt to from A in its second phrase — this melody consists entirely of eighth notes and intervals of a second that weave around G in its first phrase and around A in its second. In many ways this tune resembles the Benares vocal melody on the same page and is typical of many in his sketchbook and, according to Tiersot (1905:66), many in Tagore's *A Few Specimens of Indian Songs*. It is in two parts, each formed of a very short period which, according to Roussel, the singer repeated many times. Its range is again a sixth and its contour is that of two sine waves. This is the only tune that appears more than once in the sketchbook; in its first recurrence it is transposed up a step, and in its fourth, it is elongated and its highest note reached by a fourth rather than a second.

The remaining melodies in the manuscript have no performance instructions other than an occasional accent. Most have a key signature (one to five flats or sharps); three are marked 'en sol majeure' (pp. 15, 39) or 'en fa majeure' (p. 35). One uses an eight-note mode on A with B flat. Every tune has an implied or explicitly notated metre, usually 4/4 or 3/4 though the asymmetrical metre 5/4 appears once.

The evolution of musical thinking in this notebook suggests that Roussel was more interested in writing a composition during his trip than in recording what Indian music he heard. From page 18 on, one finds not only melody after melody but also chord structures, short passages in four-part harmony and even, toward the end of the notebook, some passages written on three and four staves (pp. 12, 21, 23, 24, 40). From the number of instruments indicated — horns, trombones, bassoons, winds and strings — it is clear that Roussel was conceiving a piece for a Western ensemble.[6] The occasional subtitles — *adagio, allegretto* and *lent* — suggest, moreover, that he was contemplating a work with three movements. Other recurring subtitles point explicitly to the three movements of his *Evocations,* the first piece he wrote upon his return to France in 1910. The name 'Ellora' (pp. 32, 36 and 45), the town 'Udaipur' (pp. 3 and 34) and the letter 'B' (pp. 4, 31 and 37) were probably shorthand ways of referring to the three images — the temples at Ellora, the cities of Rajasthan and the Ganges at Benares — that inspired its three movements, 'Les dieux dans l'ombre des cavernes' [The gods in the shadow of the caves], 'La ville rose' [The pink city] and 'Au bord du fleuve sacré' [On the banks of the sacred river]. Roussel explains in an essay published in the *Guide du Concert* on 12 and 19 October 1928:

> If I have not specified these places in the titles, it is because I do not want to impose any kind of limitation on the expression of the music. However, if one absolutely must discover some bit of local color, I can point to a theme in 'The Pink City' that was suggested to me by a scene I saw, the entry of the rajah into his palace, and in the third *Evocation,* the reminiscence of a melody that I heard sung on the banks of the Ganges by a young enlightened fakir. (Hoérée 1938:37)

In *Evocations,* one can trace the evolving nature of Roussel's perceptions in India, only some of which are captured in his sketchbook. The first movement, virtually devoid of Indian musical influences, translates his feelings of 'grandeur and mystery' before the temples of Ellora. The sounds he records in his diary — only water droplets and bird cries — may have inspired the opening, which resembles Debussy's and Ravel's water music with its impressionist harmonies and arabesque arpeggiations in the strings and harps, the pedal tone in the basses and the slowly moving melody in the woodwinds.

In the second movement, Roussel captures a more generally Eastern sound with his delicate instrumentation and the static, oscillating nature of the motives. In the middle of this movement (at 17, 20 and 21) comes the theme whose length, 6/8 metre and descending sixth were 'suggested' by those of the 'Hymne du Maharana'. Although Roussel acknowledges the source of this tune, the quotation is far from exact, as he changes its rhythmic structure, deletes the repetition and extends the consequent phrase, thus transforming it in significant ways.

Example 2 Roussel, *Evocation,* third movement, baritone solo

The third movement shows the most Indian influence, culminating in the *direct* quotation of the fakir tune (Example 2). The sliding to and away from neighbour tones in the first measures suggests the gamakas of Indian music. The rapid ornaments, syncopations and long sweeping line of the flute melody in 7 show an awareness of the improvisatory qualities in Indian music not otherwise evident in his sketchbook. The grace notes and glissandi, played by instruments of varied timbres that enter on each of the beats (as in 11), probably reflect the composer's attempts to translate the unison sound that so impressed him while respecting the timbral complexity that must have accompanied these unisons.

In the middle of this movement (31 to 36) Roussel sets verbatim his 'reminiscence' of the fakir melody. Repeating it over and over as the fakir himself did, Roussel uses it to spin out a long ballade-like setting of six four-line stanzas written at his request by the French critic M.-D. Calvocoressi. When I played this section of *Evocations* for various Indian musicians around the country during a visit in Fall 1988, they found it totally lacking in Indian elements and remarked that the text is not at all what a fakir would have sung. However, in Benares, when I sang the tune myself after playing the recording, an eminent Indian music scholar as well as my two drivers instantly recognized it as the devotional music of fakirs.[7] Roussel's recitative-like setting and the vibrato in the bass singer's voice on my recording had thrown them off; when I sang it more quickly and in an ordinary voice, they could hear the pitches. 'Jai-lan, jai-lan', they sang in response, 'Glory to Rama and Sita'. As in Roussel's sketch, their version of the melody centred on the reiteration of one pitch surrounded by an ascending and descending pattern; but, in contrast to the Roussel version, the opening of their tune spanned a third rather than a second, did not repeat the initial pitch and, what they found most significant, included an odd number of the repeated pitch in its middle section, thereby allowing the natural accent to fall on *that* pitch rather than the next higher one where it falls consistently in Roussel's version and which Roussel even notes with an accent mark in his sketchbook. In addition, they found the second part of Roussel's tune totally un-recognizable: the music they knew had no consequent phrase.

Roussel's treatment of the tune nevertheless respects the way this tune was performed and would be performed even today. Because this is devotional music, the fakirs may sing the same text and music for hours, stretching the tempo at will, giving it different colors and expressing different feelings through it: according to Dr. Prem Lata Sharma, they expect to derive some spiritual benefit from singing it thus.[8] In sections 31 to 36, Roussel likewise sets the tune, with some variations, for virtually ten minutes. Following the model of the transpositions and elongations noted in his sketchbook (pp. 4, 29, 30), he playfully varies its intervals and rhythms to allow for changes from one stanza to the next. For the first three lines of each stanza, he sets the antecedent phrase of the fakir melody (the version with the elongated second note), and for the last line, the consequent phrase. Throughout the first four stanzas, the only deviation in the antecedent phrase concerns whether it will begin on G (as in the first two stanzas) or on A flat (as in the second two). The consequent phrase, by contrast, appears in different rhythmic and intervallic forms each time, depending on the number of syllables in the verse and the syllable Roussel wishes to stress. The fifth and sixth stanzas vary the original melody more significantly, slowing it to an eighth-note pulse while maintaining the melodic contour of the source. This varia-tion technique and the timbral effects exploited in *Evocations* suggest that Roussel heard more than he actually noted in his sketchbook, but it is not clear how much more.

Yet another question persists: why did the composer not use more of these sketches in *Evocations?* His colleague at the Schola Cantorum, Vincent D'Indy, offers a clue. On 21 July 1910 he advised Roussel:

So write your Hindu symphony without thinking about this or that, nor even about including too much local color; believe me, a simple indication (like the discreet trumpets in the Agnus of the

Mass in D) is perfectly sufficient to put us in the mood, even better than a sound photograph of 'national noises'.

Look then at your India much more for the impressions it made on the man named Albert Roussel — impressions that, taken together, are a lot more European than Hindu — instead of for the orchestral imitation you might make of observed sounds; this procedure in art, inferior as it is, is becoming so commonplace that a mind such as yours could never be satisfied with it. (Hoérée 1978:46)

One direct quotation, treated appropriately, and a few vague suggestions turned out to be enough to pay tribute to his Indian voyage. *Evocations* is testimony to his interest more in feelings and visions stimulated by exotic sources than in any particular foreign musical culture per se. On 18 March 1910, he explained to the critic Georges Jean-Aubry: 'This will not be Far Eastern music but simply the sensations I felt over there translated into our ordinary musical language' (Roussel 1987:38). Two years later, in another letter to this critic on 1 May 1912, he made it clear that 'even though these *Evocations* were inspired by India, I am anxious that the country remain vague. India, Tibet, Indochina, China, Persia, it doesn't matter' (Roussel 1987:42). When Jean-Aubry reviewed the work, he pointed not to the Orientalism in the music but rather to the suave and voluptuous 'quality of the dream', and he hailed Roussel as 'one of the most truly French souls in music today' (Jean-Aubry 1916:135-6).[9] Exoticism as such remains a pretext for the painter and the poet in the composer, not yet a subtext for the musician.

*   *   *

Maurice Delage, by contrast, was not yet a fully-formed composer when he embarked on his voyage to India. He had studied with Ravel for about ten years and had completed some songs and piano works. Friends describe him as someone with a fine ear and a hatred of facility as well as a composer 'impatient with the weary discipline of technical training' (Calvocoressi 1933:61). When, in 1909, the Société Nationale rejected his first orchestral work, *Conté par la mer,* Ravel and his friends showed their esteem for Delage by breaking away and forming a rival performance organization, the Société Musicale Indépendente.

In Spring 1912, Delage's parents used the presence of their shoe polish factories in India and Japan as an excuse to travel to the Far East, and

Maurice went along.[10] According to his friend, the poet Léon-Paul Fargue, Delage left with the fervour of a pilgrim; he was not the kind of tourist who 'feels free because he is leaving and who brings along his slippers'. Although their travels took them to many of the same places as Roussel — the caves of Ellora, the city of Jaipur in Rajasthan, and the Ganges at Benares — Delage's impressions were quite different from those of his French contemporary, as were the motivations for his interest in Indian music.

In a letter from Kandy, an English colony in Ceylon, to the music journal *S.I.M.* on 4 March 1912, Delage admits not having read anything about Indian music (Delage 1912); yet his comments in this letter, in subsequent published interviews and in a radio program on Indian music he gave in April 1948 show remarkable perceptiveness. Delage underlines the ties of Indian music to religion, noting that one's caste determines what instruments one may play; he points to the differences between the music of various regions and expresses opinions about them (he found the music of Ceylon too bland and, like Tiersot (1905), that of the far north too influenced by Arab music). From what he writes about instruments and various performance practices, it is clear that Delage was exposed to Indian classical music. He explains the raga and points out that in Punjab and Gujarat quarter tones are used to soften a scale. He is aware that notes have different meanings (some joyful, others sad) and that instruments symbolize certain divinities. His conclusion: 'It is amazing that they can play together with all these contradictions.'

Indian performance practices fascinated him in particular, for such techniques seemed to be the clue to the suppleness of the musical language. He writes of a Bengali orchestra not unlike the one described by C.R. Day in 1891:[11]

> [The clarinettist] improvises extraordinarily difficult passages to make supple a scale that seems to him incomplete. He presents and interweaves his motives with a remarkable sense of tonal equilibrium, then abruptly moves away and returns by colorful modulations . . . When the musician uses a many-stringed instrument, he proceeds in the manner of a contratenor who develops his line over a basso continuo. So too in the orchestra, where the melody is led by a sort of brilliant and very voluble oboe, and the pedal is furnished by the bass clarinet only making one sound, without stopping, the very elastic cheeks of the player

replacing the sacks of our bagpipes during breathing. Add to that a drum that is really a double timpani producing the unison of the pedal and its lower octave, never exact, almost a seventh, a pair of antique cymbals . . . and you have the most pure Bengali orchestra. The drummer is the conductor . . . Sometimes [there is also] a bell, a muted drum, and what is worse in my opinion, a European violin that does just about anything. (Delage 1912)[12]

Performance on the vīnā, the oldest multi-stringed Indian instrument used principally in the South, and the vocal techniques of certain South Indian contraltos impressed him the most. The slow glissandi on the vīnā, the striking of the strings and the case, and the staccato of the performer's left-hand fingers produced effects that the composer would later attempt to imitate.[13] Likewise, the 'voluptuous tension' produced by those who sang 'with almost closed mouths a high-pitched prosody involving strange nasal sonorities, cries and breathing' captured his attention, as did 'the warm roughness of their low register where the rushed and feverish rhythms suddenly relax into a murmur full of caresses'. In his radio program he describes a singer, dressed as a tiger, who performed 'vocalises produced by a staccato at the back of the throat with a whole lemon in his mouth'. (S.A.K. Durga and V.A.K. Ranga Rao explained to me that in the 'Puli attam', a tiger's dance, performers even today place lemon wedges in each cheek so that their mouths won't get dry while they make purring/growling noises for hours.)

Unlike Roussel, Delage could not appreciate such music without comparing it to the limitations of Western music. The improvisations played on the clarinet, he writes, had an audacity that 'escaped all organization, according to our logic, of course. I'm faced then with a new instrument constructed of an unknown scale . . . With my poor ear accustomed to the almost artificial subtleties of our Western polyphony, I felt something that was beyond the notes.' The vīnā player's use of parallel fifths led him to exclaim: 'severe Academy . . . What could analysis and criticism do here, great gods! One must desire [only] to feel and love.' He rails against the presence of various European influences on Indian music, especially the use of the harmonium and, in South India, the violin, which led artists 'to lose sight of the purity of the ragas'.[14] With access to the sultans' or maharajas' palaces, he might also have been shocked by the presence of pianos in their midst (Harris 1912:425).

No sketchbook or diary remains, although Delage made some personal notations: 'prayers for a chariot stuck in the mud in Lahore' and a 'funeral chant played by some kind of a clarinet' in Benares (Delage 1912, 1948). He did collect a number of recordings during the trip[15] and on 23 October 1912 wrote to Stravinsky, 'You will see that I have been working and I will make you listen to the Hindu records, a kind of music of which you have no idea' (Craft 1982:24). These recordings document a wide range of music, from rhythmic improvisations on the iron bars, called Khattali, accompanying a wedding procession (Odeon 96. 541) and on the oboe-like Nāgasvaram, played in the temples of Ellora (Odeon 96. 453), to the complex singing of Kishori Lal (Gramo 12. 533) and Coimbatore Thayi (Gramo 5-013022) (Delage 1948). They gave him access to music he might not have been able to hear live, as much of the country's best music was performed only in private settings. During my recent trip to India, I located the most important of these records and can show that it was the Indian classical music preserved on these recordings, as opposed to the folk songs he might have heard or collected on records, that is the key to the works Delage wrote upon his return to Paris.

In Delage's Indian-inspired compositions one finds a highly original approach to Eastern materials, an intercultural influence that goes far beyond that of superficial impressionism, and a re-presentation of Indian music that empowers him to subvert traditional Western music practices. 'Trying to find those Hindu sounds that send chills up my spine', as he explained to Stravinsky (Craft 1982:33), while still writing for traditional Western instruments, Delage experimented with unusual timbres produced by altered tunings and vocal techniques, special kinds of ornaments that modify the Western sense of interval and pitch, improvisatory rhythms, new forms, and especially novel performance techniques. The works that resulted from such exploration spanned much of his career, from the *Quatre Poèmes Hindous* for soprano and small chamber orchestra (written from Spring 1912 through Fall 1913) and *Ragamalika* (1912 to 1922) to the third movement of *Contrerimes* (1927-32), the Vocalise-Étude (1929), and 'Themmangu',[16] from *Chants de la Jungle* (1914-34) (see Table 1). He also began an orchestral work, *Les batisseurs du pont,* conceived as a pantomime for the Ballets Russes, but Kipling's refusal to give him permission to use the story forced him to abandon the work.

The most interesting of the group from the perspective of Indian influence is the second of the *Quatre Poèmes Hindous,* 'Un sapin isolé' [An isolated fir tree], subtitled 'Lahore'.[17] The text is a poem by Heinrich

a. Imdad Khan, *Raga Jaunpuri Todi, Alap,* beginning, transcr. by Paul Smith

b. Imdad Khan, *Raga Jaunpuri Todi, Alap,* middle section, transcr. by Paul Smith

Example 3   TRANSCRIBER'S NOTE:
All slurred notes are played as glissandi. Portamento indicates that the marked notes are lingered on briefly in the midst of the glissando passage. A broader, more accented pause is indicated with a tenuto mark.

Heine, whom Delage also set to music in his first published song, 'Intermezzo', composed in January 1910. The thoughts expressed in this earlier song may even be responsible for drawing Delage's attention to India: 'On the wings of my songs, I will transport you all the way to the banks of the Ganges . . . and there we will stretch out under the palm trees whose shade will give us dreams of celestial bliss'. As in this song, the images in 'Un sapin isolé' invite the listener into reverie: one tree, covered with snow 'on a bare mountain in the north', dreams of another, a 'solitary' palm clinging to the edge of a scorched rock 'in the distant east'. The poem is also a metaphor suggesting that the existential human condition of feeling alone on a hill is a universal one.

For the opening cello solo, Delage inserted a direct transcription of the beginning of a recording he brought back from India, Imdad Khan's performance on the surbahār (a bass sitar with unmovable frets and a wider range) of 'Jaunpuri Todika Alap', probably recorded in 1905 (Examples 3a and 4a).[18] That Delage should attempt to transcribe this piece, as virtuosic as it is, probably arose from the fact that he himself

Example 4 Delage, 'Un sapin isolé . . .' from
Quatre Poèmes Hindous

4a. opening, cello/violin solo, m.1–19

4b. vocalise, m.1–4

4c. vocalise, m.10–16

played the cello, though only as an amateur. The performance instructions at the bottom of the page indicate that the cellist should use scordatura tuning to achieve certain kinds of resonance and to play lower notes than are normally possible. Where so marked, while strongly plucking the first note with the right hand, he or she should use the same finger of the left hand to slide between the two adjacent notes. This use of ornaments and glissandi to prolong a note, stress one or slide from one to another results in a pitch continuum, microtonal shadings and a timbre that recall those produced by sitar and vīnā players. (On the recording the notes slid through are extremely quiet, especially when there are a string of them.) When Imdad Khan shifts his melody to another string to move higher in pitch and weaves a duet between two strings, Delage gives the melodic line to the viola which then enters into a duet with the cello. The subtlety of this instrumentation very well captures that of its model.

After the first few bars of music, however, the transcription is no longer exact. Imdad Khan elaborates on the raga for almost three minutes, while Delage cuts some of the recurring passages and generally condenses the overall shape. He also alters some of the complex rhythms, although not many, and indicates a somewhat slower tempo — perhaps to give the cellist the time to execute the difficult techniques. In the last part of the cello solo before the final soprano vocalise, Delage diverges ever so subtly from his model, but in a way foreign to Indian music: he alters the order of the descending notes of the raga (from 8 b7 b6 5 4 b3 2 1 to 8 b6 b7 5 4 5 b3 4 2 1) and in so doing shifts to *Darbari,* a raga that uses the same notes but in a slightly different order.[19]

The vocal part dominates in the rest of the piece, creating confusion for the Indian listener when it is accompanied by the Indian-inspired cello-viola melody. When the Dagar brothers, famous for their singing of *dhrupad,* first heard this piece, they expressed far more interest in the cello-viola part than in Delage's vocal writing and told me they could not hear anything Indian in the singing (interview, October 1988). Most of the vocal writing is unequivocally Western when the chamber orchestra accompanies it; however, one need only refer to the same Imdad Khan recording, reexamine what Delage reports (1912, 1948) and compare his perceptions of Indian vocal techniques with those he writes into the music, to understand the Indian influence on the final two-page vocal solo. Here he uses an Indian-type scale (built on D with three sharps)[20] and borrows a quickly ascending scale of six notes and a gradually descending span of a thirteenth from the middle of the same Imdad Khan recording (compare Example 3b with Example 4c). Besides the low register, the quick, delicate staccatos throughout and the ornaments that colour the descending lines, Delage also employs closed-mouth singing in numerous places: in the second phrase to echo the major intervallic outline of the first phrase, F B C F (Example 4b); again in the two extensive descending phrases where, as Delage wrote, 'the rushed and feverish final rhythms suddenly relax into a murmur of caresses' (Example 4c); and finally in the last phrase, where the closed-mouth singing again functions as an echo, outlining the interval B F. This technique of open- and closed-mouth singing[21] was Delage's first attempt to forge a personal style inspired by the vocal techniques he heard in India and on his recordings, without attempting to retrain Western singers to produce their sounds in an Indian manner. It became a favourite in all his subsequent Indian-inspired pieces, including the Vocalise he wrote for a Paris Conservatoire competition in the 1920s.

In the third *Hindu Poem,* the 'Naissance de Bouddha' [Birth of Buddha] (subtitled 'Benares'), Delage borrows much of his thematic material from the flip side of the recording discussed above (Gramo G.C. 17364): 'Sohni', again performed by Imdad Khan (Examples 5 and 6). The raga *Sohni* is easy to recognize, as the scale occurs immediately in its entirety. Delage transcribes this quick exposition of the raga for English horn, giving it the same rhythms as in the recording. He then repeats the exposition as on the recording, has the clarinet respond with a similar virtuose chromatic descent and continues to expand on these two ideas throughout the piece. The cello's ostinato serves to recreate the sound of the accompanying strings on Imdad Khan's surbahār. This Delage accomplishes again with scordatura tuning and by asking the cellist to play the strings pizzicato. As on the recording, they function in this piece as a drone. The text, probably written by the composer, evokes the time when the gods and all of nature rejoiced at the news of Buddha's coming.

The first and last of the *Quatre Poèmes Hindous* frame the middle two and assure unity and coherence in the set. Although they set texts by Bhartrihari, an Indian king who became an ascetic, musically they express the Westerner's perspective which must frame his/her perception of Indian music or culture. Both have the tempo of $\bullet = 66$ and bear much less specifically Indian musical influence. They begin with chromatic flute arabesques à la Debussy or Ravel that conclude with the same descending gesture. The end of the first song incorporates the opening motive of the last song, and the closing measures of the last song

original tonic-B
transposed to F

Example 5 Imdad Khan, 'Raga Sohani, Drut Gat in Tin-Tala' transcribed by Paul Smith

Allegretto ♩=120
(English horn)

mp
(cello, pizzicato harmonics)

(clarinet)

poco

Example 6 Delage, 'Naissance de Bouddha' from *Quatres Poèmes Hindous,* m.1–3

incorporate the opening motive of the first one; moreover, the final measures of both songs are the same. The images and emotions described in these two songs also frame the set. In the first the image of a beautiful woman wandering through the forest is the object of the poet's contemplation, and in the last 'she' becomes the image of a memory well-cherished, perhaps India itself. 'If you think of her, you feel an aching torment. If you set eyes on her, your mind is troubled. If you touch her, you lose all reason. How can one call her the beloved?' In setting the last two phrases, the music breaks into a Western-style climax, the apex of the song's vocal line. Outside of occasional moments in the cello solo of the second song, this is the only *forte* in the whole set. Such a moment captures the pinnacle of the composer's emotional response to his Indian experiences.

Ragamalika, perhaps his most Indian-sounding piece, is indeed a transcription of an entire recording (less the last repeat of the refrain) that I recently located in a private collection in Madras: 'Rāgamālikā,

Ramalinga swamis arulpa', sung in Tamil by Coimbatore Thayi and probably recorded in 1909.[22] Thayi was a famous *devadasi* singer whom Delage had the pleasure of hearing live during a visit to the temples at Mahabalipurnam (Delage 1948). *Arulpa* are devotional songs that the *devadasis* sang for the entertainment and pleasure of the gods at the temples to which they were attached. Thayi recorded many of them,[23] and it is probable that Delage owned several of these, for he played another record which I have not yet been able to locate, 'Rāgam-Alapana', during his 1948 radio broadcast. Her voice, mezzo in its range, was a strong as opposed to a delicate one. Her recordings are full of elaborate passages of closed- and open-mouthed singing, microtonal ornaments around each of a whole succession of notes and then long stretches in which she might change the timbre but not the pitch of an important note.

In every way, *Ragamalika* reflects its model – in its changing modes (*rāgamālikā* means 'a garland of ragas'), recurring refrain, multi-partite form and tempo relationships. The piano takes the place of the tabla and the droning accompanimental string instrument. Ostinati octaves serve principally to support the vocal line, except in one very important instance. To articulate the system tonic, B flat,[24] and to bring attention to the change of mode in the middle of the piece, Delage asks that one note (the B flat in the second octave below middle C) on the *inside* of the piano be muted (see Example 7). This creates an unusual, otherworldly effect for the drone that dominates this section of the piece, and is perhaps the first example of 'prepared piano' in European music.

That Delage should transcribe these records should not surprise us, for Ravel's method of teaching involved having his students *try* to imitate models, all the while knowing that their personalities and style would shine through. Ravel himself practised this technique – perhaps the best-known example being his Piano Concerto, modelled upon one by Saint-Saëns. Furthermore in traditional models of Karnatic music-learning, one emulates a guru by imitating his or her playing. Delage made no secret of this process of composition. When invited to visit Stravinsky in Switzerland in February 1914, Delage wrote of needing a gramophone-phonograph: 'I have a lot of records with which I must work, not having done the transcriptions of the themes that I need' (Craft 1982:35). Of course, those outside Delage's inner circle of friends would never know.

With the help of these recordings, Delage succeeded better than his contemporaries in capturing both the spirit and the style of North and

Example 7 Delage, *Ragamalika*

South Indian music alike. Was it only because he was exposed to a wider range of Indian music, especially through the records, that he was more open to 'hearing what he should be hearing', in Gisèle Brelet's words, or was it because he was less attached to and more critical of the 'concepts and categories' of Western music, unlike his contemporary Roussel who taught them? In many ways it was the modernist aesthetic — with its emphasis on sound for its own sake and its sensitivity to the various contexts in which music is made — that prepared Delage to hear Indian music in its own terms.

With this understanding of Indian music, Delage was able to create a style that distinguished him remarkably from his teachers and peers. And he did not go unrewarded for his efforts. Even though the audience had little idea of the work's secret — in his 1 February 1914 review in *S.I.M.,* Jean Poueigh refers to the 'funny peculiarity' of the closed-mouth singing which he thought Delage had borrowed from its use in choruses — they demanded an encore of 'Lahore' at the first performance of his *Quatre Poèmes Hindous* on 14 January 1914. Upstaging at the same concert the premieres of Ravel's *Trois Poèmes de Mallarmé* and Stravinsky's *Trois Lyriques Japonaises,* according to Georges Auric (interview with the author, 1977), Delage's music thus stole the show and the composer knew he had found a personal voice worthy of a career.

Acknowledgements

This paper, which began with research in Paris in 1976-77 and continued throughout the 1980s, was considerably expanded after the 1988 SIMS conference by a research trip to India that Fall. I wish to thank the many people who aided me in various ways: Karuna Ahmad, the staff of the Archives and Research Center for Ethnomusicology in Delhi and the Music Department of the Bibliothèque Nationale in Paris, Kaushal Bhargava, Bob Brown, Faiyazuddin and Zahiruddin Dagar, S.A.K. Durga, Reis Flora, Rita Ganguli, Joseph Gusfield, Michael Kinnear, K.S. Kothari and A.C. Jain of the Sangeet Natak Akademi, Josef Kuckertz, Sharon Lowen, Allyn Miner, T.S. Parthasarathy, Jyoti Pande, André Peeters, N. Rajam and the staff of the Benares Hindu University Performing Arts Department, V.A.K. Ranga Rao, Manuel Rosenthal, T. Sankaran, Ravi Shankar, Prem Lata Sharma, Uma Sharma, Daksha Sheth, Steve Slawek, R.P. Subramanian, Jean Touzelet, S. Venkatraman, Vijay Verma, and most especially Joan Erdman and Bonnie Wade whose enthusiasm for Indian music infected me years ago.

Notes

1 A short note in the music journal *Courrier Musical* on 1 February 1910 reports of an 'Indian invasion . . . an orchestra composed of pure-blood Indians under the direction of M. Evans' that would be touring Europe from 15 June to 15 September (p. 128). In May 1913, the vīnā player Inayat Khan also came to Paris (Howat 1989).

2 Madame Albert Roussel gave this sketchbook to Marc Pincherle on 7 April 1951, and in 1978 its owner André Peters (founder and editor of the *Cahiers Albert Roussel*) was kind enough to allow me to consult it. Besides Indian melodies, the sketches include three tunes described as 'Thai', 'Cambodge', and 'Annadhapura'. The diary Roussel kept from 6 October through 13 November 1909 is published in Roussel 1987:178-202.

3 In *The Music and Musical Instruments of Southern India and the Deccan*, 1891, C.R. Day explained that Europeans at the time rarely had a chance to hear 'the good or classical music' of India: 'what is usually played for them consists . . . of modern ditties, sung by ill-instructed, screaming, dancing women at crowded native durbars, marriages, and other ceremonials' (p. 58). Similarly, Tiersot (1905) describes what Indian music was performed at the Universal Exhi-

bition of 1900, complaining that none of it seemed to resemble the classical music described in studies by Tagore and Day (1891). In this article, I maintain the distinction between classical and folk music not to imply that the boundaries were clear nor that folk and popular musics did not share many of the complexities of classical musics, but because it was in these terms that composers and musicologists thought at the time.

4   The presence of grace-notes and quarter tones in this music is not one that Roussel chose to address, unlike A.H. Fox Strangways (1914), who, in the musical diary he kept from his 1910-11 trip, explains that his musical sketches lack adequate indication of timbral variance and intonation. It is not clear whether the folk music Roussel heard was not performed by artful singers, as Day (1891) suggested was often the case, whether he failed to notice the subleties of timbre and intonation in this music, chose not to note them, or whether they were unimportant to him.

5   A Muslim or Hindu religious ascetic. From Arabic 'faqir', meaning poor.

6   The only reference to any other instrument is to a xylophone on the page marked 'Cambodge'.

7   I am grateful to Dr. Prem Lata Sharma, Professor Emeritus of Benares Hindu University in Benares (Varanasi), Lalta Parsad, and Jay Parkash for their help in identifying this tune.

8   I had the opportunity to hear such music sung by a group of devotees at a temple in front of the train station in Benares. The 'jai-lan' music goes on continuously until 4 a.m. every night, without even a pause between different singers.

9   Roussel wrote another Indian-inspired work shortly after his return to Paris: the opera-ballet *Padmâvatí* (begun in December 1913 but not premiered until 1923). This work has an Indian subject, the story of Padmini at Tchitor, based on a novel written in 1856 that Roussel and his collaborator Louis Laloy found in the Bibliothèque des Langues Orientales in Paris (see Hoérée 1979:73-4). Given the evidence of his diary, his sketchbook, and *Evocations* itself, one can surmise that whatever ragas Roussel used in this work he learned after his return to Paris rather than while in India.

10   A close friend of Delage's, the composer/conductor Manuel Rosenthal, provided this information to me in an interview in Paris in Spring 1977.

11 Day (1891:93) lists three strings (including a violin), a native oboe or clarinet, tabla, drone, cymbals and bells.

12 The Tanjore orchestra, by contrast, held little interest for Delage. This was basically an English-style wind band formed in the late eighteenth century at the court of Tanjore. It consisted of bagpipes, flute, brass, clarinet and drum and constituted perhaps the first 'recognizable impact of Western music' in India (Seetha 1981:111). It performed its tunes in unison, accompanied by the drone and drum. Delage brought back one recording by the Tanjore band (Gramo G.C. 2 10129) and, after playing 'Parathpa Varali Athi' during his 1948 radio program, he called it 'an experiment in harmony' that sounded like 'chance counterpoint'.

13 Day (1891:110) was also impressed by similar techniques of vīnā-playing.

14 The violin became popular in South India around the time of the first Tanjore Palace Band and has remained so ever since; the use of the harmonium, however, has been a subject of much debate, particularly around the time that Delage visited the country. Those in favour of this three-octave keyboard tuned in equal temperament argued for it being cheap, portable, and easy to learn — a means of introducing more people to music; those opposed, including Delage, thought it would kill their music by limiting the use of quartertones, imposing the equal-tempered scale, and thereby spoiling their sense of pitch. Fox Strangways led the discussions in his 'Indian Music and Harmoniums', published in *Dawn*, Vol. vii, no. 1, part III [N. series] (August 1911): 65-88. Ananda K. Coomaraswarmy and the editors of the journal *The Modern Review* also devoted a series of articles to the topic: P.R. Bhandarkar, 'Abolish harmoniums', Vol. xii, no. 10 (October 1912): 420-28; U. Ray, 'Abolish harmoniums', Vol. xii, no. 11 (November 1912): 497. There were additional responses in Vol. xii, no. 12:53-5. The use of harmoniums in classical music remains a concern in India, as one can see in the full issue of the *Journal of the Sangeet Natak Akademie* 20 (April-June 1971) dedicated to this theme.

15 Recordings were introduced in India around 1902 and the first factories opened in Calcutta in 1908. In his 1948 radio program, the manuscript of which is in the Bibliothèque Nationale, Delage listed eight recordings that he played at that time. Given what he writes to Stravinsky (Craft 1982), I have assumed that these recordings were among those he collected while in India in 1912.

16 Means 'southern style, a vulgar phase of the Dravidian style over which the Aryan breeze has already begun to flow' (Ramaswami 1923:319).

17 There are two manuscripts of this song in the Bibliothèque Nationale, ms 17644 and ms 9177. The former is bound with the other songs, forming the basis for the printed edition; the latter is a separate manuscript. While the former is dated November 1913, it is full of erasures. By contrast, the latter, though dated January 1912, is a clean copy of the score, with ink written over pencil. The latter also differs from the former in the case of one clef, some rhythms, dynamics and phrases (ms 9177 breaks up some long phrases), the addition of more passages of 'open-mouthed' singing and a lower line giving the aural effect of the scordatura tuning of the cello, none of which has been incorporated into the printed score. For these reasons, I question the dating marked at the end of these songs. Moreover it seems improbable that Delage would have transcribed the recording he found during his first month in India (see note 15). Therefore, I assume that the January date indicates the time when he began work on the song, and that ms 9177 is a copy that postdates November 1913.

18 A North Indian *ālāp* is a slow exposition without a fixed pulse. When I played this Delage piece for numerous musicians in India in Fall 1988, most responded after the first minute or so with a nod and a smile. But few recognized that Delage was using an Indian raga. I am indebted to Vijay Verma for pointing out the presence of *rāg jaunpuri* in the cello part. As I was already seeking the Imdad Khan recording that Delage played in his 1948 radio program (Gramo G.C. 17364), I set about also looking for all recordings Imdad Khan made using *rāg jaunpuri*. (According to Bonnie Wade, Imdad Khan [b. 1848] was a musician in the entourage of Maharaja Sar Jyotindra Mohan Taigaur of Benares.) At the suggestion of Michael Kinnear, I consulted the Gurtu Collection, one of the most important collections of old recordings in northern India, presently at the Benares Hindu University Museum. I am grateful to the staff of the Music Department of B.H.U. for help in locating two Imdad Khan recordings, both Gramo G.C. 17364 and that which proved to be the source of the 'Lahore' opening, Gramo G.C. 17365. Kinnear kindly provided me with the probable date of these recordings. Paul Smith transcribed the recordings and offered valuable suggestions regarding folk music.

19 I am grateful to Dr. Allyn Miner of the Department of South Asia Regional Studies, University of Pennsylvania, for pointing out this change in the raga.

20 Bonnie Wade finds 'the nature of the melody very Indian' (cf. Examples 4a and 4b):

> the conjunct melodic motion within the established 'raga' (consistently avoiding D in descent *as might happen in the raga* . . .) until a large leap creates a dramatic melodic effect (top of the second page). And slipping into a G natural when G# is otherwise the pitch of the raga, as a really accomplished musician might (if he is sure the audience knows he really knows the pitches of the raga!). The melodic descents such as on the first page, brace 3, last measure and the second brace of the second page are really like a particular type of tan that makes a vocalise (exercise)-type of effect utilizing every pitch of the raga in some pattern or another. (Letter to the author, 1 July 1986.)

21 Delage was perhaps the first French composer to use such a technique for solo singing but not for choral singing. His friend Florent Schmitt used closed-mouth singing in some choral sections of his 'Danse des Devadasis', Opus 47 (1900-08), a work also based on an Indian subject, as did others.

22 Gramo G.C. 8-13793. I am grateful to S.A.K. Durga for suggesting I consult the collection of V.A.K. Ranga Rao and to Mr. Rao for allowing me to peruse his collection on the morning of Diwali. The text is virtually incomprehensible on the recording, so that Delage's transcription was a hindrance rather than a help in locating the recording.

23 Daniélou 1952:160-62 is a very incomplete listing of her recordings. Today they are extremely rare (I located only one in all of Delhi), but the Ranga Rao collection in Madras has a substantial collection of them including all those on Daniélou's list.

24 Daniélou (1968:23-4) notes that the system tonic used by most singers was often B flat.

Interviews (1977-88)

Georges Auric, Kaushal Bhargava, Faiyazuddin and Zahiruddin Dagar, S.A.K. Durga, Joan Erdman, Rita Ganguli, Michael Kinnear, Josef Kuckertz, T.S. Parthasarathy, V.A.K. Ranga Rao, Manuel Rosenthal, T. Sankaran, Ravi Shankar, Dr. Prem Lata Sharma, and Vijay Verma.

References

BENDER, G.
　　1956   'Entretien avec Maurice Delage'. *Guide du Concert* 6 July:
　　　　　 292-3.
BRELET, Gisèle
　　1946   'Musiques exotiques et valeurs permanentes de l'art
　　　　　 musical'. *Revue philosophique* Jan-March: 71-96.
BRUYR, José
　　1932   'Un entretien avec Maurice Delage'. *Guide du Concert* 22
　　　　　 January: 423-5.
CALVOCORESSI, M.-D.
　　1933   *Musicians' Gallery.* London: Faber and Faber.
CHALUPT, René (ed.)
　　1956   *Ravel au miroir de ses lettres.* Paris: Laffont.
CRAFT, Robert (ed.)
　　1982   *Stravinsky: Selected Correspondence,* vol. 1. New York:
　　　　　 Knopf.
DANIÉLOU, A.
　　1952   *A Catalogue of Recorded Classical and Traditional Indian
　　　　　 Music.* Archives of Recorded Music.
　　1968   *The Ragas of Northern India.* London: Barrie and Rockliff.
DAY, C.R.
　　1891   *The Music and Musical Instruments of Southern India and the
　　　　　 Deccan.* London & New York: Novello, Ewer & Co.
DELAGE, Maurice
　　1912   'Lettre de l'Inde' from Kandy, 4 March 1912. *S.I.M.* 15 June:
　　　　　 72-4.
　　1948   'Une Géographie Musicale'. Text of a radio program given in
　　　　　 Paris on 25 April. Bibliothèque Nationale, Paris, Rés. Vmc.
　　　　　 Ms. 46.
FOX STRANGWAYS, A.H.
　　1914   *The Music of Hindostan.* Oxford: Clarendon Press.
HARRIS, Clement Autrobus
　　1912   'The Bicentenary of the Pianoforte: A Link between East
　　　　　 and West'. *The Calcutta Review* No. 270 (October): 425ff.
HOÉRÉE, Arthur
　　1938   *Albert Roussel.* Paris: Les Éditions Rieder.

1978 'Lettres de Vincent d'Indy à Roussel'. *Cahiers Albert Roussel* 1: 42-8.

1979 'Lettres d'Albert Roussel à Louis Laloy'. *Cahiers Albert Roussel* 2: 72-4.

HOWAT, Roy

1989 'Debussy et les musiques de l'Inde'. *Cahiers Debussy.*

JEAN-AUBRY, Georges

1916 *La Musique d'aujourd'hui.* Paris: Perrin.

LALOY, Louis

1928 *La musique retrouvée,* 1902-1927. Paris: Plon.

RAMASWAMI, M.S.

1923 'Indian Music'. *Hindustan Review* vol. xlvi, no. 280: 316-28.

ROUSSEL, Albert

1987 *Lettres et Écrits.* Edited by Nicole Labelle. Paris: Flammarion.

SEETHA, D.S.

1981 *Tanjore as a Seat of Music.* Madras: University of Madras.

TIERSOT, Julien

1905 *Notes d'ethnologie musicale.* Paris: Fischbacher.

Discography

KHAN, Imdad (perf.)

c.1905 'Jaunpuri Todika Alap'. Gramo G.C. 17364.

c.1905 'Sohni'. Gramo G.C. 17365.

THAYI, Coimbatore (perf.)

c.1909 'Rāgamālikā, Ramalinga swamis arulpa', sung in Tamil. Gramo G.C. 8-13793.

Comparative

MAURICE DELAGE

1909

1910

1912

Jan	Begins piano-vocal score of 'Benarès, Naissance de Bouddha', 3rd of *Quatre Poèmes Hindous,* in Benares
	Begins piano-vocal score of 'Jeypur, Si vous pensez', 4th of *Quatre Poèmes Hindous,* in Lahore
Feb	Begins piano-vocal score of 'Lahore, Un sapin isolé', 2nd of *Quatre Poèmes Hindous,* in Lahore
2 Feb	Stravinsky writes Florent Schmitt of receiving letters from Delage 'who is so far from us and who does not seem to be tormenting himself over the great distance'
Mar	Begins piano-vocal score of 'Madras, Une belle', 1st of *Quatre Poèmes Hindous,* in Madras
4 Mar	Letter to the journal *S.I.M.* from Kandy
18 Mar	Letter to Léon Pivet from Agra (Ceylon), will return in June
13 May	Letter to Pivet from Banshokaku, Tsuruga, Japan

Chronology

ALBERT ROUSSEL

1909

	Visits Bombay, the grottos of Ellora, Udaipur, Jaipur, the Tchitor ruins, Dehli, Agra, Benares, Darjeeling, Madras, Madura, Ceylon, Saigon
29 Oct	Calcutta, letter to Woollett

1910

Begins work on *Evocations*

1912

---

18 May	First performance, *Evocations:*
	1. 'Les dieux dans l'ombre des caverne' (temples at Ellora)
	2. 'La ville rose (la ville en fête)' (Jaipur)
	3. 'Au bord du fleuve sacré' (the Ganges at Benarès)

Comparative

MAURICE DELAGE

1912

June	Visits Japan
15 June	*S.I.M.* publishes Delage letter from India
12 Oct	Letter to Stravinsky, 'You will see that I have been working and I will make you listen to the Hindu records of which you have no idea'
17 Dec	Letter to Stravinsky, has begun poem for orchestra based on Kipling's *Bridge-builders*
end Dec to mid-Jan 1913	Delage visits the Stravinskys in Monteux

1913

3 Mar	Russian conductor Siloti and Bakst become interested in *Bridge-builders*
Summer	Work on chamber orchestra versions of *Quatre Poèmes Hindous*
Nov	Finished orchestral score of 'Lahore'
26 Nov	Travels to London to see Kipling for permission to use his novel
9 Dec	Returns to London to see Kipling, 'utterly discouraged', abandons *Bridge-builders* project

Chronology *continued*

ALBERT ROUSSEL

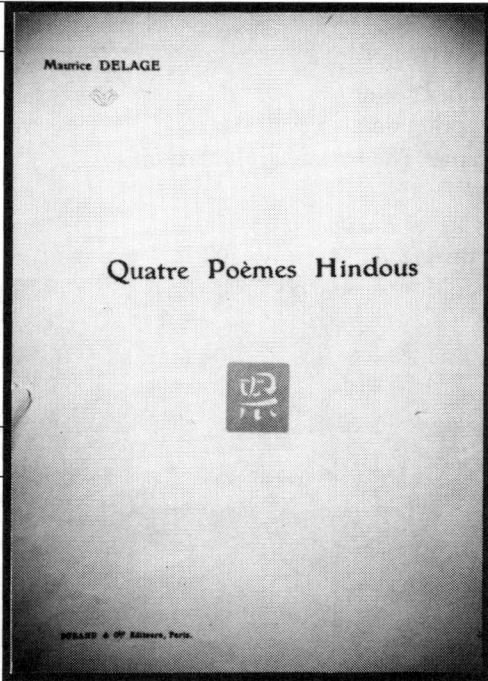

Maurice DELAGE

Quatre Poèmes Hindous

DURAND & Cⁱᵉ Éditeurs, Paris.

Dec   Begins *Padmâvatí,* based on a story at the ruins
of Tchitor

Comparative

MAURICE DELAGE

1914

14 Jan	First performance, *Quatre Poèmes Hindous*
11 Feb	Letter to Stravinsky, working on a thieves' dance and tiger's dance (later became 'Themmangu', the 3rd of *Trois Chants de la Jungle)*
May	Finishes piano-vocal score of *Ragamalika*
20 June	Durand 'enchanted' with *Ragamalika,* pays 500 fr., commissions its orchestration

1915

First performance, *Ragamalika*

1918

1920

6 Oct	Letter to Stravinsky, working on Apsaras dances

1922

Orchestra performance of *Ragamalika*

1923

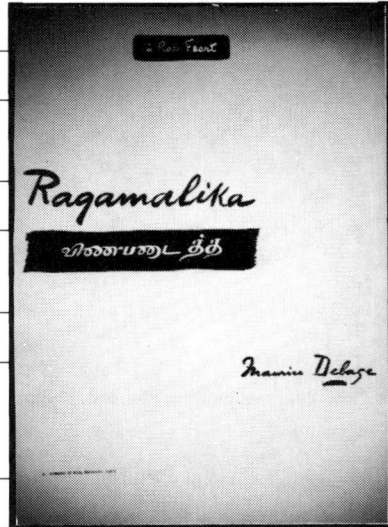

Chronology   *continued*

ALBERT ROUSSEL

1914

1915

1918

Finishes *Padmâvatí*

1920

1922

1923

1 June   First performance, *Padmâvatí,* an opera-ballet at
          the Paris Opéra

Comparative

MAURICE DELAGE

1927
Finishes piano score of *Contrerimes* whose 3rd movement 'Danse' is based on an Indian model
1929
Publishes 'Vocalise-Etude'
1932
9 June Finishes orchestration of 'Danse' from *Contrerimes*
1934
Finishes orchestral score of *Trois Chants de la Jungle*

Chronology

continued

A L B E R T   R O U S S E L

1927

1929

1932

1934

Gurus, Shishyas and Educators: Adaptive Strategies in Post-Colonial North Indian Music Institutions

Andrew Alter

Introduction

British colonialism in India incorporated a complex administrative system of native states and direct British rule. The British India map included more than 500 native states, each governed by a local ruler. These were the chief patrons of Indian music, whose wealthy lifestyles allowed for the maintenance of court musicians in a system of patronage dating from at least as early as the first Moghul rulers of the sixteenth century. While British administration supported royal aristocratic patrons, Western ideology and attitudes provided a new and modern approach to musical patronage and training which was in conflict with the traditional system.

With the dissolution of the royal princely states shortly after independence in 1947, the government of India suddenly found itself the prime sponsor of Indian musicians. Two agencies that the new independent government inherited from its colonial predecessor became the new patrons of Hindustani music. These were All India Radio and government-funded institutions of music education. In particular, institutions of music education today remain a legacy of the conflict between traditional systems of instruction and Western systems of education. The adaptive strategies employed by Indian musicians in this institutional environment demonstrate an important aspect of inter-cultural contact through music in the subcontinent.

This paper outlines the development of institutional education in North India during the end of British rule and through the first three decades of independence. Two modern institutions are isolated as case studies to show the role of institutionalized music education in North India today. The adaptive strategies that the teachers in these institutions employ are indicative of the issues currently facing the traditional music teacher in North India.

Guru-Shishya Parampara:
The Teacher-Disciple Tradition

The most important aspect of traditional instruction in North Indian music is embodied in the special relationship which exists between teacher and student, a relationship called *guru-shishya parampara. Guru* means teacher, spiritual guide; *shishya* means disciple; and *parampara* means tradition. The complete term not only describes the special relationship between teacher and student but also carries implications for the system of transmission that was dependent on that relationship. Musicians still consider *guru-shishya parampara* important today, many older musicians having received their training as *shishyas* in a *guru-shishya parampara.*[1] However, without court patronage, few are now able to teach in this traditional way. It is therefore recollections, not current practice, that provide the key elements that define a *guru-shishya parampara.* Writers such as Neuman, Owens and Deva have documented these key elements.

Social Organization of Teachers and Students

Traditionally, students lived with their teacher, ideally in the same house. They received musical knowledge from their teacher and learned a way of life that revolved around music (Neuman 1980:54). Their teacher was respected not only in musical matters but also in all aspects of moral and physical behaviour (Shankar 1968:58), and provided food and clothing for them (Nag 1985:27-8). Students were regarded as family members and the ideal teacher-student relationship was almost homologous to that of father-son (Neuman 1980:45). Many students were indeed family members, and it was not uncommon amongst Muslim musicians for nephews to learn from their uncles (Shukla 1971:19; Yodh 1978:18; Owens 1983:175). Stylistic schools, called *gharanas,* were formed around these families of musicians, and, in order to perpetuate uniqueness, students were discouraged from listening to other performance styles during their formative training (Owens 1983:171). These social conventions and obligations served several purposes. Among the most important was the creation of a total learning environment. Training was enhanced by the teacher's discussions, performances and demonstrations as they occurred during the natural course of the day's events. The training received from a teacher held special significance and was referred to as *talim*.

Talim: *A System of Oral Training*

Given the lack of documentary evidence about the essential features of any one *guru's talim,* it is almost impossible to discover any pattern for the training carried out in a *guru-shishya parampara.* Yet certain attitudes and characteristics seem to be consistent across a broad spectrum of cases.

Talim seems to have been characterized by strictness in matters of practice and in one's devotion to music (Nag 1985:78; Owens 1983:172; Deshpande 1973:9). Notation was rarely if ever used (Athavale 1970:30; Nag 1985:78); thus, the student was forced to learn everything by rote. This required much repetition in formal training methods and practice (Van der Meer 1980:139; Ranade 1984:33). Consequently, *guru-shishya parampara* embodied a process of oral transmission which necessitated constant contact between teacher and student (Deshpande 1973:9). The oral nature of this transmission explains the special relationship between teacher and student as developed in the *guru-shishya parampara.*

Orality implies the pervasive presence of sound. The student's role as listener and receiver was as important as the *guru's* in sustaining memory and recalling oral concepts (Ranade 1984:28). Learning continued outside the specific formal musical instruction (*talim*) that a student received from his *guru,* through constant interaction with a *guru* in formal instruction, accompanying him during performance, and listening to him during practice sessions. Therefore, it is hardly surprising to find almost no documentary evidence for what could be said to have comprised a traditional *talim*. It defied documentation and appeared to exhibit inconsistency because of its very nature as an element of the oral tradition.

Institutions: A Twentieth-Century Phenomenon

It is widely recognised that the early institutionalization of Hindustani music occurred primarily because of the motivation and inspiration of two musician-educators, Pandit V.N. Bhatkhande and Pandit V.D. Paluskar. The institutions set up by these two men during the early decades of this century became the models for later musical institutions. Bhatkhande, in particular, is credited with having codified Hindustani music theory, notation and practice so that curricula could be organized systematically. His familiarity with Western education models through his own training as a lawyer undoubtedly contributed to his systematic approach to institutionalized music education. His inspiration is seen as a major factor in the founding of schools in Baroda, Gwalior, Bombay, Nagpur and Lucknow during the 1920s and 1930s (Misra 1985:12-13). Similarly, Paluskar established his first music school, the Gandharva Sangeet Mahavidyalaya, in Lahore in 1901, with another in Bombay some ten years later (Van der Meer 1980:124). Paluskar's approach to institutional music education differed from that of Bhatkhande in several ways. As a deeply religious man he viewed North Indian music from the standpoint of Hindu cultural traditions and philosophies. Yet he saw the adoption of institutional education as important for the development of Indian music in the twentieth century. Bhatkhande and Paluskar's efforts were in many ways revolutionary. To some they were a necessary step in the preservation of Hindustani music.

The system of royal patronage under which musicians had traditionally worked and taught was seen as having two faults: it had kept music within the hands of a privileged few, and in the opinion of a majority of the population music had become associated with decadent court life. Music institutions, on the other hand, gave music respectability and made way for its wider appreciation (Manuel 1986:478). Paradoxically, while the British administration in India fostered the traditional aristocratic patrons, they also introduced Western ideas of institutional education and thus encouraged a new system of patronage and musical training.

Though Bhatkhande and Paluskar are often credited with starting the first schools of music in India, closer examination of the facts shows that this trend towards institutionalization began earlier. Sourindro Mohun Tagore of Calcutta, Madhavrao Maharaj Scindia of Gwalior, and Sayajirao III of Baroda were all innovative in their experiments with institutional music education. All three were influenced by Western beliefs and attitudes. Sayajirao III of Baroda founded the Bharatiya Sangeet Vidyalaya in 1886. The exact circumstances of its establishment are unknown, but by 1926 it had become affiliated to Baroda University and by 1984 it had been elevated to the Faculty of Performing Arts within that university. Similarly, the Maharaja of Gwalior founded the Madho Sangeet Mahavidyalaya during the early part of this century, soliciting Bhatkhande's help. The Maharaja sent seven musicians to Bombay to learn Bhatkhande's notation system, so that it could be used in instruction at the school (Misra 1985:45).

The earliest known music institution in India was established by the wealthy landowner Sourindro Mohun Tagore in 1871, in Calcutta. This Bengal Music School employed at least five faculty members who taught both vocal and instrumental music to over fifty students in one location. Though fifty years span the period between the founding of the Bengal Music School and the Bhatkhande Sangeet Vidyapeet in Lucknow, there are certain similarities between the structures of these and other early music schools. This similarity resulted from the common purpose for which they were set up as well as the Western attitudes that began to permeate many areas of Indian society at this time.

Institutional music education sought to increase and preserve the appreciation of music throughout the larger Indian public. It also sought to give music the respectability of an academic discipline (Shankar 1968:51; Neuman 1980:198). Therefore schools had to cater somewhat indiscriminately to large student bodies. By the 1920s curricula were established in an effort to systematize assessment of students and to provide a basis for the awarding of degrees and diplomas. The completion of a three-year degree course became a means to increase one's prestige (Neuman 1980:208). Numerous teachers were collected in one location so that they became accessible to a large number of students. Classes of ten to eighteen students were taught in scheduled, time-bounded sessions, reducing individual teacher-student interaction.[2]

For this system to succeed, Bhatkhande and others thought it necessary to incorporate notation into teaching practice. This innovation not only contributed to the systematization of teaching, but also provided a means for preserving many compositions that might have been lost through the oral transmission process. Students were taught notation and tested on it. Examinations became an integral part of a student's life and Bhatkhande's books were widely used as references.

Adaptive Strategies: Two Case Studies

During the 1950s and 1960s music schools were established at an unprecedented rate. Most of these early post-independence schools chose to copy the Bhatkhande model. Set curricula and examinations were the basis for awarding degrees (Deva 1970:8). Not long after the rapid establishment of these schools in the 1960s, dissatisfaction with the new institutional patron began to grow amongst musicians. This growing sentiment can be seen in a variety of articles and books as well as in comments by musicians and scholars throughout the decades since independence (for example, see V.G. Jog quoted in Misra 1985:69; Van der Meer 1980:118; Athavale 1970:30; Deva 1970:7; Deshpande 1973:95-6; Neuman 1980:50). These comments do, nevertheless, acknowledge the function of institutions in promoting music appreciation amongst a wider audience. However, music appreciation and music performance do not require the same kind of training. Musicians over the past two decades have found it increasingly necessary to readopt aspects of the *guru-shishya parampara* to train competent performing musicians, thus conjoining two models — one a conceptual remnant of the *guru-shishya parampara,* and the other a legacy of early twentieth-century Westernization in education.

Changes occurring in music schools today demonstrate the adaptive strategies employed by traditional musicians in a modern environment — an environment that has been influenced by India's colonial past. They also highlight the aspects of the *guru-shishya parampara* that are relevant to the teaching of Hindustani music today. These adaptive strategies allow one to study an important aspect of intercultural contact through music in North India.

The Sangeet Research Academy, Calcutta

The Sangeet Research Academy was established in 1978 as an institution for the preservation and transmission of Hindustani music. Wholly funded by the India Tobacco Company, it is located in the southern area of central Calcutta. Its objectives, quite simply, are to recreate the atmosphere of the *guru-shishya parampara*. There are six teachers at the academy, each representing one vocal genre or *gharana*. *Tablā* accompanists may be hired to accompany formal instruction and performances, but there is no solo instrumental teaching.

The campus includes the main administration building and adjacent housing for faculty and student-scholars. Each faculty member has his or her own house or flat, which often includes rooms for student accommodation. Students who cannot be accommodated with their teachers are given rooms in an adjoining hostel. The academy covers all lodging expenses in addition to the regular faculty stipends.

Students must undergo an audition before a panel of expert musicians prior to entering the academy. A student selected by this panel must choose a teacher, who may then accept or reject the student. Students are called 'scholars' and receive a stipend and free accommodation. A scholar has indefinite tenure and continues studying with the same teacher as long as the teacher wishes; the scholar receives formal instruction only from the initially selected teacher. Thirteen scholars were enrolled at the time of my research in 1988. Some teachers had only one scholar studying and living with them. However, any teacher may accept general students who come to the house for intermittent formal instruction. These students do not live on campus, and do not pay fees or receive a stipend.

All formal instruction occurs in the houses of faculty members. No syllabus is followed. Once a year each scholar must give a performance that is recorded and evaluated by a panel of expert musicians, to ensure progress. Apart from this performance there are no examinations.[3] The academy does not award a degree or diploma.

Sri Ram Bharatiya Kala Kendra, New Delhi

Pandit[4] Amarnath, a vocal teacher at the Sri Ram Bharatiya Kala Kendra, offers an interesting comparison to the Sangeet Research Academy. The Kendra was organized by the central government's music bureau — the Sangeet Natak Akademi — as a centre for the teaching of the performing arts. It is largely funded by government grants, though students pay fees. Solo instrumental music and vocal music are taught in addition to three types of classical dance. Pt. Amarnath is the leading vocal teacher at the Kendra.

Pt. Amarnath is in full control of the selection of his students. A student he accepts receives automatic clearance from the administration. The Kendra refers all students directly to Pt. Amarnath if they wish to study with him. Students may continue to study with Pt. Amarnath for as long as they are able and for as long as Pt. Amarnath wishes. Therefore, no formal convocation marks the end of training.

In 1962 the Kendra became affiliated to a larger institution to facilitate the awarding of degrees. The examinations set by this larger institution are offered to all Kendra students. However, Pt. Amarnath does not allow his students to take these examinations. This is made clear at the time of a student's enrolment and is one of the criteria by which a student is accepted.

A building adjoining the main teaching studios provides accommodation for approximately twenty students and five faculty. The majority of faculty and students live off campus as hostel space is given on a priority basis to foreign students. Pt. Amarnath lives off campus and travels to the Kendra every morning six days a week to teach from 9.30 am to 12 noon. Students are scheduled to receive formal instruction only two or three times in a week but are encouraged to attend as many classes as they wish. An average of five students are present in class even while only one pupil receives formal instruction. The class is structured to allow learning through observation and discussion as well as individual formal instruction. I observed class discussion on such diverse topics as health, homeopathy and religion in addition to questions of general musical knowledge. Pt. Amarnath has approximately twenty-five students, four of whom also study at Delhi University in various degree programs. Most students study only with him, and none attends other classes at the Kendra.

Pt. Amarnath claims to teach his students in the *guru-shishya parampara* manner. It is apparent from a variety of sources that Pt. Amarnath's own training under Ustad Amir Khan followed this traditional model (Van der Meer 1980:139; Saxena 1974:11; and personal communications). However, the presence of the Kendra constrains several aspects of his teaching.

Conclusions

Teachers in the Sangeet Research Academy and the Bharatiya Kala Kendra believe that the modern/Western institutional system has significant ills that must be redressed through the adoption of the *guru-shishya parampara*. The assimilative process rejects those elements of an institutional education that are incompatible with the *guru-shishya parampara* while maintaining elements required by changing circumstances. The two institutions take different approaches to this assimilative process. Yet the musicians at each school have adapted to the institutional system in similar ways. They have all accepted an administration as a necessary element in management; maintained teacher control over student selection; eliminated time-bound classes in formal instruction; eliminated curricula, examinations and degrees; and tended toward a complete training atmosphere conducted by a single teacher.

Most noteworthy in both cases is the elimination of curricula, examinations and degrees. For Pt. Amarnath and the teachers at the Sangeet Research Academy evaluation is acceptable, but it is never an ultimate recognition of the completion of study. For them, the transmission of knowledge cannot be structured into the time-restricting framework of a degree course, and, therefore, even examinations that include a practical performance component can show little about a student's achievements as a performing musician. The highest accolade for which students strive is the positive appraisal of teacher and peers, not a Bachelor of Music degree. Yet, the acceptance of an administration is an acknowledgement that institutionalization holds certain benefits in an environment of government and private corporate patronage. Were a teacher to teach privately, certain necessary financial restrictions would be placed on both student and teacher that would hinder the transmission process.

The remaining areas of assimilation indicate the particular structures in these two situations that maintain the dominance of a single teacher over a given student's training. This occurs in both student selection and formal instruction. At the Sangeet Research Academy the residential *guru-shishya parampara* situation is approximated, thereby enhancing this total learning environment. While Pt. Amarnath cannot create this same residential atmosphere, he has at the very least structured his classes to enhance student-teacher interaction.

The adaptive strategies seen in these two case studies show an assimilation of elements of the *guru-shishya parampara* that arise from and are compatible with the oral nature of Hindustani music. The complete learning atmosphere that existed in the *guru-shishya parampara* is still considered the best means for transmitting an oral tradition, consequently the teachers in both cases rejected certain features of institutionalized music education that had compromised the oral transmission process.

Notes

1   For both Hindu and Muslim musicians, the teacher-disciple tradition was an important social relationship in which musical knowledge was transmitted. The term *guru-shishya parampara* has

predominantly Hindu connotations but nevertheless is often used by both Hindu and Muslim musicians.

2   Many people are now realizing that Bhatkhande's education ideals have in some cases been misconstrued. Class size may by necessity have been close to twenty, but Bhatkhande himself never believed all twenty students should sing in unison. In most institutions today, a great deal of unison singing occurs. A reappraisal of Bhatkhande's works might well show other such examples.

3   This matter was coming under review while I was visiting the academy in January 1988.

4   *Pandit* is an honorific term for a Hindu teacher and is often abbreviated as 'Pt'.

References

ATHAVALE, V.R.
    1970   'The Improvisation of the Musical Composition'. *Journal of the Indian Musicological Society* 1/3:30-2.
DESHPANDE, Vamanrao H.
    1973   *Indian Musical Traditions: An Aesthetic Study of the Gharanas in Hindustani Music.* Bombay: Popular Prakashan.
DEVA, B.C.
    1970   'A Decade of Indian Music'. *Journal of the Indian Musicological Society* 1/4:5-16.
MANUEL, Peter
    1986   'The Evolution of Modern *Thumri*'. *Ethnomusicology* 30:470-90.
MISRA, Susheela
    1985   *Music Makers of the Bhatkhande College of Hindustani Music.* Sangeet Research Academy.
NAG, Deepali
    1985   *Ustad Faiyaaz Khan.* New Delhi: Sangeet Natak Akademi.
NEUMAN, Daniel M.
    1980   *The Life of Music in North India.* Detroit: Wayne State Univ. Press. Repr. Chicago: The Univ. of Chicago Press, 1990.
OWENS, Naomi
    1983   'The Dagar Gharana: A Case Study of Performing Artists'. In *Performing Arts in India: Essays on Music, Dance and Drama,* ed. Bonnie C. Wade. Monograph Series no. 21, Center for South and Southeast Asia Studies, University of

California Berkeley. New York: University Press of America, pp.158-237. Repr. in *Asian Music* 18/2, 1987.

RANADE, Ashok D.

1984   *On Music and Musicians of Hindoostan.* New Delhi: Promilla.

SAXENA, S.K.

1974   'Ameer Khan: The Man and his Art'. *Sangeet Natak* 31:5-12.

SHANKAR, Ravi

1968   *My Music, My Life.* New Delhi: Vikas Publications.

SHUKLA, Narendrarai N.

1971   'Alladiya Khan — As I Knew Him'. *Journal of the Indian Musicological Society* 2/3:14-25.

VAN DER MEER, Wim

1980   *Hindustani Music in the Twentieth Century.* The Hague: Martinus Nijhoff.

YODH, S.N.

1978   'Vilayat Hussain Khan of the Agra Gharana'. *Journal of the Indian Musicological Society* 9/3:17-38.

American Midwestern Schools of Music as Venues of Musical Mediation and Confrontation

Bruno Nettl

In ethnomusicological literature, the concept of a meeting of musical cultures has ordinarily suggested large-scale events such as the confrontation of Western and Indic musics in modern India, or of sub-Saharan and Middle Eastern-based traditions in pre-modern West Africa. They have usually been sketched with a wide brush drawing movements of societies, large repertoires, generalized and widely shared elements of style. It is instructive also to consider the meeting of musics in venues such as concerts, weddings, radio programs, films, night clubs, stores, publishing houses and schools, all of them microcosms, as it were, of the total cultural system. This essay considers schools of music at large American universities as places of both convergence and collision of many musics.[1] These include standard Western art music (principally composed between 1720 and 1920, the 'common-practice' period, here labelled 'central classical music'); 'early' music (Medieval, Renaissance, early Baroque); 'new' or experimental art music (largely music composed after 1960); jazz; folk and ethnic music of European-derived cultures; non-Western traditions; and some musics that make rare appearances in the academic sector of Western musical culture — popular music including rock and country-and-western, and light classical music. Some of these would be accepted as distinct musics by measures conventionally used by musicologists and theorists. Others are clearly considered to be separate by the members of Music School society despite their stylistic similarity. The interaction of these musics in an American institution is not unlike the meeting of cultures on a broader scale.[2]

Venues and Basic Assumptions

Schools of Music in 1950 and 1990

The poly-musical situation as it existed in the 1980s is the principal focus of this essay. The world of music school musics about 1950 was substantially different, as these same institutions were then essentially unimusical. Despite their substantial size (ca. 300-700 full-time music majors), the students and teachers of that era were devoted to the propagation of Western classical music. There was, to be sure, some musical experimentation in the sense of a development of 'new' music within the sociocultural framework of the classical, incorporated into the general classical performance framework and repertoire and not treated as a separate music. Thus, works of Bartók, Stravinsky and Webern were performed in concerts along with older music. 'Early' music (pre-1650) was hardly performed except as a classroom exercise, and there were no concerts of non-Western or ethnic music and no folk music perform-ances, except strictly outside the School of Music, sponsored by and located in other units of the university. Jazz was barely beginning to make inroads, but only on the assumption that it would be integrated into the classical framework — the large band, with conductor, printed music and hardly any improvisation. The unimusical conception of the school was not questioned, and the suggestion that one might introduce musics outside the central classical into the concert schedule or the curriculum was greeted as a joke. Music education, music appreciation and music theory courses concentrated totally on the so-called common-practice styles. Theory courses were almost exclusively devoted to functional harmony along with a little sixteenth-century counterpoint. In contrast to the more multicultural leanings of departments of visual art and literature, within the School of Music one found the basic assumption that the culture's central music was the European art music mainly of the late Baroque, Classical and Romantic periods — the music of the composers whose names were engraved on the outside of the building and whose works were listed under the heading 'Music' in the library's catalogue, in contrast to 'Folk music', 'Popular music', 'Music,

Indic', or 'Music — to 1800'. Other music was kept away: ignored; relegated in courses to special short bits somehow to underscore its inappropriateness; kept out of the lives of students by the active discouragement of participation in dance bands and popular entertainment. It was not an institution in which musical cultures met.

Forty years later, the midwestern university School of Music, typically doubled in size through economic prosperity and population growth, has become one of the institutions in American society in which musics meet, but an institution that makes judgments about the ways in which these musics, and the societies they reflect, are related.

The World of Musics, Bimusicality and Polymusicality

For the reader who may wonder about the appropriateness of ethnomusicological perspective in a discussion of an American academic institution, let me first point out that musicologists (including ethnomusicologists) have typically seen the world of music as a group of discrete musics which have a structure, provenance and relationship to society somewhat like those of languages (see, further, Nettl 1985:18-19). The guiding basic assumption is that a society — a discrete population — has *a* music, or at least a principal music, which consists of a set of rules and principles governing ideas about music, musical behaviour and musical sound, a repertoire of some degree of consistency, with a hierarchy of central and peripheral phenomena. In general, a 'society' is a people with distinct culture, what we usually regard as a nationality. There is Italian music, Chinese music, Arapaho Indian music, Ewe music. This homology of society and music is of course an oversimplification and subject to criticism, but it may be helpful here at least as a point of departure.

If we build on the analogy with languages, we see bi-musicality and polymusicality playing a greater and more complicated role in musical culture than their linguistic counterparts. For while linguistic competence can be more or less easily established (see, e.g., Labov 1972:186, 191), it is difficult to determine just what is required for a person to 'have competence in', participate in, 'understand', possess or 'identify with' a music. While languages are moderately close to equal in complexity and amount of content such as size of vocabulary, musics differ enormously at least in quantity — length of units (pieces, songs), desirable timbres such as instruments, number of available textures and, most of all, size of repertoire. Beyond that, a 'polymusical' person may participate in a variety of musics to very different degrees and in very different ways. Assuming — as we will in the rest of this essay — that a large culture such as that of the United States has a considerable number of musics, we can imagine a professional clarinettist who plays in a symphony orchestra and teaches clarinet (his main music is 'central classical'), occasionally sits in a jazz ensemble but is not considered very good, tries to listen occasionally to records of rock music in order to empathize with his teenage son, once took a course in Indian music and occasionally tries *kriti*-s on his instrument. He participated in a tour of Peru where he heard a good deal of Quechua and Aymara music and liked it, and he plays, but generally dislikes and claims not to understand, some works of post-1960 'new' music. How polymusical is this musician? His musical life could be described as a set of concentric circles, with Western classical music in the centre. Analogous situations may exist in linguistic participation, but the complex type of situation just described and probably quite common in American culture would tend to be rare in language behaviour.

A Blackfoot man claimed to have two musics central in his life — the intertribal powwow repertoire of Plains Indian cultures, and the country-and-western music which he plays in a small band in a bar. He was also trying to learn, but slowly, some older and explicitly Blackfoot ceremonial music. He played trumpet in a high school band and learned the typical repertoire of such institutions (marches and some concert music), he goes to Methodist church and can sing several hymns from memory, and, a person with a sense of curiosity, he has seen two opera productions at a nearby college. This structure, with dual centre, shares characteristics with the concentric circle format.

This type of musical persona has become increasingly the norm in the cultures of the world. But if individuals are now frequently polymusical, institutions and contexts for musical performance may be either uni-musical or polymusical. The Blackfoot powwow; the Metropolitan opera house; the First Lutheran Church; the *dowreh* in north Tehran devoted to Persian classical music; Sastri Hall, of Karnatic concerts, in the Mylapore district of Madras; the Rose Bowl in Urbana, Illinois (home of 1950s country music); the typical American radio station, devoted to jazz, heavy metal, 1960s rock, rap, or church music; the violin lesson; the rehearsal of the big-band jazz organization: these are all examples of principally unimusical institutions.

Organizations and Institutions that Mediate Among Musics

There are also organizations and institutions whose function, and sometimes purpose, is to effect mediation among musics. In the music histories of some cultures, such units seem in the last several decades to have gradually increased in significance. Let me give some examples.

Concerts. The public concert in Europe gradually (and no doubt with exceptions, detours and reverses) moved from the presentation of music in one style, or by one composer, to something requiring diversity and synthesis. But typical concerts around 1840 in Western European cities consisted of music from the present and the immediate past (e.g. a concert of a variety of works by Beethoven); representative orchestra concerts today include music from a span of 200 years, and many choral concerts, material from the early seventeenth century to the late twentieth. Even so, these concerts are not mediators among musics in the larger sense; they include only the central art music. But they may provide a mix of materials that were at one time incompatible: symphonies and concertos written for a court along with overtures from operas and works originally regarded as sacred, for example.

The introduction of the public Western-style concert in other societies had a similar effect in more emphatic form. The concerts of Karnatic music that take place in Madras afternoons and evenings during the so-called Music Season, in December and early January, consist of songs and improvisations in all sorts of ragas, some of them traditionally winter or summer ragas, some morning and some evening ragas, all at the same time and season, and in new sorts of juxtaposition to each other.

A traditional Persian performance, typically taking place in a private venue, would consist of a lengthy exposition of a single *dastgah* or mode; but modern public concerts, given in evenings in a concert hall, complete with printed program and intermission, might provide short performances of two to five *dastgahs*. Or, going further afield in synthesis and combination, a concert by the North American Indian Dance Theater combines many kinds of Indian music and dance — material from different culture areas, from different times, and with varying degrees of phantasy and Westernization. Thus, a concert itself may be seen as a mediating institution among musical cultures.

Recordings. The existence and ready availability of recordings has actually and potentially broadened the musical experience of many millions of individuals, in effect making the private home a kind of venue for the meeting of musical cultures. More obvious as a mediating locale is the record shop, in North America for example, but also in Indian cities, in pre-1978 Tehran, and even on Indian reservations. The typical record shop sells musics of various sorts. In Iran, twenty years ago, one would find (in separate sections) Iranian popular music, Western popular music, some (though admittedly little) music from India, Afghanistan and Arab nations, some Persian classical music, Islamic sermons and Koran reading, and Western classical music. In record stores of Madras, a city in which patrons of live performance concentrated on Karnatic music and some film music performed in night clubs, some record stores would additionally carry Hindustani music, a large quantity of film music in various languages and from various parts of India, and a small amount of music from outside India. The American record store has its separate sections: rock, pop, 'soul', rhythm-and-blues, country, folk, classical and 'international'. On Indian reservations, stores selling records — usually those that also sell other kinds of specifically Indian artifacts — provide recordings of music by a variety of Indian peoples in a number of styles and with various degrees of modernization, and music in totally Western styles performed by Indians. Although I know little (and there seems to be no literature)[3] about the ways in which record store patrons interact in stores and to what extent they are stimulated to permit musics to meet in their experience, these shops at least provide the opportunity for musical cultures to meet.

Other Contexts. Without going into detail, we may consider certain films and film music traditions (for example, the multi-stylistic film repertoire of the Indian film industry); certain radio stations (but not the typical American music stations, which specialize in narrow repertoires such as classical, recent rock, older rock, Beatles only, jazz, country-and-western, bluegrass); and libraries.

Finally, *Music Schools.* In certain respects, an American university School of Music in the period ca. 1980-90 has also been an institution that mediates among many musics. It does this by welcoming, in its peculiar way, a number of distinct musics into its scope of activity and providing a taxonomy for them, permitting them to interact, but finally, also, providing roles and functions for them and their adherents that present them in a hierarchy and suggest ways in which the 'highest form' — central classical music — may, as it were, be served by the others.

The Musics of the School of Music

What justifies the description of a School of Music as inhabited by different musics, and how can we establish the boundaries among them? Examining performances — concerts — is most immediately helpful. We may ask whether the somewhat vague and broad taxonomy based on aspects of style and sound, presented above and common to the terminology of the school's citizens, is reflected elsewhere. One kind of answer comes from examining the costumes of the performers and their interaction with each other and with the audience. The main types of music, or the musics, are as follows.

A. Classical music from the period 1720 to 1920 or a little later, already labelled as the 'central classical' repertoire. Male performers dress in tuxedos (or dark suits) and women in modestly formal dress. Musicians interact with each other not at all or in accordance with prescribed ritual, thus: the conductor, upon entering, shakes hands with the concertmaster, asks the orchestra to rise to acknowledge applause, etc. Interaction with the audience is similarly formal. Performers do not speak to the audience except sometimes to announce encores, and even this is done with some visible embarrassment. Otherwise, interaction is through applause and bows, and at most goes as far as calls of 'Bravo!' and presentation of flowers on stage. Members of the audiences dress (not uniformly, of course) with relative formality. One sees many men in suits and few without neckties. There is approximate correlation between formality of audience dress, cost of tickets and size of the production. Thus, the most formal dress is found in opera audiences, followed by symphony orchestra, chamber music and finally solo piano recitals.[4]

B. 'New' music, clearly distinguished by its style at least most of the time, is performed by musicians dressed more informally. A typical outfit is slacks and a turtle-neck sweater (for some women as well as men), but others, with or without jacket, may be found. The performers in an ensemble try not to appear in perfect uniform. The relationship between musicians and audience is usually as formal as in the central classical music performances, although during some of the pieces the relationship among performers and even between performers and audience may, by exception, occasionally be very close and informal. In contrast to central music, 'new' music scores sometimes include directions to that effect and in other ways provide for non-sonic aspects of the music, such as the measurement of the piano with a tape measure by the soloist in John

Cage's Piano Concerto. Audiences at new music concerts dress informally but not casually; indeed, many individuals dress rather as do the performers, and while there is much variety, this similarity may have to do with the desire of the audience to show its identification with the musicians, in what is sometimes considered a downtrodden and neglected sector of the musical world. Indeed, the audience consists substantially of composers and performers of 'new music'; to a greater degree than in the other genres, the composers, performers and listeners are the same people. Even when this is not the case, the impression of unity of performers and audience in new music concerts is remarkable, and comparable to that of 'ethnic' concerts.

C. Although the type of jazz performed in a university does not really correspond to the important types of jazz heard in the public sector, jazz is regarded as a separate category. One rarely hears solo or small ensemble performances in a School of Music; normally it is the so-called 'big-band' jazz. Musicians dress in uniform, but it is normally non-matching trousers and sports jackets or blazers. In general, the performances are formal, and the musicians in dress and behaviour share the characteristics of their tuxedo-clad colleagues. However, the leader or conductor addresses the audience, announcing pieces (there is no printed program), giving some background about individual musicians and works, telling about recent and forthcoming tours of the group, and making occasional jokes. After a number he calls out the names of soloists as they rise or walk forward to take bows. During a piece, soloists move from their seats and walk to the front of the ensemble, facing the audience while playing.

The audience dresses informally, and there are more children than in central classical or new music audiences. In particular, many men wear sweaters, some of the same men, indeed, who may have been seen wearing suits at the previous night's symphony concerts.

D. 'Ethnic' concerts include some performed by members of the school and others brought in for education and entertainment, and include events such as the following: folk song concerts; performances by a resident Russian folk orchestra populated by Americans; a chorus of African Americans (and a few others) labelled the 'Black Chorus'; a visiting chorus of gospel singers. What distinguishes this group from the others, including concerts of non-Western music discussed below, is the real or at least presumed identification of the performers and their music with the audience in not only musical but also social and cultural senses.

The basic assumption is that an 'ethnic' concert is directed to a particular audience comprised of members of an ethnic or racial group or of a social or political movement — at least so it is perceived by many participants.

Performers' dress is in some way symbolic of the ethnic group in question — traditional rural folk costumes are most typical, but 'mod' dress, brightly coloured choir robes, uniformly plaid shirts may appear. The leader of the group usually addresses the audience before the performance and between the numbers, in a tone that assumes performers and audience to be an exclusive group and the event a kind of conspiracy against the establishment. Not usually explanatory of the music, the remarks introduce individuals, delve (by implication) into their personal lives and attitudes, include anecdotes, and may be mildly deprecatory — with a wink — of the music being performed. There are jokes and expressions thought to be intelligible only to the ethnic audience. All together, in contrast to the central classical concert which maintains distance between performers and audience, the people present at an 'ethnic' concert seem to feel themselves more of a group. Informal dress of the audience is characteristic — blue jeans, leather jackets, no neckties; or sometimes conspicuous formal dress.

E. Concerts of non-Western music, particularly of university groups such as a gamelan, by local faculty such as a sitar teacher, or by visiting groups such as a Japanese classical ensemble, share characteristics with both the ethnic and classical concerts. Audiences include many members of the nationality whose music is being performed, and to them it is in part an 'ethnic' event. For the other members of the audience, they are essentially educational experiences. An Indian concert is seen as a way of drawing the local Indian community together and of fostering respect for Indian culture; thus, dress is very formal, and members of the audience interact before the concert and in the intermission in a particularly enthusiastic manner. American members of the audience, faculty and students, exhibit no consistency in dress. The performers wear traditional Indian costume, whether they are in fact Indians or Americans, and whatever they may wear in everyday life. The interaction with the audience is a mixture of traditional and educational. For example, someone introduces the Indian performers — a non-Indian faculty member or administrator is regarded as ideal — giving, in Indian style, the musical genealogy of performers, but also providing some factual material about the music, as one might do in a classroom. Communication between performers and audience is generally like that of Western classical concerts.

F. 'Early' music, Medieval, Renaissance and early Baroque, is performed at special concerts, by ensembles generally called Collegia Musica. This repertoire is kept quite separate from the central classical repertoire, whose concerts hardly ever include Renaissance or even early Baroque pieces. Special instruments (although this early repertoire could also be played on standard instruments), special costumes often based on dress in Elizabethan England, and attempts to make these events partially into educational events relate early music concerts to those of non-Western music. The two types also share patterns in audience behaviour and the relationship between performers and audience.

G. This listing accounts for the vast majority of concerts in the music building. Musical life in the surrounding university and local community includes other kinds of music and social contexts, primarily rock and related genres, and country music, performed in bars or night clubs. They too have their traditional costume — unpredictable in the case of rock, though no two members of a group dress identically — and farm or work clothes or spectacular outfits related to these in the case of country music. The point is that groups of this sort occasionally appear in the music building, where we may associate them in behaviour and in performer/relationship with musics mentioned already — new music in the case of rock, ethnic concerts in the case of country-and-western.

The Musics Meet: Collision or Convergence?

The music building absorbs all of these kinds of music and thus provides a venue for musical cultures to meet. It does this, however, by continually asserting the hegemony of the classical music, in two ways: (1) the taxonomy symbolized by dress suggests a hierarchy; and (2) the various musics and their events are permitted into the music building if they conform to standards developed in the classical concert.

In what is a complex set of relationships, various kinds of encounters might occur. For example: individuals attend all or several of the concert types. There is overlapping and borrowing of musical styles. The various kinds of music are performed in identical performance contexts. The types of concerts are governed by similar sets of values.

A. *Audiences.* A Music School[5] and its associated performance institutions have a large potential audience, a community of perhaps 100,000, all of whom are welcome. In fact, while a precise count is not available, concert-goers of some regularity are far fewer: in highly approximate estimate, some 300 music students (out of 800 in residence) may attend concerts regularly, along with 80 music professors and about 100 students from other departments plus about 300 non-music university employees and townspeople who appear occasionally. Although there is significant overlapping, the tendency is for each concert type to have a specialized audience, divided along various lines – ethnicity, level of education, political attitude, and most obviously by age. Indeed, if we can describe American society as comprised of a multitude of ethnicities, white American 'Anglo' cultures are importantly divided by age, each age group having its typical ethnic music. For example, the audience of central classical concerts is oldest, and that of new music and ethnic events, youngest. Within the classical repertoire, chamber music and organ concerts attract older audiences than symphony concerts. Jazz concerts have an older audience than does the concert band. In the meeting of musical cultures in the music building, there is only a small group of people who attend performances of all or several of the musics.

B. *The Ensemble Requirement.* The interaction of musics takes place in a hierarchical system which is symbolized in several ways. First, the clearly upper-class dress of performers in concerts of central classical music supports its elevation, as does the formal dress and relatively higher age of the audience. Related to this most obvious correlation are some fundamental issues in the debates that determine the day-to-day business of the music school. For example, one of the most prominent aspects of the school is the large number of ensembles which it sponsors. These are said to exist for the training of students in repertoire and performance practice, but in large measure their purpose is to provide musical entertainment and edification for the university and local community. Each student is required to perform in a 'conducted ensemble'.

The issue of which ensembles actually count as 'conducted' is one of the points of debate. Among the ensembles are the following: symphony orchestra; concert band; marching band; several choruses; wind ensemble; jazz band; Russian folk orchestra; gamelan; opera company; Peruvian panpipe ensemble; southern African mbira ensemble; new music ensemble; string quartets; small jazz bands; clarinet choir. The great majority of these work under a conductor and perform music from the period 1700-1930.

The jazz band, gamelan, string quartet, mbira and panpipe ensembles, and the new music ensemble either perform music outside this period or do not clearly have a conductor (although leadership by a faculty member is present). To have these ensembles accepted as fulfilling the requirement has always been difficult for students and faculty (although in the end they succeed), and it is made clear that 'the School' would prefer to have students perform in symphony orchestra, band and large chorus. Ensembles outside the central classic framework must fight for inclusion and must prove their worth either by performing music that is in some ways similar to the central art music or at least by operating in ways similar to the large ensembles — using printed music and having a conductor. Thus, the Russian folk orchestra is successful because it plays from scores and parts, has a conductor, and uses functional harmony in arrangements of traditional Russian folk tunes. The gamelan succeeds because its adherents argue that there is actually a conductor (even though he does not stand in front beating time in the air), and they point out that among non-Western ensembles, it comes closest, in its internal structure and that of its music, to the large Western ensembles. Peruvian and African ensembles are included because they are large enough; string quartets, small jazz bands, sitar-and-tabla are not included because they have no conductors. Rock and other popular ensembles meet none of the criteria. A conducted orchestra playing light music would be included.

The importance of large ensembles with conductor seems to me to be related to fundamental values of Western urban and middle-class culture (see Nettl 1989) — the homology between symphony orchestra and factory, military organization and hierarchical social structure (Small 1987). The fact that the symphonic repertoire includes some of the music regarded as greatest by Western audiences and critics revolves in part from the acceptance of this value structure by composers, performers and audiences. The way in which the Music School permits musics to meet but also to retain their proper relationships is by privileging the large ensembles and accepting those of other musics — new, old, jazz, popular, ethnic, non-Western — grudgingly, and if at all then to the degree that they adopt the values of the central music. This is, of course, also a process to be observed in Asian and African nations that have developed orchestras of traditional music and instruments for just this competitive function (Nettl 1985:57-61).

C. *The Results of the Meeting.* The influence of non-Western, folk and earlier music on the central classical repertoire and its composers since the Renaissance (but mainly in the last 150 years) is often mentioned in music history courses, but not much is made of it in the Music School's world of performance. No thought, for example, is usually given to arranging works so as to emphasize the influence, such as the use of strange vocal styles or costumes (if one can imagine that), or more realistically, to arranging programs that exhibit the influence specifically (e.g., for Hungarian folk music, a concert of relevant works by Bartók, Liszt, Brahms, Haydn and Schubert). In the central classical concert, the meeting of musics is effected totally on the terms of the central repertoire. A folk tune is a theme in a symphony, harmonized and performed by the traditional woodwinds. An African drum is integrated into the standard percussion section.

In concerts outside the central classical framework, the sounds of musical cultures meet by approximating classical ideals. The very concept of concerts is not compatible with the traditional performance contexts of most or much non-Western music, but for that matter also not of Medieval, jazz and folk performance. The traditional three-hour concert of Madras (already in part a product of Westernization) and the three sets of jazz at a club become in the music school ninety-minute concerts with intermission. The concert band too is structured as an analogue of the symphony orchestra. Emphasis is on ensembles comparable to the orchestra (the gamelan, large jazz band) or Western chamber groups. There is no thought of having a jazz club or an African ceremony in the gym. The various musics meet in part by being placed in a common concert format, having some overlapping of audience and being subjected to the system of values governing the culture of classical Western music. But in terms of musical style, they do not really meet. For one thing, there is the matter of purity.

D. *The Importance of Purity.* The concept of purity, in various respects, plays a substantial role in the Music School, though the 'impure', the stylistically and culturally mixed, has its place as well. In important ways, what is in some sense 'pure' is privileged. Thus, concerts remain inside their taxonomic boundaries; you do not find a string quartet before intermission and a sitar after, or, contrary to Beethoven's time, an orchestra preceded by solo piano. There is great interest in authentic performance, rendered in accordance with composers' intentions and historical performance practice. In historical teaching and scholarship, there is emphasis on periods of stylistic stability, the centres of stylistic periods and the periods in a composer's career, and some neglect of the unclear boundaries between them. Students are discouraged by their primary teachers from performing or hearing music outside their major field of interest. Attention is focused on the static, not on the changing. The meeting of musics is somewhat inhibited by these attitudes.

Considering the co-existence in the music school of a group of musics, all under the hegemony of the classical system, one might expect to see the emergence of performances in which are found combinations of musical style or repertoire. Analogous combinations (sometimes including elements of Western music) have been found in the concert performances by national or nationalistic music and music/dance ensembles in Asian and African nations. Actually, the influence flows mainly from the central style to the peripheral ones. East European folk music is accepted in that aspect of it that is performed by large ensembles — the Russian folk orchestra, its organization analogous to the symphony; the Balkan choir, analogous to the concert choir. The large jazz band, a miniature of the concert band, is there, playing a substantial amount of music that lacks important characteristics of jazz such as improvisation; playing from music, it doesn't swing. The point is not that this kind of jazz does not exist in the outside, 'real' world of jazz, but that the school selects it to be the exemplar of jazz within its walls.

Convergence or Collisions?

Let me summarize with the characterization of the musics of the music school as if they were groups of people in society. Its centre, the central classical music and the students and teachers most associated with it, welcome the peripheral musics under particular conditions. These must change to conform to the centre's standards in behaviour and conception in order to maintain their distinctive sound; this includes the concert format, audience behaviour in the most general sense, the privileging of large ensembles and conductors. They are encouraged to maintain stylistic consistency. They do not share the stage with the central classical music, and only rarely with each other. They avoid the promulgation of mixed styles, of musical pidgins (such as certain styles of Indian film music or African popular music).

In their social context, they are permitted entry to the music building as long as they do not threaten the central music, as they might, for instance, if they had a major impact on the ensemble requirement or the sequence of required music history or theory courses. They are optional adjuncts to the curriculum of the centre, while the central repertoire is anything but optional in the curricula where the peripheral musics are a specialty.

We return to the macrocosm of world music seen as a confrontation of musical systems resulting in convergences and collisions. On the world scene these meetings exhibit a variety of results: the total abandonment of genres, styles, repertoires, entire musical systems; the development of syncretic styles and repertoires; the increased diversity of musical opportunity for certain individuals; the artificial and compartmentalized preservation of older traditions; transfer of discrete traits of music; pluralistic coexistence of music; embracing or rejection of the new. In any one meeting of cultures, a variety of musical results may ensue, but occasionally one predominates.[6] The processes and results mentioned may be helpful in characterizing the meeting of musics in the music school.

In the microcosm of the music school, repertoires are not lost or abandoned, and syncretic styles do not often result. The individual is given increased opportunity to become polymusical, and at the same time, artificial preservation of musics — 'early' and non-Western musics in particular — sometimes occurs. In the juxtaposition of the central classical repertoire to its less significant satellite styles, the parallel to the relationship of a dominant culture to its satellites, or of a major power to Third World colonies, is unavoidable. The traditional culture of the dependent societies must conform to the values of the central power while yet maintaining its distance. This might mean adopting Christianity but eschewing industrialization, or imitating Western-style family life but avoiding intermarriage. The minority or peripheral musics in the Music School tend to maintain separation; jazz and Indian music and even 'new' music do not enter the framework of the concerts or curricula of the central classical repertoire. On the other hand, they are not permitted life in their own cultural contexts but, to exist at all, must imitate the contexts of the central music.

The university Music School is a place of musical mediation only to a degree and is a venue of both convergences and collisions. Convergence: individuals are free to participate at least as listeners and passive students in courses in a number of the musics that inhabit the building, and there is a modest degree of stylistic overlap and fusion. But collision: the musics, as it were, repel each other, maintaining distance, coexisting in the hierarchical social structure that Western academics have long taken for granted, permitted to maintain a modest spot in the institution if they bow to the values of the centre.

Notes

1   The data for this essay, largely the author's personal experience, come from Schools of Music at the Universities of Illinois and Michigan, and Indiana University, but are generally indicative of schools of music or large music departments at other major institutions in the United States. For corroborative data and a somewhat different view of American conservatories, see Kingsbury 1988.

2   In this discussion, I refer, for purposes of theoretical abstraction, to musics and musical systems as if they had, as it were, lives of their own, realizing that they are the results of human decision and action but also that they constitute, for societies and their subdivisions, powerful symbols of identity, relationship, and cultural locus (see Powers 1980:8).

3   An interesting exception was a paper presented by John F. Szwed and Morton Marks at the 31st Annual Meeting of the Society for Ethnomusicology, Rochester, New York (Szwed & Marks 1986).

4   See Kingsbury 1988:111-41, Small 1987 and Finnegan 1988. My own data come from three years of systematic observations in Krannert Center for the Performing Arts and other concert venues at the University of Illinois and other midwestern schools of music.

5   The data in this paragraph refer specifically to the community of Champaign-Urbana, Illinois, and the University of Illinois student body and faculty.

6   The literature on this subject is large; but see in particular Kartomi 1981; Shiloah & Cohen 1983; Blum, Bohlman & Neuman 1991. A summary of research with bibliography is found in Nettl 1986.

References

BLUM, Stephen, Philip V. Bohlman & Daniel M. Neuman (eds.)
     1991   *Ethnomusicology and Modern Music History.* Urbana: University of Illinois Press.

FINNEGAN, Ruth
     1988   *The Hidden Musicians.* Cambridge: Cambridge University Press.

KARTOMI, Margaret J.
     1981   'The Processes and Results of Musical Culture Contact'. *Ethnomusicology* 25:227-50.

KINGSBURY, Henry
  1988   *Music, Talent, and Performance: A Conservatory Cultural System.* Philadelphia: Temple University Press.
LABOV, William
  1972   *Sociolinguistic Patterns.* Philadelphia: University of Pennsylvania Press.
NETTL, Bruno
  1985   *The Western Impact on World Music.* New York: Schirmer Books.
  1986   'World Music in the Twentieth Century: A Survey of Research on Western Influence'. *Acta Musicologica* 58:360-73.
  1989   'Mozart and the Ethnomusicological Study of Western Culture'. *Yearbook for Traditional Music* 20:1-16.
POWERS, Harold S.
  1980   'Language Models and Musical Analysis'. *Ethnomusicology* 24:1-60.
SHILOAH, Amnon & Erik Cohen
  1983   'The Dynamics of Change in Jewish Oriental Ethnic Music in Israel'. *Ethnomusicology* 27:227-52.
SMALL, Christopher
  1987   'Performance as Ritual: Sketch for an Enquiry into the True Nature of a Symphony Concert'. In Avron Levine White, ed., *Lost in Music: Culture, Style, and the Musical Event.* London: Routledge & Kegan Paul, pp. 6-32.
SZWED, John F. & Morton Marks
  1986   'Fieldwork in Record Stores'. Paper delivered at 31st Annual Meeting, Society for Ethnomusicology, Rochester, NY.

Irish Meets Folk:
The Genesis of the Bush Band

Graeme Smith

During the 1970s a vocal and instrumental ensemble known as the bush band appeared on the Australian folk music scene. It was a group of about five musicians, who performed a combination of Australian vernacular ballads and mostly Irish dance music played in relatively unsophisticated style. While the bush band sometimes played on the concert platform, its main performance context was the 'bush dance'. Such occasions were most often urban and the dances chosen as historical Australian 'folk dances'. A dance caller would enable those unfamiliar with the dances to participate and the forms were often simplified. Throughout the evening these dances were interspersed with songs performed by the band. Over a decade these bands and their performances quickly became popular among a wide range of social groups, from inner-city students to sub-urban working class families, as well as folk enthusiasts with whom the style originated. The bush dance became a popular choice for cross-generational events like weddings and twenty-first birthday parties, and for community fundraising events (O'Shea 1988:102). The bush band reached its peak of popularity around 1980. Although less popular now, it is still well-established in Australian musical life, and its music is the most important popular public genre of Australian folk music.

As a localised popular music style, the bush band has its parallels in other regions of the world. Current fashions in the mass recording industry place these genres among world music, and they are marketed for urban western listeners as authentic and stylistically varied. In aspects of its instrumentation and origins, the bush band is comparable with bluegrass; in attitudes to its historical and social place, with Jewish-American klezmer music; in its politics, with the Chilean new song movement. Its social meaning in Australia has emerged from its unique historical and social origins, and its popularity illuminates broader issues in Australian social consciousness and cultural history.

Bush bands play Australian folk music with a strong Irish inflection. The songs celebrate and document the lives of the convicts, shearers, drovers and pioneer settlers who occupy an important role in Australian nationalist iconography. The Irish inflection is generally understood in terms of the Irish influence in Australian history and culture: it is widely seen as the source of Australian radicalism — of working-class con-sciousness, informal conviviality and egalitarian rebelliousness. Most listeners to this music have little exact knowledge of specific musical influences and origins, and most performers perform in a received style with ʾ .le conscious knowledge of the sources of the influences which figure so strongly in the public meaning of the music. In fact, the performance style is relatively recent, its musical base not in the nineteenth century but in social interactions of Anglo-Australian folk revival performers and Irish immigrant musicians in the early 1970s.

This article examines the origins of the bush band in the musical contact between Irish musicians who emigrated to Australia after World War II and those of the Anglo-Australian folk revival. It describes the historical construction of a genre of Anglo-Australian popular songs — 'Australian folk songs' — through the Australian folk movement in the 1950s and 1960s, and the parallel but distinct process in Irish dance music in Ireland in the same period. It then looks at the two groups whose interaction led to the formation of bush bands — performers from the folk music revival and immigrant Irish musicians — and describes the musical contact which occurred between them. The musical affinities of these groups and the social distance between them contributed to the form taken by the resulting genre.

Public Folk Music

The notion of folk music is no longer widely accepted by ethno-musicologists as a useful analytical category (Wachsmann 1980). It is too greatly imbued with nineteenth-century nationalisms, with élite con-descension toward subaltern musical styles, and with Romanticism (Harker 1985, Keil 1978). Even folklorists have seriously revised the object of their study and reformed themselves as a particular style of sociologist of expressive behaviour. In spite of this scholarly analysis and criticism, the concept continues to have a lively independent popular existence: musicians, record companies, performers and advertisers all know what they mean by folk music, even if they do not always agree with each other. As befits a category with so politicized a history, its meaning remains the site of ideological conflicts and dissension.

Contemporary folklorists often limit themselves to the expressive communication of small groups, or to genres of expressive communication which are independent of media industries or official institutions (Ben Amos 1971). Some musical genres, both historical and contemporary, come within this definition, but most of what is popularly considered to be folk music in Australia does not. In understanding such genres, the categories of the folksy, the folkloric or what Germans refer to as *volkstümlich* are more useful than that of folklore in the sense understood by folklorists (Smith 1988, Goertzen 1988).

The music of the bush band and similar genres can be called 'public folk music': a style of popular music which is widely practised and recognized in society as 'folk music' (with reference to its putative origin or to an imagined context of ideal performance). A public folk music depends on a recontextualization: sub-cultural, sectional, historical, or exotic musical styles are given new social meanings and new audiences within the multifaceted but coherent ideology associated with 'folk'. Public folk music is distributed and performed within socially open institutions and markets. The new contextual interpretations impute to the musical genres an inherent shared social and musical quality. Thus, at a national folk festival in Victoria in 1986 a Chinese classical orchestra may perform alongside public performances of Aboriginal music and dance, and the coherence of the 'folk' ideology ensures that audiences can with relative ease construct categories which link these genres (Stubington, 1993:141).

In some cases the creation of public folk music involves pervasive fabrication, and the term 'fakelore' is used by folklorists to describe the resulting material (Dorson 1950:343). Some historians have also shown an interest in such 'invented traditions' (Hobsbawm & Ranger 1983). A common response to such cultural processes is to expose their inauthenticity. But a critique of this nature offers us little understanding of the processes of recontextualization. Roger Abrahams and Susan Kalčik call on folklorists to shift their attention from 'the real and the fake' and become concerned with 'the change in performer audience relationship and in the setting and how these changes affect the form and content of the performance. By doing this, we will in effect describe the changeover from the folk to the popular' (Abrahams and Kalčik 1978:231).

The bush band is not a continuation or even a revival of established or historical forms of performance, and many in the folk movement most interested in historical authenticity decry its deficiencies. One such commentator notes that '"the bush band" of modern times is as much an artificial construct as is the image of the gunslinger in "the Wild West"' (McKenry 1991). The bush band is an 'invented tradition'. Yet rather than limiting ourselves to an exposé of fabrication, we should attempt to see how its social meanings have been constructed.

The Bush Band

In the following, I shall examine the historical formation of the bush band as a form of public folk music, with emphasis on the way in which its social meanings have been constructed within its public contexts. Two main sociomusical genres are significant: Australian folk song as performed in the Anglo-Australian folk revival movement; and Irish dance music and song as sponsored and promoted during the 1960s in Ireland, and as played in Australia by post-war Irish immigrants. Both genres emerged in what could be called folk revival movements, but these movements were set in different musical, social and historical circumstances, with varied cultural grievances to redress, and each addressed its own enthusiasts and participants. If the convergence between the social ideologies within which the sociomusical genres were understood enabled a musical contact to be established, the differences shaped and directed this musical interaction, resulting in the bush band.

The bush band is an ensemble of about five musicians. It contains at least one singer, at least one melodic instrument player, a rhythm guitarist, and a bass and rhythm section. The melodic instruments are usually a fiddle, an accordion, a banjo or a mandolin. The bass is usually an electric bass. The rhythm section may consist of a drummer, using a standard drum kit, or a lagerphone player. This latter instrument is an upright sistrum, set with bottletops, and struck and scraped with a serrated stick or struck on the floor.

The core song repertoire is about thirty Australian vernacular ballads popularized in the Australian folk revival. These have been frequently republished in many songbooks and are widely known (see for example

Manifold 1964, Radic 1983). More musically ambitious bands may include a number of Australian country-and-western numbers, nostalgia-tinged Australian rock-and-roll classics and recently written songs current in the folk revival movement.

The performance and arrangement style is relatively standardized. The vocal style is derived from the Australian folk revival. The vocal timbre and theatrical style is masculinist, projecting an image of aggressive independence. Singers are nearly always men, though melodic instrument players are often women. There is usually a noticeable amount of vocal tension, a relatively low level of 'sung' character in the voice, and some shifting of vowels towards what Australians perceive as Irish or British dialect forms.

The basic songs are usually symmetrical in phrasing, and most are tonal or rendered within a harmonically influenced 'modal' tonality common in folk revival performances in Britain and the United States. In general, performers use relatively limited musical structures. Performances are metrically rhythmical, accompanied by a limited number of diatonic chords. In most cases the singer is accompanied by melodic instruments in approximate unison, with strummed guitar and rhythm backing. Melodic interludes between verses are common, usually using a phrase of the sung melody.

The other important items of the repertoire are dance tunes, mainly jigs and reels, which may also be included in song arrangements for longer interludes between verses. These dance tunes are generally Irish or Scottish, with occasional tunes of similar style collected in Australia. In concert or hotel performances, the band may encourage informal dancing by the audience. At organized bush dances a number of nineteenth-century 'colonial' group dances will be demonstrated or taught by a dance caller, often the band vocalist. These dances are often line or circle dances, usually Irish ceili dances, dances common in the English folk revival, or dances noted in Australian historical sources. A few simple couples' dances, once popular in Australian rural communities, are also included. It has often been noted that this music and dance repertoire, so characteristic of the bush band, bears little resemblance to any historical Australian styles (Andrews 1988).

The Australian Folk Revival

The primary source of the bush band was the Australian folk revival movement. This movement consists of a network of music clubs and venues for the performance of genres of music styled as folk music by the participants in the movement. The formal institutions such as clubs and associations are built upon a network of individuals, many of whom have held an intense commitment to the folk music movement over the past two decades.

The historical and social construction of the folk music movement in Australia is discussed in Smith 1985. The movement grew from the activities of a group of left-wing intellectuals in the 1950s who, drawing on the models of similar concurrent radical folk revivals in the United States and Britain, forged an Australian movement within the cultural nationalism of the Australian left of this period. In this intellectual movement, radical nationalists attempted to define an Australian culture against both American popular culture and an official high culture dominated by obeisance to British traditions. Within this movement the espousal of an Australian vernacular musical tradition was particularly important. The late nineteenth century, where the potential for an Australian cultural independence was first seen, was a key source of inspiration. With this cultural aim in mind, a number of collectors such as John Meredith, John Manifold, Norm and Pat O'Connor and others recorded a body of vernacular ballads from the late nineteenth century, particularly of shearers and drovers, and publicly promoted these through publication and performance as evidence that Australia had a folk music.

The popular 'folk boom' of the mid-1960s became a marginal popular music movement and formed the basis of the folk movement of the 1970s and 1980s. In the 1960s the Australian folk movement sang British and American folk music or traditional song; 'singer-songwriter' songs, particularly of the protest song and related genres; and nineteenth-century Australian vernacular song which had been collected and promoted by the founders of the folk revival in the 1950s and early 1960s.

Predominantly middle-class in its clientele, this folk revival attracted many immigrants from the British Isles who were part of the folk-club movement in Britain. In the late 1960s this movement and these immigrants provided much of the musical inspiration in the developing circuit of Australian folk clubs. Amongst the genres listed above, Australian songs were relatively little performed. They had less dramatic breadth than many songs popularized in the British revival, such as the long narrative ballads and erotic and tender love songs which found favour with the new romantically serious-minded folk club audience.

The performance genre of 'folk music' actively defined itself against what it saw as mindless industrially-mediated popular music, and the literary credentials of the British folk song tradition were an important justification of its appeal. Though there were some continuities, the activists of the 1950s were not among the most active participants in the folk revival of the 1960s. Few were competent performers within the new styles of presentation of the folk boom, and the cultural preoccupations of the 1960s were less with Australian cultural nationalism than with a cosmopolitan bohemianism. Within this the exotic played a large part, but the exoticisation of the Australian past was not widely pursued. Thus Australian folk song, though of symbolic importance, was less performed than other styles and genres.

This balance was challenged by developments in the student anti-war movement of the late 1960s and early 1970s. A number of radical activists saw Australian involvement in the Vietnam war as evidence of imperialist domination, and raised the slogan of Australian independence, seeking analogies with the nationalist liberation movements of Third World countries (see for example, *The Builders' Labourers' Songbook* 1975). With inspiration from the apparent mass democracy of the Chinese Cultural Revolution, the espousal of a strident Australian nationalism became possible once again. Thus, although Australian songs had relatively little status among the folk club performers and audiences, a growing number of listeners with less focused tastes were once again prepared to promote and listen to them. With the dismissal of the Whitlam Labor Government in 1975 by the vice-regal Head of State, Governor-General Sir John Kerr, many on the left were further spurred towards seeing Australian republicanism as an important political issue. The images of the Eureka Stockade goldfields uprising of 1854 and the nationalist republicanism of the 1890s, powerfully represented in the folk song revival movement, once again became widely-used political symbols. The bush band was able to appeal beyond dedicated folk enthusiasts to an audience influenced by the new radical populism. This audience had also witnessed the growth of indigenous Australian rock music in the second half of the 1960s and early 1970s, and was less likely to be satisfied by the solo individual artist of the 1960s folk revival.

The Irish Folk Revival

The 1960s in Ireland were a time of considerable social change and of a new national confidence which challenged the conservative ideology of

Gaelic, Catholic, rural and parochial Irish culture. Quite suddenly, new government policies encouraged foreign investment, and the fortunes of the nation, which had long been in economic decline, seemed to be improving. Three major musical movements developed within this new social mood, and by the end of the decade these had significantly altered the way Irish traditional music was perceived and practised. The first of these was *Comhaltas Ceoltóirí Éireann* (the Irish Musicians' Association). After a steady expansion through the 1950s, this organization grew spectacularly in the 1960s. By 1964, the annual *Fleá Ceoil* (traditional music festival) was drawing an audience of 50,000, and was seen by a contemporary commentator as 'one of the greatest and most original features of Irish life' (MacMathuna 1965).

The second new approach to Irish dance music originated with the academic composer Seán O'Riada, who was the first person to organize traditional musicians into concert performance formats. His musical innovations were continued in the studied musical approach of the Chieftains.

The third musical movement of the 1960s was the ballad revival, inspired by the singing group the Clancy Brothers. These young men, who had emigrated to America in the early 1950s, were on the fringe theatre scene in New York. Inspired by the theatrical styles and image management of performers of the American folk revival, they developed an Irish version of this cultural strategy. In doing so, they brought genres of Irish popular domestic and local song into public forums and displaced the respectable models of Irish song established in the nineteenth century (Moloney 1982:94-6).

The Clancy Brothers used scarcely any traditional dance music in their repertoire, but their followers, the Dubliners, did. This group's most significant achievement was to bring together the image of the Dublin urban working class – plebeian, rebel, tough but eloquent – and that of traditional dance music which Dublin taste had hitherto regarded as irredeemably 'cultchie' music. This is a Dublin derogatory term for an Irish countryman, with all the stereotypical connotations of the rural fool. The Dubliners included both a talented fiddle player and a virtuosic banjo player, and introduced a new combination of musical genres. Vernacular ballads, nationalist rebel songs and defiantly plebeian narrative ballads, often of urban Dublin origin, were combined with Irish traditional dance music.

Each of these three developments offered a new interpretation of Irish dance music. For *Comhaltas Ceoltóirí Éireann* the music was a traditional skill, capable of development to an extremely high level, and it was incorporated into a relatively conservative nationalist ideology which stressed the idealized moral framework of a rural society. National culture was a defence against the threats posed by modernity and cosmopolitanism (Henry 1989). Seán O'Riada's concert-based groups suggested the potential of Irish dance music as a musical form within the social and formal structures of Western art music, performed for contemplation within a concert setting. In the ballad revival, Irish traditional music was constructed as a popular 'folk music', with its power resting in a nostalgic affirmation of lower-class culture reacting defiantly to oppression.

How did these movements enter Australia, and what was their effect there?

Irish Music in Australia

Ireland was a major source of European immigrants to Australia in the nineteenth century, providing about a quarter of Australia's white population. Throughout the first half of the twentieth century Irish-Australians were a distinctive group in Australian society, united by religion and a perceived social disadvantage. Although an Irish cultural heritage became an important rallying cry for this group in the twentieth century, for second and later generations of Irish-Australians Ireland was a site of fantasies and images. The contemporary circumstances of post-independence Ireland were not part of this identification. Consequently, when Australia's postwar immigration program brought a new group of Irish amongst the enormous influx of new European immigrants, these Irish immigrants in many ways were as foreign to established Anglo-Australians and Irish-Australians as were their fellow immigrants from continental Europe. Rather than being absorbed into Australian social institutions, many of them relied on enclosed social networks of friendship and employment. An immigrant Irish community formed, with links to wider social institutions, especially through the Catholic Church, but with an inner cohesion of its own (Grimes 1986).

Many competent and active Irish dance musicians had come to Australia since World War II, and many of those who came in the 1960s had participated in *Comhaltas Ceoltóirí Éireann* in Ireland. But though they shared musical experiences, some were isolated in Australia through the dislocations of emigration. Those who continued to perform tended to play for Irish community organizations such as sporting clubs and social clubs, and with each other, at parties in private homes. They scarcely ever played to audiences beyond the social circles of Irish immigrants.

The first Australian branch of *Comhaltas Ceoltóirí Éireann* was established in Melbourne in 1970, bringing to Victoria the confident new approaches to Irish music. In early 1970 a public meeting was called, advertised through the Catholic media, and about fifty people attended, including a number of active musicians (Loughnane 1985). Many of the musicians who attended had experience in *Comhaltas Ceoltóirí Éireann* in Ireland. They formed a branch and began to hold fortnightly meetings in a city hall, which consistently attracted audiences of about five hundred.

As well as informal concerts, dances and sessions, *Comhaltas Ceoltóirí Éireann* organized classes where many children of postwar immigrants were taught to play Irish music. In most cases this teaching was only effective for those children who came from active musical families, but the formal organization of *Comhaltas* considerably strengthened the power of their parents' social model of playing Irish music, and resulted in a strikingly high standard of musicianship in this second generation of players.

The Emergence of the Bush Band

In the late 1960s, patterns of entertainment in Australia were changing. In Victoria, this was particularly associated with changes in liquor licensing laws which allowed longer opening hours for hotels, some of which began to supply entertainment and encourage independent musical entrepreneurs and groups to use the relatively under-used facilities of large lounge bars. The folk movement was one of the first groups to move into these larger hotel venues. In contrast to the coffee shop folk singer, hotel performers needed a style of presentation with the musical and theatrical presence and volume to be effective in these new settings. The bush band was the response to the demands of the new venues.

Bush bands were not the first vocal and instrumental groups to perform the repertoire of Australian folk song. In the 1950s, the first activists of the folk song revival had formed groups with which to create an image of social performance of the songs which they were promoting. Most of the repertoire was collected from singers who were not public performers, and the first collectors, inspired by historicist definitions of folk song, had little interest in the social contexts of performance of the songs. We can assume, however, that these vernacular songs were performed unaccompanied to small groups of close associates, and, notwithstanding the possible skills of performers in this style, there was no precedent for organized formal performance with a theatrical sense which extended beyond this ambit.

The first of these bands of the 1950s, the (original) Bushwhackers, used the most prominent instruments of Australian rural performers, the accordion and the mouth organ, together with the 'bush bass' (a tea chest bass), and the 'lagerphone'. These improvised instruments were included to provide a good-humoured image of rural resourcefulness (Meredith 1986:8). Such groups, stressing the universality of the repertoire, never moved beyond a simple and direct presentation of songs, with simple guitar accompaniment and unison instrumental melodic support. However, whatever success these bands had in bringing historical material to the attention of a wider public, they never managed to overcome a fancy-dress, 'colonial' image, and could not address the audiences of the folk movement which developed in the 1960s.

The new bush bands of the 1970s used some of the instrumentation and style of these bands, but tended to drop the more emblematic and improvised instruments: an electric bass usually replaced the tea chest bass, and the lagerphone was supplemented, but not supplanted, by a standard drum kit. The survival of the lagerphone owes a great deal to the influence of one player, Dobe Newton, who transformed the instrument from a 'sort of overgrown tambourine given to a vocalist if he or she couldn't play guitar'. It became a loud and versatile rhythmic instrument, delivering syncopated accentuation within a powerful continuing rhythmic structure, and it was an important part of the stage presence of the bush band (Newton 1991).

However, the main inspiration of the bush band of the 1970s was not its Australian predecessors of the 1950s revival, but the Dubliners. Most members of the Australian folk revival had heard the marrying of Irish genres of vernacular song and dance music achieved by the Dubliners. Records of the Clancy Brothers and the Dubliners were widely available, and the Clancy Brothers were one of the most influential groups to tour Australia at the height of the folk boom around 1964. For the more dedicated followers of the Irish folk revival, Chieftains records began to appear around 1970. For young Australians the new reconstructed 'Irish music' of the Dubliners, shorn of sentimental and nostalgic songs, had the ring of authenticity: it seemed a true folk music springing from a creative and unified lower class, and it was consonant with the image of the legendary Australian rural worker, the supposed originator of Australian folk music. As well, Australian radical historiography, which had participated in the construction of Australian folk music, had always stressed the Irish influence on the ethos of the Australian rural worker (Ward 1966 (1958):46-57, 165-8). Thus, contemporary Irish models of performance were particularly attractive for Australian folk revival performers.

Inspired by these performance styles, the first Australian bush band, the Wild Colonial Boys, was formed in 1969 around a talented Irish emigrant singer, Declan Affley (Bourke 1985). He gathered a number of other performers including a Scottish country dance fiddler, an Australian piano accordion player and a Dublin-born singer, and attempted to create the effect achieved by the Dubliners in a performance of Australian songs. Though the band lasted scarcely a year, it released one LP, *Glenrowan to The Gulf,* appeared in the Tony Richardson film *Ned Kelly,* and had a powerful influence on the folk revival.

The bush bands formed in the image of the Dubliners and the Wild Colonial Boys included the Colonials, the Bushwackers and the Cobbers, in Melbourne, and the Ranting Lads in Perth. These used a powerful masculinist vocal delivery and fast instrumental dance tunes supported by a strong rhythm section. The repertoire was two-sided, with Australian bush songs alternating with Irish dance tunes, and occasionally Australian rural waltzes. The virtuosity of the dance music players was an important counterbalance to the studied unsophistication of the vocal style. The combination enabled these groups to move their historicist romanticism into the world of the counterculture.

That the Irish dance music was crucial to the success of these groups is demonstrated by the comparative lack of success of Australian rural dance music. Australian-based vernacular dance music, of parallel provenance to the vocal repertoire of the folk movement, is in the main rather sedate and unprepossessing to an audience, and was judged to be inadequate for the construction of this public repertoire. The radical commitments of many of the participants of the Australian folk revival led them to favour songs which could be seen as expressions of the conditions and resistances of historically distant lower class groups; the verbal content of these songs was thus of paramount importance. Much Australian traditional dance music, however, was too close to other, more familiar musical genres to attract interest. The image was 'old time' rather than 'folk'. Australian waltzes and closed couples dances sounded suspiciously like Edwardian popular music, and faster dance music indistinguishable from the records of Jimmy Shand and his Scottish band to which they had been drilled in folk dancing at primary school. For a young generation on the eve of political commitment, bohemian lifestyle and sexual adventure, extant Australian traditional instrumental musical genres held little attraction.

Irish dance music, particularly as presented by Irish vocal and instrumental groups, was thought to be a more appropriate musical partner for Australian traditional song. This interest in Irish traditional music led members of the folk revival to musical activities in the Irish community, and to Irish players resident in Australia.

The Irish Community Meets the Folk Revival

Postwar Irish immigrant musicians, on the whole, had little contact with the folk music movement, and where contact occurred, the two groups maintained a social distance. Contrasting socioeconomic backgrounds set them apart. The typical folk enthusiast is Australian-born, tertiary-educated, lower middle class, in white-collar employment, socially radical, non-conformist, and generally anti-religious. Players from the Irish community are more often working-class, employed in manual labour, socially conservative, and by Australian standards devoutly religious.

Although most members of the Australian folk revival movement had no contact with the social institutions of Irish immigrants, nor had the social background easily to enter their world, there were a few Irish immigrants influenced by the ballad revival who were in both groups. This enabled a handful of Australian-born instrumental players from the folk revival movement to make contact with Irish traditional players, particularly in Melbourne after the formation of *Comhaltas Ceoltóirí Éireann*.

When learning music of technical difficulty such as Irish traditional dance music, a live model is of enormous help to demonstrate tech-niques and to suggest ways of achieving a certain sound, better than even the clearest recordings can do. The Australian folk revival audience now expects a high level of instrumental technique and skill from its per-formers. This was not the case in the late 1960s, and there were then few, if any, instrumental performers with highly developed musical technique; Irish traditional dance players were, by these standards, conspicuously brilliant.

The *Comhaltas Ceoltóirí Éireann* meetings allowed a number of interested young players from the folk revival this access to Irish dance music. Because this was a formal open organization, it enabled enthusiastic young Anglo-Australian musicians to listen to and play in sessions with highly skilled players of Irish traditional music.

Although both Anglo-Australian performers and Irish immigrants saw their preferred genres within a 'folk' ideology, the inflections of this differed. The history and politics of Australian radical nationalism on which Australian folk rested were not identical to those of the populist versions of institutionalized Irish nationalism which founded Irish music movements. The social and political contradictions inherent in the three Irish music movements described above were invisible to Australians, and Irish music served communal and personal needs for its immigrant audience which were irrelevant to Anglo-Australians. Nonetheless, the Irish had a well-established position in Australian national mythology, and Anglo-Australian folk performers were able to use this to situate Irish music within their own repertoire.

In this way Irish traditional dance music came to be accepted as an essential part of an Australian folk repertoire, though it had little connection with the historical styles of Australian vernacular music-making which formed the repertoire's professed core. The musical and social contact continued as a few members of the Irish immigrant community began to 'cross over' between the genres of Irish music and Australian folk and were recruited into bush bands as key instrumentalists. These have usually been the talented children of the generation of postwar immigrants and they have a comfortable relationship with both musical worlds.

These musicians provided powerful musical inspiration to Australian players in the folk revival movement, influencing the basic instrumentation, musical repertoire and aspects of playing style. As well, the Irish 'session', an informal meeting of musicians to play instrumental dance music for their own enjoyment, has become part of the musical culture of the folk revival in Australia.

Conclusion

The bush band has moved into social environments beyond the closed groups which provided the initial audiences and the reservoir of musicians for the genre. These formative groups in the folk revival and the Irish community established both the musical styles and techniques which formed the basis of the genre and the grounds whereon the social meaning of music would be established. The bush band became a public folk music. Its significance was read within the ideology of public folk, as a historicist and communalist music, giving a musical expression to Australian radical nationalism. The wide acceptance of its public folk music ideology is evidenced by the continuing popularity of the bush band.

However, despite the durability of the frameworks of meaning within which this music is performed and listened to, it does not command a simple interpretation. Performers, especially those from professional groups, provided inflections of these meanings, blending Australian nationalism with images from live rock music and other popular music styles. In addition, the growth of feminist and non-anglophone cultural perspectives amongst audience and performers has called much of the symbolic structure of the bush band into question, and responses vary from outright rejection of the style to modifications of repertoire and performance style. As in any successful musical genre, the coexistence of elements with diverse social meanings enables the music to become a site of social debate. It is this, as much as the populist musical simplicity of the basic genre, which has enabled the music of the bush band to become a widespread amateur genre, and to continue to influence allied popular music styles.

References

ABRAHAMS, Roger & Susan Kalčik
>   1978   'Folklore and Cultural Pluralism'. In Richard Dorson, ed.,
>   *Folklore in the Modern World*. The Hague: Mouton, p. 223-36.

ANDREWS, Shirley
>   1988   'Why not Appreciate Australian Folklore as It Really Was
>   Rather than How You Think It Should Have Been?' In
>   Edwards 1988:31-6.

BEN AMOS, Dan
>   1971   'Toward a Definition of Folklore in Context'. *Journal of
>   American Folklore* 84:3-15.

BOURKE, Colleen
>   1985   Sleeve notes to LP recording *Declan Affley*. TAR 020,
>   Sydney: Tradition Australian Records.

The Builder's Labourer's Songbook
1975   Melbourne: Widescope.
DORSON, Richard
1950   'Folklore and Fakelore'. *American Mercury* 70:335-43.
EDWARDS, Ron
1988   *Proceedings of the Third National Folklore Conference.* Canberra: Australian Folk Trust.
GOERTZEN, Chris
1988   'Popular Music Transfer and Transformation: the Case of American Country Music in Vienna'. *Ethnomusicology* 32:1-22.
GRIMES, John James
1986   'Irish Immigrants in Sydney in the Twentieth Century'. In Colm Kiernan, *Australia and Ireland 1788-1988:* Bicentenary Essays. Dublin: Gill and Macmillan, pp. 215-26.
HARKER, Dave
1985   *Fakesong: the Manufacture of British 'Folksong' 1700 to the Present Day.* Milton Keynes: Open University Press.
HENRY, Edward O.
1989   'Institutions for the Promotion of Indigenous Music: The Case for Ireland's *Comhaltas Ceoltóirí Éireann. Ethnomusicology* 33: 67-95.
HOBSBAWM, Eric & Terence Ranger (eds.)
1983   *The Invention of Tradition.* Cambridge: Cambridge University Press.
KEIL, Charles
1978   'Comment: Who Needs "the Folk"?' *Journal of the Folklore Institute* 15:263-5.
LOUGHNANE, Vincent
1985   Interview with author, Melbourne, 5 Dec. 1985.
MACMATHUNA, Ciaran
1965   Sleeve notes to *Fleá Ceoil.* Gael-Linn CEF 013.
MANIFOLD, John (ed.)
1964   *The Penguin Australian Songbook.* Melbourne: Penguin.
MCKENRY, Keith
1991   Insert notes to CD *Battler's Ballad.* CD FWD 001, Canberra: Fanged Wombat Productions/National Library of Australia.

MEREDITH, John
  1986   'John Meredith Speaks for Himself' (interview). *Stringybark and Greenhide 6/2: 4-9.*
MOLONEY, Mick
  1982   'Irish Ethnic Recordings and the Irish-American Imagination'. In *Ethnic Recordings in America: A Neglected Heritage.* Washington: American Folklife Centre, pp. 85-101.
NEWTON, Dobe
  1991   Interview with author, 20 Feb. 1991.
O'SHEA, Helen
  1988   'Dancing and Romancing in Australian Country Halls'. In Edwards 1988: 102-5.
RADIC, Therese (ed.)
  1983   *A Treasury of Favourite Australian Songs.* Melbourne: Curry O'Neil Ross.
SMITH, Graeme
  1985   'Making Folk Music'. *Meanjin* 44:477-505.
  1988   'Folklore, Fakelore and Folkloric'. In Edwards 1988:42-5.
STUBINGTON, Jill
  1993   'Folk Music in Australia: The Debate'. In Gwenda Beed Davey & Graham Seal, *The Oxford Companion to Australian Folklore.* Melbourne: Oxford University Press: 132-43.
WACHSMANN, Klaus
  1980   'Folk Music'. In Stanley Sadie, ed., *The New Grove Dictionary of Music and Musicians.* London: Macmillan. Vol. 6:693.
WARD, Russel
  1966   *The Australian Legend.* Melbourne: Oxford University Press. First published 1958.

Discography

AFFLEY, Declan
    1985   *Declan Affley.* Sydney: Tradition Australian Records TAR 020.

THE BUSHWACKERS BAND (The Original Bushwhackers and Bullockies Band)
    1974   *The Shearer's Dream.* Melbourne: Picture Records 1007. Reissued by Larrikin Records, Sydney: LRF 019.
    1976   *And the Band Played Waltzing Matilda.* Melbourne: Image ILP 753.
    1978   *Murrumbidgee.* Avenue Records PC 7881.
West Australian Bush Bands. Vol. I. Perth: Tempo TP 109.

THE WILD COLONIAL BOYS.
    1970   *Glenrowan to the Gulf.* EMI SOEX 9631.

Cultural Contact Through Music Institutions in Ukrainian Lands, 1920-1948

William Noll

Introduction

Most nation-states have a network of organizations that establishes or maintains a wide variety of institutionalized links between regions, between urban and rural populations, and between various social groups. In the twentieth century rural-urban culture contact has become increasingly prominent and complex in most states, as population groups have been brought into a common national fold in decisive ways.[1]

Much of this contact is formalized and legitimized through the assumption that the state has an inherent right to develop and extend a network of institutions over its territory. One upshot of this is to link urban and rural areas in complex patterns that carry social, economic and political implications as well as implications for expressive culture, including music. Most twentieth-century states tolerate or promote a wide variety of music institutions, including national networks that help to foster a national musical vision. These networks are usually only one of several aspects of a given population's musical culture, although the importance and influence of any music network can be enormous. In a few twentieth-century states the music network is a domain reserved exclusively for the state. The specifics of these and other music networks vary through time and from state to state, and the differences reflect not only various kinds of musical thought but wider social and political constructs as well.

In Ukrainian lands, national music institutions were created in the early twentieth century for the explicit purpose of linking urban and rural populations. Two different sets of music institutions were developed in the two large Ukrainian ethnographic zones (of unequal size), western and eastern, which have had significant historical differences (see map). From the late 1300s, most of western Ukraine was a part of Polish or Austrian states; in 1920 it was incorporated into the interwar Polish state. Much of the western zone was never a part of any Russian state until World War II, when it was incorporated into the Soviet Union. Regions of eastern Ukraine have at various times been a part of Ukrainian, Mongol, Ottoman Turkish, Cossack, Polish and Russian states. In 1920 the eastern zone, about 80% of Ukraine, was incorporated into the Soviet state. The short-lived Ukrainian Republic (1917-20) encompassed regions of both western and eastern Ukraine (see Magocsi 1985).

Map of Ukraine

In both western and eastern zones, Ukrainian populations in 1920 became citizens of states dominated by non-Ukrainian populations:

Poles in the west and Russians in the east. This geographic and political situation was important in the development of Ukrainian music institutions, as contacts between urban and rural populations increased within the contexts of the legal and political norms of each state, and as each state allowed or promoted the extension of a network of music institutions. A comparison of the music institutions of western and eastern Ukraine reveals similarities and significant differences in the patterns of culture contact, especially that generated or initiated by urban élites in their dealings with rural populations.

Music Institutions in Western Ukraine

Among the most significant urban-rural links in Ukrainian lands, as well as in most of Central and Eastern Europe in the late nineteenth and early twentieth centuries, was the establishment of self-help societies. Through their agencies, village libraries were founded, improved personal hygiene was promoted, and new agricultural techniques for increasing crop yields were introduced to rural areas, largely by national activists. In Ukraine these societies were initially conceived and propagated by the clergy and the urban intelligentsia (Himka 1979:5). The self-help societies were not connected to any state institution but were created in part to help bring a Ukrainian state into existence. Specifically, they helped to encourage a national consciousness among all Ukrainian social groups. In time a complex identity emerged among the peasantry, part of which can be described as national. By the end of World War I, millions of peasants in Ukraine and all over Central and Eastern Europe carried a sense of national identity that had been foreign or barely known to their grandparents or even their parents (Sanders 1958:46; for studies of peasant identity in Ukraine, Poland, Slovakia and Romania see Himka 1984:449-51, Narkiewicz 1976:38-64, Kieniewicz 1969:118-20, Brock 1976, and Mitrany 1968:546-66).

The most influential of these self-help organizations in western Ukraine was the *Prosvita* ('Enlightenment') Society. Established in 1868 in the city of L'viv (Polish Lwów) by a group of young Ukrainian intellectuals, by 1920 Prosvita had grown into the largest and probably the most significant national network in Ukrainian lands. Urban activists, priests and rural gentry helped to establish thousands of village institutions that included reading clubs, choirs, temperance societies, schools, cooperative stores and the like (Himka 1979:5-6). Village reading rooms were especially important as centres of education and development of rural-urban culture contact. The number of reading rooms in western Ukraine increased steadily from the late nineteenth century to World War II, from a few hundred to over three thousand (Doroshenko 1959:24). Millions of people made use of the facilities. The village reading room housed space for rehearsing theatrical and musical events as well as a library with books and newspapers. It was in the reading rooms that a new music reached the western Ukrainian village.

Until the early twentieth century the efforts of urban Prosvita members with regard to music were limited. In 1909, at a Congress of Prosvita activists in L'viv, new proposals were put forward to create a network of music institutions in western Ukrainian villages. Especially significant were the statements of the composer and ethnomusicologist Filaret Kolessa (1910:238), who proposed that Prosvita create an explicit urban-rural link in musical practices by helping to establish village choirs, to be housed in the reading rooms.

Over the next few years a music section was developed at Prosvita in L'viv. Here urban professionals helped to arrange, notate and distribute to more and more village choirs versions of Ukrainian melodies, mostly in arrangements for four voices (soprano, alto, tenor, bass). Some of the repertoire from which these arrangements were drawn utilized collections made in the field by ethnographers and others, including transcriptions notated from recordings. The melodies were typically arranged in a choral format, sometimes including piano accompaniment, although *a cappella* arrangements were the most common. The collections from which the arrangements were drawn included music of both western and eastern Ukraine. In this way the Prosvita urban activists were creating a national practice that encompassed music of both western and eastern zones, and that could be utilized by both urban and rural populations. This music was not intended to supplant the regional village musical norms of long standing but was regarded as a supplement to these norms (Kolessa 1910:235-36).

In fact, the music network of Prosvita was self-limiting in its aims and specific in its preferred musical contexts. The network was designed to promote primarily choral music, arranged according to urban fashions, as a national repertoire that could be shared by all Ukrainians in both urban and rural settings. The primary context was the stage (or something resembling it) on which a local ensemble performed for neighbours, friends and family. This was a grass-roots organization in which local amateurs participated at their discretion.

Ukrainians whom I interviewed in Poland and who were active Prosvita participants in the western Ukraine of the 1920s and 1930s (then a part of the Polish Republic) describe the music scene of that time in their villages as multifaceted.[2] The national repertoire of the music network was but one aspect of village music culture, and many musical practices of long standing were not directly affected by the new institutions. The Christmas season still included the regional melodies of the *koliady,* sung by carolling villagers, and the winter songs, *shchedrivky* ('carols of the Epiphany'). Easter and spring included such music as the *vesnianky* and the *haivky* ('spring ritual songs'), the latter realized by girls and boys in informal settings. The village instrumental ensembles that performed at weddings, christenings, evening social gatherings and the like were still active. Their repertoire consisted of a smattering of melodies and genres from various generations, and included older regional melodies from the nineteenth century as well as recent radio-derived fare such as tangos and foxtrots. The village ensemble most typically consisted of two, three or four musicians, mostly farmers with small holdings who played music as a part-time craft, to supplement their primary farm-derived income. At weddings and other music contexts such as evening dances at the village inn, men and women danced and sang to the music of the village ensemble.[3] The Prosvita music network had no direct influence on this music, nor does it seem that the amateur choristers tried to influence such genres of rural musical practice. Notated choral arrangements of Christmas, Easter, spring and wedding melodies were available through the Prosvita network but were only occasional curiosities. The music of the national network was only a small, if socially significant, part of the total musical culture. The village had its own local musical life that was still very much alive.

The directors of the reading room choirs were volunteers who, like their choristers, received no payment for their services. Participation in the choir usually carried a high degree of prestige, however. The choir directors were trained in courses held in L'viv by the music section of Prosvita, usually lasting for one month. They were responsible for choosing the repertoire for their choirs, from a large assortment of arrangements of village-derived music and works by Ukrainian and other composers. These arrangements were published by commercial enterprises, and Prosvita helped to distribute them. Other active village volunteers included young women who taught choreographed versions of the national dances (e.g. *kolomyjky* and *kozaky*) as they had learned them in courses developed by Prosvita, usually held in provincial capitals and also lasting about a month. The young women taught the dances to both children and young adults in the village reading room or in a nearby open space outside.

Both the village choir directors and the village dance instructors used material that was processed in and distributed from urban areas. The urban professionals in L'viv, including folklorists, musical ethnographers and dance specialists, helped to collect, collate, arrange and then distribute material for amateurs who brought back to the village a national practice. Although based to a certain extent on rural music, this national practice was created in the context of an urban-rural link that was part of a broad-based national vision.

The Polish state of the time tolerated Prosvita (in some regions) as a Ukrainian cultural organization operating in the Polish Republic,[4] but Prosvita was self-financed and managed; members paid a yearly fee. These fees, with the revenues from concert and theatre tickets, produced the money to continue the village institutions. Although a self-financed cultural network, Prosvita can be viewed as a de facto political institution in that it encouraged, and even helped to create, a national identity among western Ukrainians. That identity was not limited to the western regions, as evidenced by the use of eastern Ukrainian music and dance as Prosvita materials.

To my knowledge there is little data concerning Prosvita and its musical activities during World War II. According to those whom I interviewed, musical activities all but ceased. After the war, a period of turmoil and bloody conflict accompanied the process of relocating millions of Poles and Ukrainians along either side of the new political borders. This process was largely completed by 1948.[5] Those Ukrainians who remained in the post-War Polish state were forbidden for several years to reestablish a cultural or music network; this applied to all Ukrainians, not just to those from the border areas (cf. Mróz 1979:186). In those western Ukrainian areas until recently in the Soviet Union, all Prosvita and village institutions from before the war were prohibited, and the musical life of the village was brought under state authority and control.

Music Institutions In Eastern Ukraine

In the late nineteenth and early twentieth centuries the important centres of Russian imperial administration were located in urban areas, most of which had only a small Ukrainian population. Most of the urban population spoke Russian, Polish or Yiddish, and many other aspects of urban life were non-Ukrainian in character. Surrounding the cities was a mostly Ukrainian rural population, of which the urban citizens knew little and with which most had limited contact. The urban Ukrainian intelligentsia was small, and imperial policy was designed to prevent, if not destroy, any chance of an intensified Ukrainian national identity. Early in the nineteenth century Ukrainian was declared to be a dialect of Russian, and it was banned from use in most schools until the upheavals of 1917. Ukrainian schools were few in number; in 1897 more than 90% of the village population was illiterate (Krawchenko 1985:20-28).

Although the establishment of national networks (such as Prosvita) was difficult in such circumstances, here, as elsewhere, efforts were made to improve the living standards of the rural population by founding self-help societies. The most prominent of these, the Kachkovskyi Society, was not the flourishing concern that Prosvita became in western Ukraine: despite the much larger population of eastern Ukraine, the Kachkovskyi Society was only about half the size of Prosvita. Eastern Ukraine had approximately ten times fewer village institutions per capita than western Ukraine in the late nineteenth century (Himka 1979:5). Chapters of Prosvita were allowed to be organized in eastern Ukraine in a limited fashion after the uprisings of 1905.

During the brief existence of the Ukrainian Republic (1917-20), Prosvita institutions were established in hundreds of villages throughout eastern Ukraine (Kytasty 1954:1). With the fall of the Ukrainian Republic and the incorporation of eastern Ukraine into the Soviet Union in 1920, existing village institutions were liquidated. A new 'red Prosvita' (*chervona prosvita*) was founded with the aim of organizing village institutions for 'mass-culture activity' (*kul'turno-masova robota*), directed by state concerns (Chepeliev 1979:30). As in the past, the most important village institution with respect to an organized music network was the reading room. Communist Party cadres established music clubs in these, in an effort to promote what was described as a new musical culture. The Soviet researcher Shevchuk describes this perceived division between past and future rural culture (1963:112-13): 'the liquidation of the older primitive village culture' was one of the main objectives of the party. That which was to supplant the village cultural norms was to be initiated and distributed by the party in both urban and rural areas, in order to create a national culture on the Soviet model. Music was one aspect of the larger ideological campaign.

As early as 1920 a performance context for the new music had been created in Kiev, where a series of concert-meetings (musical events interspersed among political speeches) included performances of art music, folk music and revolutionary songs. This was part of a 'village week', designed to promote rural-urban political solidarity (Chepeliev 1979:32). Few peasants participated, however, perhaps because of the difficulties in transporting large numbers of people from villages to the city. Therefore, the new music was taken to the villages. A series of publications was established with the aim of propagating the new musical culture throughout rural eastern Ukraine.

One of the first of these was *Muzychne mystetstvo na seli* ('Musical Art in the Village'), a publication of the Leontovych Musical Society (1921-28).[6] The efforts of this society included written guidelines for village choir directors and instrumental ensembles, along with a repertoire list that was widely propagated as the norm in the 1920s (Kytasty 1954:2). Other publications followed, mostly for purposes of establishing the new music institutions in villages.[7] A collection of articles, *Mystetsvo v klubi* ('Art in the Club', 1926), described how to make choral arrangements that would find a wide common denominator appealing to public taste. A brochure, *Masovyi spiv* ('Mass Song', 1926), gave advice on methods of music education in villages. The journal *Muzyka mac* ('Music of the Masses', 1926-31), described the formation of large village music ensembles, among other topics.[8]

By the mid-1920s musicians who specialized in the new musical culture were organized into collectives. Few in number for the first several years, some of these collectives were large touring ensembles that went from village to village, performing song, dance, and instrumental music interspersed with political lectures (Kuven'ova et al. 1971:29). By the late 1920s these ensembles had helped to establish dozens of non-touring village ensembles. The style and repertoire were taken from the larger touring ensembles, and some of the village participants became professionals in their own right. Members of the ensembles took part in 'political, cultural and anti-religious campaigns in the village, conducted an evaluation of the music collectives, taught in accordance with their work [and] helped in the creation of a new revolutionary repertoire' (Chepeliev 1979:34).

By 1930 most village reading clubs were officially known as 'Houses of

Folk Art'. Party activists saw them as 'an excellent means to organize ideologically, to lift aesthetic perception and the level of creative activity of the masses' (Chepeliev 1982:62). Each village choir or ensemble and its House of Folk Art was part of a provincial music network which organized regional musical events, such as performances and competitions. Another, separate network was (eastern) Ukraine-wide, mainly involving folk music specialists trained in Kiev. This central music network was one of the most prominent features of music organization in Soviet Ukraine, especially its training centre in Kiev for professional folk music practitioners and authors: *Tsentral'ne instruktyvno-metodychna stantsiia pry sentori mystetstva Narkomosvity URSR* ('The Central Training Compound for Instruction and Method, under the auspices of *Narkomos,* Ukrainian SSR'). Responsible for implementing the general policy on music, *Narkomos* ('the People's Commissariat of Education') was the arm of the party that helped to create cultural policy and that carried out political programs in the provincial as well as in the central music networks (Kytasty 1954:2-3 and Chepeliev 1979:35).

The large touring collectives/ensembles were organized under the auspices of *Narkomos.* Participants received the bulk of their instruction at the Central Training Compound, after which they were deemed qualified to work as professional folk music practitioners. Performance and publication were the two main areas of instruction. Materials on musical practice and methods were prepared in and distributed from the Central Training Compound, including collections of songs, lists of the recommended repertoire, instruction sheets for song and dance ensembles (choreography, staging large ensembles, etc.) and pre-printed programs. New music by Soviet composers and written material by professional mass-culture activists were also published, in the following journals among others: *Radians'ka muzyka* ('Soviet Music', 1936-41), *Sotsiialistychna kul'tura* ('Socialist Culture', 1937-41), *Narodna tvorchist'* ('Folk Creation', 1939-41), and *Ukrains'kyi folklor* ('Ukrainian Folklore', 1937-39) (Chepeliev 1982:64).

The touring musical ensembles of the central network took their directions from specific administrative units within *Narkomos.* From 1923 one such prominent unit was the Council of Repertoire, whose members decided such matters as which pieces to allow in public performance and which to proscribe. Hryhory Kytasty was a participant in one of the early, and most famous, instrumental ensembles in Soviet Ukraine during the 1920s and 1930s, the Bandura Chorus. He notes

(1954:2) that the Council of Repertoire determined the percentage of a performance that would be devoted to revolutionary melodies. Over the six or seven years of the late 1920s and early 1930s, the Council of Repertoire proscribed most of the Ukrainian content of the repertoire of the Bandura Chorus, substituting revolutionary and mass song fare that was being widely propagated throughout the Soviet Union.

One of the main provincial network performance contexts of the new musical culture was the 'musical olympics' (*muzychna olimpiada*), where song and dance ensembles competed for awards and placement. Appointed judges assessed the quality of the staged music and dance performances. The first competition, held in Kharkiv in 1931, included 61 ensembles with about 2000 participants.[9] The musical olympics became a common feature of the various provincial networks, and numerous regional events were established. In 1937 perhaps as many as 482 musical olympics took place in Soviet Ukraine with 360,000 amateur musicians as participants (*Statystychnyi dovidnyk* 1940:68). The primary repertoire for these was that distributed by the Central Training Compound. The repertoire also included new songs composed by members of the various ensembles, with texts on socialist themes (Kuven'ova et al. 1971:151). This practice remained common, with old or new melodies in a wide variety of genres being used to set new texts, e.g. '*Kolomyjky about the Party*' (Pravdiuk 1958:120).

In addition to the amateur village ensembles of the provincial network and the large professional touring ensembles of the central network, student ensembles at urban universities were active in amateur performances. Like other ensembles, they used the material prepared in the Central Training Compound. Some were quite large, with many dancers and singers as well as instrumentalists. They have long been known for their highly stylized, if energetic, performances. In the 1920s and 1930s, many student ensembles were sent to rural areas, both as representatives of the new musical culture and to work as party organizers (Shevchuk 1963:289-99 and Kytasty 1954:8). Since the 1930s student ensembles have been one of the most visible and widely touted performing media, often featured in newsreel and television programs, and participating in well-publicized youth festivals (cf. Zaiets' 1982:85-6).

World War II interrupted the publishing and performing activities of the new cultural specialists. All their journals had ceased publication by 1941, and the musical olympics of the provincial networks were suspended. During the war a few of the virtuosi from the professional folk music ensembles were organized, for purposes of entertainment, as part of touring 'concert brigades'. These were groups of classical musicians, professional folk musicians, actors, dancers and others who travelled together and staged performances for Soviet military audiences (Chepeliev 1982:64).

After the war the musical olympics and other aspects of the pre-War new musical culture were renewed. The political situation in the post-War Stalinist period included an effort to intensify the centralization of village culture. In 1948, over most of the Soviet Union (including Ukraine), party music activists gathered in a series of republic-wide seminars in which they were given new instructions concerning musical contexts and the participation of village amateurs. The style and repertoire were to be more tightly controlled and further standardized, and larger numbers of villagers were to participate (Stel'makh 1970:94, Kuven'ova et al. 1971:78-86 and Chepeliev 1982:64). From this intensification of the music networks came more ensembles, more music collectives and more new performance contexts — all of which were to lead to a massive increase in the use of state institutionalized music over the next two decades.

Summary

The networks of music institutions in the two zones of Ukraine in the first half of the twentieth century were largely conceived and implemented by urban-born and/or urban-trained activists who were consciously creating institutionalized links with rural populations. The music and dance practices that were developed and distributed through these institutions were more or less derived from rural populations, although they were stylized, notated and arranged by urban dwellers in ways that were thought to appeal to both population groups. Most of the musical performances took place in local centres (such as the reading rooms and Houses of Culture) that were part of a widespread national network. Staged performances and amateur participation were the norm.

There were significant differences between the music institutions of western and eastern Ukraine. Activists in western Ukraine used music to help establish and maintain a national identity among a large rural population with ethnic minority status in the Polish state. The music network was not a part of state institutions but was funded by participants. The village reading room and most aspects of the local music institutions were largely under the control of local members, people who were born and raised in a particular village. Their participation in the music network was regarded as a local activity in the context of national institutions. The choir directors chose their own material from a range of publications. Virtually no one in the village who participated in the music network was a professional; rather, they were farmers and the like. Their music network did not directly affect other village music activities, such as religious music and the rituals of the wedding sequence, including the music of the village instrumental ensemble. In this sense the institutions of the music network of western Ukraine were self-limiting and specific to certain contexts. The national musical practice derived from the network was not intended to monopolize the village music culture.

In 1920 there were far fewer national Ukrainian institutions in rural areas of eastern Ukraine. The party cadres of new musical specialists in many villages were working with less experience than most of the Prosvita activists of western Ukraine. Nevertheless, they were establishing not only national (Ukrainian) cultural institutions, but also supranational (Soviet) institutions, the policies of which were at least partially directed by party professionals in faraway urban areas. The music networks were largely created by touring professional activist-musicians, trained in a central compound, who in turn passed on aspects of this training to village ensembles. The music networks were not grass-roots organizations but were initiated, funded and controlled in urban political centres. They were state institutions, subject to administrative and party authority. The repertoire and other practices were largely created and directed by urban folk music specialists, from whose recommended repertoire there was only occasional deviation. Finally, the music network in eastern Ukraine was intended to be the primary shaping force of village musical culture. Religious music was considered to be an unacceptable practice for public display, and instrumental ensembles were as highly organized and standardized as the vocal music. In this sense the music of the network in eastern Ukraine was intended as the model for most of the musical life of the village.

Notes

1   National activities that came to be shared by urban and rural populations in twentieth-century Europe include widespread or universal education, voting rights (real or illusory), celebrations of national holidays, and participation in national and international

economies, as opposed to sectional or regional economies that have a narrow range of dispersal for most goods and services.

2   I conducted fieldwork in Poland in 1980-83 among both Ukrainian and Polish villagers. The research was supported in part by grants from the Wenner-Gren Foundation for Anthropological Research and the Polish Academy of Sciences.

3   The older part of the ensemble repertoire, that which stemmed from the nineteenth century or earlier, was highly regionalized, even localized, and could differ greatly between villages only a few miles apart in terms of melodic types and scales, size and composition of the instrumental ensemble, dance genres and dance steps, and metro-rhythmic norms (among other features).

4   The Polish state did not tolerate the establishment of Prosvita institutions in all regions. In the region Volyn' (northwestern Ukraine by current borders), for example, Prosvita was actively suppressed by the State.

5   For three years after World War II, millions of people clogged the roads and rails of much of Europe. Some were returning home after captivity or exile during the war, some were being expelled from their homes, other were fleeing particular ideologies, some wished to emigrate to faraway lands, and still others were being forcibly returned to lands from which they had already fled. The historian Norman Davies (1984:563) calls this 'one of the greatest demographic upheavals in European history'. The relocation of millions of people along the Polish-Soviet border can be viewed as part of this upheaval.

6   This society was named after the Ukrainian composer Mykola Leontovych (1887-1921), choirmaster at the Imperial Chapel in St. Petersburg. The Leontovych Musical Society was suppressed by the Soviets in the late 1920s as part of a broad program of national suppression.

7   None of these was a scholarly publication. They were designed to promote a standardized musical practice throughout rural Ukraine and were part of an enormous standardizing effort that was virtually Union-wide. In the early 1930s most ethnographic research institutions in Ukraine were closed, not to be revived until after World War II.

8   A large part of the party's rural music organizational effort of the 1920s took place in the heavily populated forest-steppe regions of

central Ukraine, along the Dnieper River. Far less such activity seems to have occurred in the southeastern regions that were to become industrial centres.

9   From these statistics it seems that the performing ensembles at the musical olympics were large, perhaps averaging more than thirty people per troupe.

References

BROCK, Peter
  1976   *The Slovak National Awakening: An Essay in the Intellectual History of East Central Europe.* Toronto: University of Toronto Press.
CHEPELIEV, V.I. and O.H. Myroniuk
  1979   'Propahanda muzychnoho mystetstva sil's'kymy kul'turno-osvitnimy zakladamy Ukrainy v 20-30-kh rokakh'. *Narodna Tvorchist' ta Etnohrafiia* 5:30-36.
  1982   'Muzychne mystetstvo v sil's'kykh klubakh'. *Narodna Tvorchist' ta Etnohrafiia* 1:62-4.
DAVIES, Norman
  1984   *God's Playground: A History of Poland.* Vol. 2. New York: Columbia University Press.
DOROSHENKO, Volodymyr
  1959   *Prosvita, ii zasnuvannia i pracia.* Philadelphia: 'Moloda Prosvita' im. Mytr. A. Sheptyts'koho.
HIMKA, John-Paul
  1979   'Priests and Peasants: The Greek Catholic Pastor and the Ukrainian National Movement in Austria, 1867-1900'. *Canadian Slavonic Review* 21/1:1-14.
  1984   'The Greek Catholic Church and Nation-Building, 1772-1918'. *Harvard Ukrainian Studies* 8/3-4:426-52.
KIENIEWICZ, Stefan
  1969   *The Emancipation of the Polish Peasantry.* Chicago: The University of Chicago Press.
KOLESSA, Filaret M.
  1910   'Pohliad na teperishnyj stan pisennoi tvorchosty ukrain-s'koho narodu'. *Pershyj Ukrains'kyj Pros'vitno-Ekono-michnyj Kongress, Protokoly i Referaty.* L'viv: Tovarystvo Pros'vita.

KRAWCHENKO, Bohdan
   1985   *Social Change and National Consciousness in Twentieth Century Ukraine.* Edmonton: Canadian Institute of Ukrainian Studies, University of Alberta.
KUVEN'OVA, O.F., O.M. Kravets', T.D. Hirnyk & V.T. Zinych
   1971   *Sviata ta obriady radians'koi Ukrainy.* Kyiv: Naukova Dumka.
KYTASTY, Hryhory
   1954   *Some Aspects of Ukrainian Music Under the Soviets.* New York: Research Program On The USSR (Mimeograph Series No. 65) [title page in English, text in Russian]
MAGOCSI, Paul Robert
   1985   *Ukraine: A Historical Atlas.* Toronto: University of Toronto Press.
MITRANY, David
   1968   *The Land and the Peasant In Rumania.* New York: Greenwood Press. First published 1930.
MRÓZ, Lech
   1980   'Contemporary Transformations in Lemko Tradition'. *Ethnologia Polona* 5:183-90.
NARKIEWICZ, Olga A.
   1976   *The Green Flag: Polish Populist Politics 1867-1970.* Totowa, NJ: Rowman & Littlefield.
PRAVDIUK, O.A.
   1958   'Suchasni narodni pisni'. *Narodna Tvorchist' ta Etnohrafiia* 3:120-25.
SANDERS, Irwin T.
   1958   'The Peasantries of Eastern Europe'. In Irwin T. Sanders, ed., *Collectivization of Agriculture in Eastern Europe.* Louisville: University of Kentucky Press, pp. 24-48.
SHEVCHUK, H.M.
   1963   *Kul'turne budivnytstvo na Ukraini u 1921-1925 rokakh.* Kyiv: Vydavnytstvo Akademii Nauk Ukrains'koi RSR.
Statystychnjy dovidnyk
   1940   Kyiv: Kul'turne Budivnytstvo Ukrains'koi RSR.
STEL'MAKH, Adelaida
   1970   'Kozhnomu sil's'komu klubovi khudozhniu ahit'ryhadu'. *Narodna Tvorchist' ta Etnohrafiia* 1:94.

ZAIETS', O.S.
   1982   'Stydents'kyi fol'klorno-etnohrafichnyi ansambl'. *Narodna Tvorchist' ta Etnohrafiia* 2:85-6.

From Syncretism to the Development of Parallel Cultures: Chinese-Malay Interaction in Malaysia

Tan Sooi Beng

One of the first questions that came to mind while seeing Chinese opera in Malay last Sunday on TV3's *Sekapur Sireh* was why did it take so long to think of the idea.

What we saw was merely an excerpt lasting less than ten minutes that amounted to perhaps two episodes in the projected drama about the legend of Hang Li Po in Malacca.

Both of the scenes were mainly musical events, the first showing the Chinese princess at sea and the second narrating her meeting with Sultan Iskandar Shah.

One of the leaders of the opera class, Richard Foo, said the rehearsal process leading to the performance took about three weeks. The event was especially staged for the TV3 Sunday morning broadcast and was designed to coincide with the Chinese New Year celebrations over the inauguration of the Year of the Goat.

And for a few minutes of TV time, history was made as a group of Chinese opera performers for the first time told one of the most charming tales of 15th-century Malacca in Bahasa Malaysia.

(Utih, New Sunday Times, 24 Feb. 1991)

The above quotation illustrates the nature of Chinese-Malay cultural interaction in Malaysia today. The question posed by Utih, one of Malaysia's foremost theatre critics, is timely. Why has it taken so long to think of the idea of performing Chinese opera in Malay?

This essay aims to answer questions of a similar nature by looking at Chinese-Malay musico-cultural interaction in Malaysia from the pre-colonial fifteenth century to the present. It attempts to show that while, in the past, cultural interaction between the two ethnic groups occurred in urban areas leading toward intermixing of musical and cultural forms, such is not the case today. In recent decades, there has been a reemphasis on maintaining individual Chinese and Malay cultural forms. I shall argue that this shift is mainly a result of responses to government policies.

The impetus for Chinese-Malay musico-cultural change in Malaysia has been extra-musical, namely socioeconomic and political. Combinations of positive and negative results have emerged.

Chinese-Malay Cultural Interaction
Before Independence

The first Chinese settlements in Malaysia date from the period of the Malacca Sultanate of the fifteenth century. At that time, the number of Chinese domiciled in the peninsula was small and consisted mainly of men. They intermarried with Malay women, learnt to speak Malay and adapted to the Malay sociocultural environment (Tan, C.B. 1988:ch. 1). By the eighteenth century, there had emerged a group of Chinese who spoke a version of Malay (see Example 1) and adopted certain features of Malay dress and cooking (*ibid.*:108-14); they called themselves 'Baba'. The Babas learnt English and sent their children to English schools set up by the British.

During the colonial period, when large numbers of Chinese migrated to Malaya in search of employment, the Babas formed an influential class of businessmen and emerged as a special group of people who formed a link between the British and the Malays. As they could speak both Malay and English, the Babas acted as translators for the British and spokesmen for the Chinese. European merchants preferred to make business transactions with Baba businessmen who could speak English. With their knowledge of English, the Babas could also easily find employment in the commercial sector as clerks and brokers (*ibid.*:50-51).

Chinese-Malay cultural interaction continued to take place under

British rule. In music, the Babas developed *dondang sayang,* an elaborate form of Malay poetry or *pantun* singing. *Pantun* has an ABAB rhyme scheme with the first couplet alluding to the meaning of the verse (Example 1):

Tukar baju pakay seluar
Chobak chobak menanam padi
Saya sorang orang di luar
Chobak chobak menabor budi

Orang berayat bernama tinggi
Tangkap buaya tidak bergigi
Orang hidop tidak berbudi
Sebagi kapal tiada kemudi

Changing clothes wearing trousers
(I) try to plant rice
I am from outside
(I) try to sow kindness

Educated people are looked up upon
(Like) catching crocodiles without teeth
People who live without good deeds
Are like ships without rudders

Example 1: *Pantun* in Baba Malay with
ABAB rhyme scheme and the first couplet
alluding to the meaning of the verse
(Koh and Co. 1920:16)

Singing in antiphonal style, the Babas improvise verses, each trying to outwit the other. Through the Malay *pantun,* the Babas debate topics such as good deeds (*budi*) (Example 1), love (*kasih*), business (*niaga*) and the sea (*lautan*) (Low 1976:ch.3).

Dondang sayang is accompanied by two Malay drums (*rebana*), a Western violin (*biola*) and a *gong*. Sometimes, other instruments such as guitar, maracas, accordion or harmonium may be included (Thomas 1986:3, 8).

All the songs are based on one melody sung to the Malay *asli* dance rhythm (Example 2):

---

d t t t   tt t .d d d

g

(d = drum syllable 'dung', an undamped stroke played
by the right hand striking the drum head towards
its centre and producing a deep, resonant sound;
t = drum syllable 'tak', a light sharp stroke
near the rim of the drum; g = gong.)

Example 2: Malay *asli* rhythm played by *rebana*

As in traditional Malay singing, the vocal line is fairly independent of the violin line. The performer improvises freely (see Example 3).

Example 3: Vocal, *biola* and *rebana* lines of section of *dondang sayang*

Malay dances, music and theatre were also popular among the Babas during the colonial period. Malay *keroncong, asli* and *joget* were performed at weddings and other occasions of celebration of the rich Babas (Tan, C.B. 1988:124). *Asli* pieces such as *Mas Merah, Tudung Periuk* and *Anak Raja Turun Beradu* were popular as many of them had Chinese elements incorporated. For instance, in *Tudung Periuk,* melodic interludes and cadential phrases (*patahan lagu*) use pitches 3 and 5 together with 2 and 1 (see Example 4):

Example 4

and pitches 3 and 5 with pitch 6 (Example 5):

Example 5

In *Mas Merah,* pitches 5 and 6 are played with pitches 1 and 2 (Example 6):

Example 6

These melodic phrases emphasize the minor third intervals (between pitches 3 and 5 and 6 and i) characteristic of the Chinese pentatonic scale (which can be represented as pitches 1 2 3 5 6 from the diatonic major scale; see Examples 5 and 6).

The Babas were so fond of the Malay *bangsawan* theatre that they set up their own amateur troupes. For example, the Chinese Babas of Penang performed a Malay *bangsawan* play called *Princess Nilam Cahaya* to collect money for the Chinese Flood Fund on 28 May 1918 (*Straits Echo*). A review article commented that even 'the Malay professionals present' admitted that 'the piece . . . was fairly well performed'. In 1918, the same group performed *Nyai Dasimah* (*ibid.*, 12 Oct. 1919) and in 1920 *Ginufifah* or *Herto Brabant* (*ibid.*, 13 July 1920).

Within the Malay community in urban areas, borrowing of Chinese elements also occurred. For instance, Malay *bangsawan* performers staged stories of different ethnic origins. Chinese plays were adopted and shown in areas with predominantly Chinese populations. On such occasions, costumes and musicians were borrowed from the Chinese opera troupes. During their season in Penang, Wayang Kassim performed *Sam Pek Eng Tye* (*Straits Echo*, 15 Dec. 1909) and *Lo Fen Koie* (*ibid.*, 19 Dec. 1909). The Grand Opera Co. staged *Boo Seong* and *Pow Kong Un* (*ibid.*:28, 29 Jan. 1914).

Bangsawan theatre provided the arena for musical change and promoted musical interaction. Although *bangsawan* music basically mixed Malay and Western elements, Middle Eastern and Indian rhythmic patterns and modes were often added to this mix (Tan, S.B. 1989a:237-48). When Chinese plays were performed, music with Chinese characteristics was incorporated. As in the *bangsawan* song 'Shanghai Street', melodic phrases which emphasized the minor third interval (6 and 1̇) characteristic of the Chinese pentatonic scale, were often used. 'Meaningless' syllables such as 'hai-lah' and 'a-hai-a-hai' (see Example 7) and melodic contours common in Chinese folk songs were also included (see Example 7).

Hai-lah - - u-la - san a-hai a-hai   Ber-ti-ba-lah Ra - ja   a - hai

Example 7: Minor third interval and 'meaningless' syllables in *Shanghai Street*

Even though the British practised 'divide-and-rule', keeping rural Malays in agriculture and importing Chinese immigrants as labourers in the tin mines, some Chinese-Malay cultural interaction took place in urban areas, especially among the Babas and the Malays.

Assertion of Divergent Parallel Cultures
After Independence

Since Independence in 1957, there has been a reassertion of divergent cultures instead of syncretic ones. This development has paralleled a resurgence of ethnic consciousness in Malaysia.

Ethnic division, which was promoted by the British before Independence, has been reemphasized by clauses in the new constitution which give special privileges to Malays and other indigenous groups (Bumiputra). With the implementation of the New Economic Policy (NEP)[1] in 1971, the government has attempted to restructure society and create a Malay commercial and industrial community so that the Bumiputra can become full partners in all aspects of Malaysian economic life (Sundaram 1984:163). To achieve this objective, public corporations and statutory bodies have been set up for the Malays. Special privileges, such as quotas in connection with scholarships and admission into universities and colleges, admission to public service, and the issuance of licences and permits for the operation of certain businesses, have been given to Malays.

The NEP, which does not allow the Chinese to enjoy the same opportunities and rights as the Bumiputra, has made the former even more aware of their identity. For the Chinese who feel their identity and dignity threatened, traditional emblems such as Chinese festivals, Chinese opera and Chinese orchestra music are very important and are retained to stress their distinctiveness.[2] Festivals such as the Phor Tor Festival (the feast of the Hungry Ghosts), the Goddess Kuan Yin's Birthday, Chinese New Year and Chap Goh Meh are celebrated on a grand scale.

Such festivals also thrive because they provide rallying points for Chinese of different class, educational and language backgrounds to unite as a 'community' and to help one another. As a consequence of the NEP and the special privileges granted to the Bumiputra, the Chinese not only feel that they are denied equal opportunities with the indigenous people, but that they are being neglected by the government. Therefore, they have no choice but to take care of themselves. Through festivals, money is collected for the poor and the sick, for schools and hospitals. For instance, through the Phor Tor festival, funds have been raised for the rebuilding of the private Lam Wah Ee Hospital, the Chinese Assembly Hall (*Da Hui Tang*), and the expansion and upgrading of National-Type Chinese primary schools[3] in Penang (Tan, S.B. 1988). Those who can afford it contribute to social welfare projects and the building funds of hospitals and schools at festivals so that the needs and welfare of the poorer Chinese are taken care of.[4]

Besides the proliferation of festivals, Chinese opera and musical performances have also increased in number in recent years. Although there was a decline in operatic performances in the 1950s and 1960s as a consequence of competition from the film industry, today at least one opera is performed each day somewhere in Malaysia throughout the year. In Penang, over one hundred areas each offer several nights of opera performances during the Phor Tor Festival. As local troupes are few in number, whole troupes are imported from Thailand while individual Hong Kong actors and actresses are hired to perform with local Cantonese troupes and musicians (Tan, S.B. 1980:36, 37).

In recent times, even the Babas are being motivated to identify with the non-Baba Chinese and drop their Baba identity. Although the Babas speak Malay and have lived in Malaysia for generations, they have not been granted Bumiputra status. They do not receive any special privileges in terms of educational opportunities, civil service appointments or loans for business. At the same time, private Chinese businessmen are unwilling to take in Babas who cannot speak or write Chinese. Given the circumstances, it is not surprising that the Babas are seeking non-Baba Chinese identity (Tan, C.B. 1983:73). Consequently, *dondang sayang,* which was once so popular among the Babas, is disappearing quickly.

Many Chinese also hold on to traditional symbols because they feel threatened by official cultural policies which are perceived as assimilationist. In 1967, the National Language Bill ensured that Malay rather than English, Chinese or Tamil became the national and sole official language. Since then, Bahasa Malaysia, the national language, has also become the medium of instruction in national schools and universities. Islam was also established as the official religion in the present constitution, meaning that considerable government funds are made available for the construction of mosques and support of both Islamic culture and religion. While other religions and languages are regarded as permissible, they are not granted official status.

Increasingly, following the 1969 racial riots when ethnic relations in

Malaysia broke down, the Malaysian Government has also called for all communities to accept a national culture based on a core of Malay characteristics. In the government's eyes, the riots had erupted due to a 'crisis of values' resulting from the existence of divergent cultures (Ghazali Shafie 1979:6-7). To the government, a common national culture which would promote a common national identity was required to avoid further racial riots. At a nationwide congress held in August 1971 at the University of Malaya, three main principles of what constituted national culture were outlined (Kementerian Kebudayaan, Belia dan Sukan 1973:vii):

> a) the national culture of Malaysia must be based on the cultures of the people indigenous to the region;
> b) elements from other cultures which are suitable and reasonable may be incorporated into the national culture; and
> c) Islam will be an important element in the national culture.

Since the outlining of these principles, government officials have been emphasizing that national culture should be based on a core of Malay characteristics. In 1982, the Prime Minister Dr. Mahathir Mohamed himself declared that:

> . . . unity and stability should be built and nurtured through one language, that is, the national language based on the Malay language, and through one culture, that is the national culture based on the culture of the indigenous people of Malaysia. (*New Straits Times,* 19 December, 1982)

The creation of a national culture as defined above is perceived as a threat to the identity and culture of the Chinese, especially in a country where they are hardly a small minority. According to the 1980 Population Census, 55.3% of the population of Peninsular Malaysia are Malays while Chinese and Indians account for 33.8% and 10.2% respectively (Jabatan Perangkaan Malaysia 1983). To many, the concept of a national culture will mean the demise of existing non-indigenous cultures. Inevitably, the Chinese cling to traditional emblems as forms of resistance.

Hence, when the Home Affairs Minister of 1979, Tan Sri Ghazali Shafie, suggested that the lion dance as it had originated in China be changed to a tiger dance, to be accompanied by music played on the gong, flute, tabla or gamelan, there was widespread protest from Chinese cultural organizations. To Ghazali Shafie, 'the tiger, unlike the lion, is found in Malaysia' (Ghazali Shafie 1979:7). Since then, a statewide association, the Penang Chinese Martial Arts Association (with about forty lion and dragon dance troupes as members), has been formed to offer protection against harassment by police, especially in the application of performance permits, to provide solid bases for protest and to promote the sharing of musicians, performers and skills.

Conclusion

Cultural and musical interaction took place between Chinese and Malays during the pre-colonial and colonial periods. Cultural changes were promoted mainly by social and economic gains that could be acquired through culture contact. The Baba continued to retain Baba identity as it was economically and politically advantageous to do so. *Dondang sayang* was promoted as entertainment for the Babas. At the same time, the Malay *bangsawan* theatre acquired Chinese elements in order to attract Chinese and Baba audiences.

While in the colonial days Chinese-Malay interaction was towards adaptation and syncretism, today there is a shift towards the development of parallel divergent cultures. The overall effect of heightening ethnic consciousness and adopting an economic policy which provides privileges to Malays has promoted greater integration among the Chinese and an emphasis of Chinese identity. Policies which are seen as attempting to assimilate the Chinese into the dominant Malay culture have resulted in the stressing of Chinese traditional culture as emblems of ethnicity.

This is not to say that no musical or cultural interaction is taking place among Chinese and Malays in Malaysia. There are a few attempts at mixing Chinese and Malay musical and theatrical elements. In Malay popular music, for instance, Hang Mokhtar sings Malay songs using Chinese tunes, syntax and sentence construction (Tan S.B. 1989b:157). Well-known for its jazz fusion, Asiabeat combines gamelan, tabla, *kompang* and Chinese drums in its compositions. Some Chinese cultural groups have incorporated Malay music, dances and dramatic themes into their performances. Many play Malay folk songs such as 'Tanah Air Ku', 'Air Didik' and 'Inang Cina' (arranged by Lee Soo Sheng), and new compositions incorporating local dance rhythms like 'Malay Dance' based on the *ronggeng* rhythm (by Saw Yeong Chin). Contemporary dance choreographers such as Marion D'Cruz (Five Arts Centre), Ramli Ibrahim (Suasana Dance Co.) and Leong Wai Kein (Kwangsi Association) have also combined Chinese and Malay movements and music in their works. Leong Wai Kein recently produced 'The Romantic Batik' which mixes traditional Malay movements and Malay music with Chinese dance movements (*New Straits Times,* 14 July 1990).

Although the trend is towards the development of parallel divergent cultures in Malaysia, a few artistic forms which are syncretic or adaptive have emerged. This is a result of the indefatigable human spirit and unfailing creativity of some individuals.

Notes

1   The NEP aims to (i) eradicate poverty by raising income levels and increasing employment opportunities for all Malaysians, irrespective of race; and (ii) accelerate the process of restructuring Malaysian society to correct economic imbalance, so as to reduce and eventually eliminate the identification of race with economic function (Government of Malaysia 1971).

2   Jayawardena (1980:430-50) claims that Fiji Indians who have had to accept being defined as Indians, together with the restricted rights of immigrants that this entails, maintain identity in several significant respects, e.g. marriage patterns, some distinctive form of religious worship and retention of Tamil and Telugu as domestic languages. On the other hand, in Guyana, immigrant Indians who were not declared to be separate and were not encouraged to keep apart, have merged with other Guyanese Indians and have almost lost their separate identity.

3   In National-Type Chinese primary schools, Chinese is the medium of instruction while Bahasa Malaysia and English are subjects taught. On the other hand, in National primary schools, Bahasa Malaysia is the main language of instruction while English is a subject. (Chinese may be taught but students must make special applications to the schools if they wish to study Chinese. However, as Chinese is not a compulsory subject in National primary schools, these classes are often held after school hours. According to many parents, they are often not well organised.)

4   For discussion of the assertion of Chinese ethnicity and the collection of funds through the Phor Tor Festival, see Tan, S. B. (1988).

References

GHAZALI SHAFIE Tan Sri
    1979   'Keperibadian Nasional Belum Lahir'. *Dewan Masyarakat,* 15 August: 6-9.

GOVERNMENT OF MALAYSIA
    1971   *Second Malaysia Plan, 1971-75.* Kuala Lumpur.

JABATAN PERANGKAAN MALAYSIA [Department of Statistics, Malaysia]
    1983   *Banci Penduduk dan Perumahan Malaysia 1980.* Kuala Lumpur.

JAYAWARDENA, Chandra
    1980   'Culture and Ethnicity in Guyana and Fiji'. *Man* 15: 430-50.

KEMENTERIAN KEBUDAYAAN, Belia dan Sukan [Ministry of Culture, Youth and Sports]
    1973   *Asas Kebudayaan Kebangsaan.* Kuala Lumpur.

KOH AND COMPANY
    1920   *Pantun. Dondang Sayang Baba Baba Pranakan.* Vol. 1. Singapore: Koh and Company.

LOW Kim Chuan
    1976   *Dondang Sayang in Melaka.* B.A.(Hons) thesis, Monash University, Melbourne.

SUNDARAM, Jomo K.
    1984   'Malaysia's New Economic Policy: A Class Perspective'. *Pacific Viewpoint* 25(2): 153-72.

TAN Chee Beng
    1983   'Acculturation and the Chinese in Melaka: The Expression of Baba Identity Today'. In L.A. Peter Gosling & Linda Y.C. Lim (eds.), *The Chinese in Southeast Asia,* Vol. 2. Singapore: Maruzen Asia, pp. 56-78.

    1988   *The Baba of Melaka: Culture and Identity of a Chinese Peranakan Community in Malaysia.* Kuala Lumpur: Pelanduk Publications.

TAN Sooi Beng
    1980   'Chinese Opera in Malaysia: Changes and Survival'. *Review of Southeast Asian Studies* 10, December: 29-45.

1988   'The Phor Tor Festival in Penang: Deities, Ghosts and Chinese Ethnicity'. Working Paper, Centre of Southeast Asian Studies, Monash University.

1989a   'From Popular to "Traditional" Theatre: The Dynamics of Change in *Bangsawan* of Malaysia'. *Ethnomusicology* 33: 229-74.

1989b   'The Performing Arts in Malaysia: State and Society'. *Asian Music* XXI (1): 137-171.

THOMAS, Philip

1986   *Like Tigers Around a Piece of Meat: The Baba Style of Dondang Sayang.* Singapore: Institute of Southeast Asian Studies.

Newspapers

New Straits Times
New Sunday Times
Star
Straits Echo

Discography

Muzik Tarian Malaysia. WEA Records WG M 93402B.

Album Melayu Deli. EMI Records EMG S 5588.

Malam Keroncong Asli. Polygram Records PHIL PY 833553.

Kocik Kocik Jago Kobau. Cassette. Lyrics by Hang Mokhtar; distributed by Suara Cipta Sempurna, 1987.

Asiabeat. Cassette. Music by Asiabeat, distributed by CBS, 1983.

The Dynamics of Change in
Huê and *Tài tu* Music
between 1890 and 1990

Lê Tuân Hùng

Nhac Huê (Huê music) and *nhac tài tu* (amateur music) are the two types
of classical chamber music in central and south Vietnam, respectively.
Huê music originated in the city of Huê, an important cultural and
political centre in central Vietnam between 1678 and 1945. It was
favoured among mandarins and aristocrats in Huê from the late
seventeenth century, and was introduced into south Vietnam in the
nineteenth century. It was then modified and became known as *nhac tài
tu* (amateur music).

From the late nineteenth century contact with Chinese and Western
cultures has had a significant impact on the development of *Huê* and *tài
tu* music. The influx of foreign cultural and musical ideas and practices
motivated different responses from *Huê* and *tài tu* musicians. In my
opinion, it was mainstream sociopolitical changes in Vietnam from the
late nineteenth century that initiated and sustained the specific
responses of *Huê* and *tài tu* musicians to Chinese and Western musical
ideas. In this essay, I examine musical and extra-musical changes in *Huê*
and *tài tu* music which resulted from contact with Chinese and Western
cultures and delineate the sociopolitical motivations behind these
changes.

Indigenous Aspects of *Huê* and *Tài tu* Music

In the *Huê* and *tài tu* traditions, the indigenous concept of music as a means for emotional expression played an important part in the formation of various musical and extra-musical features. Masters of *Huê* music such as Hoàng Yên, Buu Lôc and Nguyên Huu Ba who learned their art in the late nineteenth or early twentieth century tended to use emotional terms such as sadness, happiness and tranquillity in their descriptions of the extra-musical characteristics of classical pieces (Hoàng Yên 1921b:52; Nguyên Huu Ba 1969:33-4; and Buu Lôc n.d.: tape D.39). *Tài tu* musicians also associate music with feelings. According to these musicians, compositions are designed to convey different feelings such as joy, anger or lamenting (Bùi Văn Hai n.d.:1).

The design of the modal systems and the important role of improvisation in *Huê* and *tài tu* music appear to correlate with this concept. In fact, each modal system in *Huê* and *tài tu* music is associated with a specific emotion as follows:

Modal system	Emotional association
Huê music	
Khách or *bắc*	Happiness
Thiên or *thuyên*	Solemnity
Xuân	Tranquillity
Ai	Melancholy
Qua Phu	Extreme sadness
Tài tu music	
Bắc	Happiness, gaiety
Ha or *nhac*	Reverence
Xuân	Serenity
Ai and *oá*	Sadness
Dao	Restlessness

These extra-musical meanings are generated from a set of technical conventions related to tonal material, melodic construction, and the use of ornaments and tempo. By applying these conventions, performers can evoke a recognizable emotion associated with a specific modal system. Furthermore, the important role of improvisation in performance of *Huê* and *tài tu* music enables musicians to bring out their personal feelings in the performing process, for a piece of music provides performers only with a melodic framework. Performers must elaborate a piece's framework in their own style.[1]

Influence of Chinese Culture

In the late nineteenth and early twentieth centuries there was a strong tendency among *Huê* and *tài tu* musicians to graft Chinese extra-musical features on to the above indigenous musical and extra-musical features. The re-interpretation of the meanings and function of *Huê* and *tài tu* music from the Confucian view of music was an example of this practice. The notion of *Huê* and *tài tu* musicians that music is a part of nature and expresses the harmony between heaven and earth is the basis of their belief that the five main musical tones are associated with five materials (metal, wood, water, fire and earth) (Hai Biêu n.d.: tape D.59; Nguyên Văn Thinh 1963:103; Tân Viêt Điêu 1961:371). This notion is a direct borrowing from the Confucian cosmological concept of music.

In addition, a number of musicians borrowed the Confucian concept of music as a means for ethical and educational guidance in their interpretation of the social functions of *Huê* and *tài tu* music. In China, music was regarded as one of the four noble arts by which an individual could purify his or her thought and spirit.[2] Music was also one of the six essential subjects of a Confucian education.[3] Thus, some *Huê* and *tài tu* musicians asserted that 'wise men of ancient time invented music as a means to correct man's thought and character' (Hoàng Yên 1921a:371), and that it was through the study of music that one 'learned the spirit of orderly organization and disciplinary practice' which was embodied in the organization of musical materials and the execution of these materials (Hoàng Yên 1921c:370).

Some *Huê* musicians borrowed the Confucian view of emotional restrictions on music in their theoretical writings. According to the Chinese classic *Yueh Chi* [Record of Music], if music is to serve as a means of ethical guidance, it should be emotionally restricted. The 'right music' should bring neither sadness nor too much joy (Kaufmann 1976:36). Music that expresses extreme sadness or cheerfulness was considered to be 'evil music', which could have bad effects on humankind's virtue (Kaufmann 1976:39). Vietnamese musicians adopted this view by stating that *Huê* music expresses joy but not license, sorrow but not defeat. Such statements certainly contradict the indigenous concept of music as a means by which to express personal feelings.

Huê musician Nguyên Huu Quát harshly criticized the adoption of these Chinese views and maintained that they had nothing to do with *Huê* music (1921:176). His view is supported by the fact that none of the musicians who borrowed Confucian concepts of music actually abandoned the indigenous concepts of music as means for personal expression. They tended to graft Confucian concepts onto the indigenous ones, despite the contradiction between the two ideals. In my opinion, it was the sociopolitical conditions of the Vietnamese society of that time that motivated *Huê* and *tài tu* musicians to adapt Confucian views of music.

Between the fifteenth and nineteenth centuries, the Vietnamese monarchies adopted Chinese, especially Confucian, ideals as the principal guidelines for social, cultural and political activities. Government organization and the system of education were closely modelled on their Chinese counterparts. In addition, the Vietnamese monarchies adopted Chinese as the official written language for all government documents and communications.[4] As a result of these policies, the Chinese language and Confucian values were highly respected among the Vietnamese élite and literati. This sociocultural trend was further intensified by the pro-Chinese, anti-Western policy implemented by the Nguyên kings between 1802 and 1883 in order to protect the Vietnamese Confucian culture from being corrupted by the influx of Western ideals. Despite the fact that the Vietnamese monarchy lost most of its power to the French in 1884, Confucian thought continued to dominate sociocultural activities and became a patriotic symbol in the fight against the colonial forces until the early decades of this century. Thus, it is possible to argue that the aims of *Huê* and *tài tu* musicians in adopting the Confucian concepts of music were to increase the social value of their art, to heighten their social status, and to enable their art to function effectively in the sociocultural conditions of Vietnam in this period. As Chinese and Confucian ideals were highly respected by the Vietnamese, the reinterpretation of the meanings and functions of *Huê* and *tài tu* music from the Confucian viewpoint would certainly have helped to heighten the social value of these two types of music and the social status of musicians.

Huê and *tài tu* musicians' use of Chinese loan words in the making of titles of their compositions can also be seen as an attempt to increase the social value of their music. In fact, all compositions in the classical repertoire of *Huê* and *tài tu* music have Chinese loan words in their titles. Some of these titles, such as *Luu Thuy* [Flowing Water] and *Phung Câu*

Hoàng [The Male Phoenix Courting The Female] are direct trans-literations of the titles of well-known pieces mentioned in Chinese literature. In the nineteenth century, there was also a tendency to create song-texts in Chinese. In a collection of twenty-five pieces of *Huê* music dating from c. 1863, the song-texts of ten pieces are in Chinese (Trân Văn Khê 1961:69). Even though Chinese has no longer been used in song-texts written in the twentieth century, the practice of using Chinese loan words in the titles of compositions prevailed until the 1970s.

The preference for Chinese loan words was certainly motivated by the promotion of Chinese as the offical written language by Vietnamese monarchs before the twentieth century. This practice led to the rise of the belief among the Vietnamese that Chinese loan words sound more respectable than their indigenous counterparts. Therefore, most of the important terms in arts, music, literature, science, technology, economics and politics were derived from Chinese. This practice continued in Vietnam until the 1980s.

Besides using Chinese loan words in titles of compositions, *tài tu* musicians tended to create song-texts based on Chinese stories, legends and historical accounts. None of the song-texts of *Huê* music that I have collected so far are based on Chinese stories. This suggests that the level of Chinese influence in *tài tu* music was greater than in *Huê* music. The influx of Chinese refugees and migrants in the provinces of south Vietnam since the seventeenth century is probably the main reason for this higher level of Chinese influence in *tài tu* music.

After China had been taken over by the Man Chu in 1680, thousands of Chinese fled to Vietnam and resettled in My Tho, Biên Hoà and Hà Tiên. From 1778, many Chinese merchants and migrants came to Gia Đinh and Biên Hoà and developed Chinese zones in these areas (Vuong Hông Sên 1968:41-5). The policy of the Vietnamese monarchs of favouring the Chinese culture enabled that culture to flourish in these areas. By the end of the nineteenth century, Chinese tales and historical accounts had become very popular among the south Vietnamese. In the first decade of this century, publications of verse narratives based on Chinese stories and translations of Chinese historical novels were in great demand in south Vietnam (Son Nam 1974:118-20). The popularity of Chinese stories explains why *tài tu* musicians of this period based their song-texts on these stories.

Chinese musical styles began to play an important part in the transformation of *tài tu* music from the 1910s. Around 1908, a number of *tài tu* musicians began to organize public performances in hotels in My Tho and Saigon to raise funds for the nationalist movement (Son Nam 1974:123). The success of these performances introduced *tài tu* music as a form of entertainment in restaurants, hotels and movie theatres in south Vietnam around 1913 and 1914 (Trân Văn Khai n.d.:83 and 85). From 1915, public performances of *tài tu* music were gradually transformed into a new form of performing art called *ca ra bô* ['singing with gestures'] in which singers performed pieces or sections of a piece of *tài tu* music using dialogues with gestures. By the end of the 1910s, this form of singing had developed into a new form of music-drama called *cai luong* ['renovation']. As the number of pieces in the classical repertoire of *tài tu* music was very limited, there was a heavy demand for the composition and adaptation of new pieces for use in the *cai luong* in its early stage of development. Between 1920 and 1960, Mông Vân, Ba Chôt, Huỳnh Thu Trung, Xuân Phát and others composed and adapted many pieces for use in different dramatic situations on stage. Many of the adapted pieces are Chinese folk and theatrical songs. *Tài tu* and *cai luong* musicians classify these adapted melodies into the *quang* and *triêu châu* styles according to their geographical origin. The terms *quang* [from Guangdong] and *triêu châu* [from Chiu Chow] designate the Chinese provinces of Guangdong and Chiu Chow where these melodies originated.

The preference for Chinese culture among the population was the main motivation for the adaptation of these Chinese pieces. As Chinese historical and classical novels were very popular in south Vietnam, a number of *cai luong* troupes adopted Chinese stories in their performances in the late 1920s (Pham Duy 1975:141-3). In order to emphasize the Chinese character of these performances, *cai luong* performers adopted the style of make-up, costumes, acrobatic acts and music of the Chinese theatrical troupes in Cho Lón (the Chinese area of Saigon) (ibid.). Many of these Chinese tunes, such as *Manh Lê Quân* (name of a Chinese lady), *Không Minh Toa Lâu* [Không Minh Sits on the Dais] and *Trang Nguyên Hành Lô* [The Departure of a Mandarin] are still in use in *cai luong* performance of either Chinese or Vietnamese stories. As the *cai luong* developed, Vietnamese musicians formulated two modal systems which incorporate stylistic melodic motives and tonal ornaments of *quang* and *triêu châu* melodies. They designated these new systems as the *quang* and *triêu châu* or *tiêu*.[5] Between 1930 and 1960, musicians such as Mông Vân, Sáu Hai and Ba Chôt composed many pieces in the *quang* system for *cai luong* performances. Nowadays, these pieces are also played by *tài tu* musicians who do not associate themselves with *cai luong* activities.

Influence of Western Culture

From the 1920s, drastic sociopolitical changes in Vietnam also motivated a number of *Huê, tài tu* and *cai luong* musicians to initiate other new practices and to adopt new instruments. These musical changes show a strong interest in aspects of Western music among Vietnamese musicians.

The first decade of the twentieth century witnessed the rise in Vietnam of modern nationalist movements which initiated a drastic change in the attitude of the Vietnamese toward Western culture and values. Before the 1900s, Western culture and language were considered by the Vietnamese as 'barbaric' and 'inferior'. Despite the fact that the Vietnamese monarchy lost most of its power to the French in 1884, French efforts to spread their language, thoughts and ideals among the Vietnamese encountered great difficulties because the local people were uncooperative. Until the 1910s and 1920s, French schools were regarded as places for traitors and for the propagation of anti-traditional values (Nguyên Hiên Lê 1968:107). These schools never succeeded in enrolling the required number of students, despite attractions such as scholarships, free books, papers and pens (ibid.; Nguyên Anh 1967:40-1). This anti-Western attitude began to change in the early years of this century because of the rise of modern nationalist movements. In fact, by the end of the nineteenth century, all resistance movements which had maintained Confucian and indigenous ideals as their fundamental guidelines had been crushed by the French. The disastrous failure of these movements forced Vietnamese patriots to re-evaluate traditional ideals and to look for alternatives in their fight for independence.

In the 1900s, Vietnamese patriots became aware of the success of the Meiji restoration in Japan. The fact that the Japanese had succeeded in protecting their own interests against Western colonial forces and won the war with Russia in 1904 and 1905 motivated Vietnamese patriots such as Phan Bôi Châu, Luong Văn Can and Nguyên Quyên to adopt the Japanese model of modernization as one of their anti-colonial aims (Nguyên Hiên Lê 1968:26). In 1904, Phan Bôi Châu formed an organization called Duy Tân Hôi [Modernization Association], which aimed to promote the adoption of Western ideals and practices through the activities of its schools and commercial associations. In 1907, Luong Văn Can, Nguyên Quyên, Hoàng Tăng Bi and others established the Đông

Kinh Free School in Hanoi. This school was modelled after the famous Keiō Gijuku school of Fukuzawa Yukichi in Japan. Its aims were to expose young Vietnamese to Western education and to spread literacy and Western ideas throughout society. A number of schools with similar aims were also founded in central and south Vietnam in the early years of this century (Nguyên Hiên Lê 1968:137-42). As a result of these activities, Western science and culture were gradually accepted by the Vietnamese as the main means to revitalize their own society.

This new sociocultural environment motivated a number of *Huê* and *tài tu* musicians to adopt Western notation and/or instruments. From 1920, a number of south Vietnamese musicians began to use Western instruments such as the acoustic guitar and violin to play *tài tu* and *cai luong* music (Nguyên Thuyêt Phong 1989:75-6; Trân Thanh Long 1987:24). In using these instruments, *tài tu* and *cai luong* musicians tended to modify their construction and playing techniques to enable them to produce the different types of glissando ornaments which are typical of *tài tu* and *cai luong* music. For example, guitar fingerboards were filed into a wavy shape to enable performers to produce ornaments by pressing a string after plucking. The resulting instrument was named *luc huyên câm* [six-stringed instrument] or *dàn ghita móc phim* [guitar with curved fingerboard] (see Figure 1). Nowadays, it is a principal instrument in the performance of *tài tu* and *cai luong* music in south Vietnam.

Apart from adopting Western instruments, a few musicians began to show an interest in Western notation. In the 1940s and 1950s, Nguyên Huu Ba developed two systems with which to notate pieces of *Huê* music. These systems were called *ký âm Viêt Nam khoa hoc hoá* [renovated Vietnamese notation] and *ký âm tây phuong Viêt Nam hoá* [Vietnamized Western notation] respectively. In these two systems, the pitches were notated as in Example 1. In scores using these systems, each musical line was notated in two forms of notation and performers could choose the system that they wished to use (see Example 2).

What Nguyên Huu Ba meant by the Vietnamization of Western notation was the use of special signs to indicate microtonal ornaments such as *rung* (vibrato) and *mô* (perk) (see Example 3). In a vibrato, the discrepancy of pitch between the original tone and the ornamental tone ranges from a quarter of a tone to three-quarters of a tone. In a perk, the original pitch is raised approximately a quarter of a tone.

These systems provide a much more detailed notation of rhythm than the traditional systems, in which only the main beats were indicated.

Fig. 1. The fingerboard of
the *Luc huyên câm*

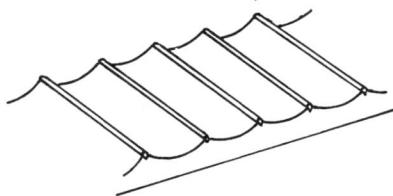

Ex. 1. Notational system developed by Nguyên Húu Ba

Ex. 2. Notated versions of the first phrase of the pieced *Lúu Thúy*
(Flowing Water) (Nguyên Húu Ba 1969:52).

Ex. 3. Notation of
microtonal
ornaments.

Ex. 4. Notational
system of
rhythmic patterns.

Nguyên Huu Ba used a number of signs to indicate rhythmic patterns, as shown in Example 4.

The advantage of these notational systems is that they provide performers with more information about technical aspects of a piece and thus assist the process of learning. However, as these systems began to be used in the teaching of *Huê* and *tài tu* music in the newly-established National School of Music in Saigon from 1956, a problem arose: in practice they discouraged students from developing skills in improvisation. In addition, the lack of proper instruction in improvising techniques and the deliberate intention of the teaching staff to require students to follow faithfully the notated versions in examinations and school concerts gradually encouraged students to adopt the practice of treating pieces of *Huê, tài tu* and *cai luong* music as fixed compositions.

The use of Western notation also initiated a tendency among students and graduates of the National School of Music to temper the pitches of pieces of *Huê, tài tu* and *cai luong* music. My examination of the playing style of well-known graduates who later became teachers at the National School of Music in the 1960s such as Pham Thúy Hoan and Phuong Oanh indicates that these performers tended to tune their instrument to pitches of the tempered scale. Only in the glissando ornaments did they produce the proper non-tempered pitches of *Huê* and *tài tu* music by manipulating the tension of the string before or after plucking.

Another Western-orientated innovation introduced by teachers of the National School of Music in the 1960s and early 1970s was the formation of large-scale ensembles. In general, the format of these ensembles (i.e. the number and types of instruments) was very flexible and tended to vary from one performance to another. On one occasion, the school presented an ensemble of eight zithers *dàn tranh* and four four-stringed lutes *tỳ bà* (Thái Văn Kiêm 1969:98, photograph). On other occasions, it presented ensembles comprising twenty zithers *dàn tranh* and two-stringed lutes *dàn nguyêt*, or ten *dàn tranh*, seven *dàn nguyêt*, four *tỳ bà*, two two-stringed fiddles *dàn nhi* and one bamboo flute (Nguyên Ngu Í 1964:91; Trân Thanh Tâm 1964:88). The use of two or more instruments of the same type in these large-scale ensembles is quite unconventional. In fact, in typical *Huê* and *tài tu* ensembles, each instrument must have a distinctive timbre. This practice does not encourage the use of two or more instruments of the same type in an ensemble.

Western influence is explicit in the use of imitative and antiphonal passages and in the employment of two or more instruments to play one part in unison in musical arrangements for these ensembles. Without the use of the newly-developed systems of notation and the acceptance of the concept of fixed composition, it would not be possible for two instrumentalists to play one part in unison.

Compositional Activity since 1975

The tendency among teachers and graduates of the National School of Music to adopt aspects of Western music was further intensified during the socialist revolution in Vietnam between 1975 and 1990. The year 1975 marked the establishment of a unified Vietnam under the leadership of the Vietnamese Communist Party. Since then, the government has carried out many programs of social, political, economic and cultural reform in order to turn Vietnam into an ideal socialist state. One of the most significant reformation programs of the post-1975 period was the Cultural and Ideological Revolution, the aim of which was to 'build a new culture' (Anon. 1976:5) by blending indigenous and Soviet sociocultural concepts and practices.

Regarding artistic creativity, the government has encouraged artists and musicians to formulate a new language which is described as *dân tôc hiên dai* ('modern national'). This language is supposed to be a synthesis of indigenous and 'progressive' non-indigenous means of expression (Hô Chi Minh 1977:30 and 90). The aim of the adoption of technical features of foreign arts is to enrich the expressive capability of Vietnamese arts and music (Phuong Thuy 1986:16). This attempt to renovate Vietnamese arts and music can be viewed as a continuation of the modernization movement which was initiated in the early decades of this century. The belief that Vietnamese culture and arts are at a 'lower' stage than those of foreign nations (Hô Chi Minh 1977:52) could have been the main motivation behind the decision to adopt foreign cultural features to 'improve' indigenous arts.

In their response to the official call for the creation of a modern national language in music, teachers at the National School of Music (now known as the Conservatorium of Music) have attempted to blend aspects of Vietnamese and Western music in their new compositions for traditional instruments. Structures, textures, harmony and orchestration of Baroque, Classical and Romantic music have been preferred. The reasons for this are, firstly, that these are the only types of Western music to have been taught in the Vietnamese conservatoires and are thus the only types of foreign music that Vietnamese musicians know quite well.

Contemporary music and art are considered 'poisonous' and 'dangerous' (Hô Sĩ Vinh 1988:16). Secondly, as many musicians still believe in the superiority of Western classical music, they have tended to adopt its technical features to 'improve' Vietnamese music.

New composers have based their works on sonata, variation, ternary and other Western forms. Chordal, multipart and contrapuntal textures borrowed from Baroque and Classical music have become increasingly popular. Many new pieces have sections which are dominated by these Western textures.

A number of composers, such as Nguyên Văn Đoi and Quang Hai, have tried to combine traditional and Western instruments in orchestras. Perhaps the best-known examples of this practice are Nguyên Van Đoi's *Concerto for zither đàn tranh, strings and percussion* and Quang Hai's Concerto *Quê Tôi Giai Phóng* [The Liberation of My Fatherland] for zither *đàn tranh* and full symphonic orchestra.

Besides making technical changes, new composers have also tended to abandon the traditional concept of music as a means by which to express personal feelings. From 1975, the government has continuously propagated the Marxist-Leninist concept of art. The fundamental idea is that arts should serve the political needs of the proletariat and the Party (Tô Huu 1973:345). New compositions should therefore 'reflect faithfully the reality of the new life and new man in order to educate and stimulate the masses in the socialist struggle' (Tô Huu 1973:280). Artistic representation of reality must be linked with the task of ideological and political education. As a result, post-1975 composers have begun to compose many original works with sociopolitical or patriotic titles, such as *Quê Tôi Giai Phóng* [The Liberation of My Fatherland] and *Tình Ca Quê Huong* [Love Songs for Motherland] for traditional instruments. By cultivating such new musical and extra-musical concepts as well as a considerable body of compositions, musicians of the National School have developed a new idiom of music which differs from *Huê, tài tu and cai luong* idioms.

Conclusions

Despite the development and popularization of the national and *cai luong* idioms, many *Huê* and *tài tu* musicians have continued to maintain their former playing style and repertoire. Their practice of keeping music as a form of private entertainment protected their art from being affected by sociopolitical policies. Furthermore, the government's respect for old, skilled traditional musicians has effectively encouraged them to preserve their playing style and repertoire. However, unlike the *cai luong* and National schools, the classical schools of *Huê* and *tài tu* music have gradually lost their popularity. Before the nationalist and socialist revolutions, *Huê* and *tài tu* music served as entertainment for the intellectuals in central and south Vietnam. The playing or enjoyment of these types of music was a symbol of social prestige. With the rise of modern nationalism and socialism in Vietnam, a new generation of Western-orientated intellectuals replaced the old generation. For these new intellectuals, Western values, practices and arts have greater appeal than those of their own tradition. As a result, support for activities of *Huê* and *tài tu* music has gradually decreased.

The preference for Western values and arts among the new upper classes and intellectuals has also led to a decrease in the social value of the music-drama *cai luong*. Despite its extreme popularity in south Vietnam, *cai luong* is nowadays regarded as being non-progressive by many intellectuals in Vietnam.

In conclusion, sociopolitical developments motivated the responses of *Huê* and *tài tu* musicians to the influx of Chinese and Western culture. The variety of their responses led to the transformation of *Huê* and *tài tu* music as well as the development of new musical styles. These responses include (1) the grafting of non-indigenous extra-musical features onto indigenous ones, (2) the rejection of non-indigenous traits, (3) the adaptation of non-indigenous traits, (4) the abandonment of pre-existing traits, and (5) the simultaneous development of musical styles.

The development of *Huê* and *tài tu* music also indicates that two or more responses can take place simultaneously in each historical period. Multiple responses can be set in motion under various circumstances. First, multiple responses may occur when the native population is in contact with two or more cultures simultaneously, in which case the sociopolitical environment can motivate different responses to the influx of different cultures. In fact, the pro-Chinese, anti-Western policy of the Nguyên kings between 1802 and 1883 and the promotion of Confucian values as symbols of patriotism by the resistance movements between 1884 and 1905 motivated *Huê* and *tài tu* musicians to reject aspects of Western music and to adopt musical and extra-musical features from China before the 1920s.

Multiple responses can also take place when different groups of musicians react to sociopolitical change and intercultural contact in different ways. Some musicians reject non-indigenous aspects and

continue to maintain their traditional practice. Others combine indigenous and non-indigenous musical aspects in order to formulate new
styles of music. Such responses lead to the simultaneous cultivation of
two or more styles of music by different groups of musicians. The coexistence of the *Huê, tài tu, cai luong* and national styles in central and
south Vietnam between 1956 and 1990 presents a convincing example of
such a case.

Notes

1   For a detailed examination of the modal systems and the importance
    of improvisation in *Huê* and *tài tu* music, see Lê Tuân Hùng 1990:71-
    133.
2   The four noble arts are *câm* (music), *kỳ* (chess), *thi* (poetry) and *hoa*
    (painting or calligraphy).
3   The six essential subjects of Confucian education are *lê* (ritual lore
    and practices), *nhac* (music), *xa* (archery), *ngu* (riding), *thu* (literature
    and philosophy) and *sô* (mathematics).
4   Only the Hô dynasty (1400-1407) and the Tây Son dynasty (1788-
    1802) promoted the use of Vietnamese as the official written
    language.
5   For a detailed examination of the musical characteristics of the
    modal systems *quang* and *triêu châu*, see Lê Tuân Hùng 1990:157-9.

References

ANONYMOUS
    1976   'Outline of the Draft Political Report of the Central
            Committee of the Vietnam Worker's Party to the Fourth
            Party Congress'. *Vietnam Courier* 55:1-28.
BÙI VĂN HAI
    n.d.   *Đàn Tranh.* Manuscript.
HÔ CHI MINH
    1977   *Vê Công Tăc Văn Nghê* [On the Artistic Tasks]. Hanoi: Su
            Thât.
HÔ SĨ VINH
    1988   *'Chung Quanh Vân Đê Đôi Moi và Nâng Cao Su Lãnh Đao cua
            Dang'* [Reformation and the Leadership of the Party in the
            Arts]. *Nghiên Cúu Văn Hoá Nghê Thuât* 2(85):15-20.

HOÀNG YÊN
  1921a 'Câm Hoc Tâm Nguyên' [Origin of Musical Instruments], Part I. *Nam Phong* 47:370-86.
  1921b 'Câm Hoc Tâm Nguyên', Part III. *Nam Phong* 49:44-61 and 88.
  1921c 'Ít Loi Ngo Voi Ông Thân Đúc Nguyên Huu Quát' [A Few Lines to Mr. Thân Đúc Nguyên Huu Quát]. *Nam Phong* 52:369-72.

KAUFMANN, Walter
  1976 *Musical References in the Chinese Classics*. Detroit Monographs in Musicology no. 5. Detroit: Information Coordinators Inc.

LÊ TUĂN HÙNG
  1990 *Music and Socio-Political Change: A Study of Đàn Tranh Music in Central and South Vietnam Between 1890 and 1990*. Monash University: Ph.D. dissertation.

NGUYÊN ANH
  1967 'Vài Nét vê Giáo Đuc O Viêtnam Tu Khi Pháp Xâm Luoc Dên Cuôi Chiên Tranh Thê Giói Lân Thú Nhât' [Education in Vietnam from the Beginning of the French Invasion to the End of the First World War]. *Nghiên Cúu Lich Su* 98:39-51.

NGUYÊN HIÊN LÊ
  1968 *Đông Kinh Nghiã Thuc* [The Đông Kinh Free School]. 2nd edn. Saigon: Lá Bôi.

NGUYÊN HUU BA
  1969 *Đàn Tranh: Nhac Cô Truyên Trung Phân Viêt Nam* [Đàn Tranh Music from Central Vietnam]. Saigon: Tỳ Bà Trang.

NGUYÊN HUU QUÁT
  1921 'Tra Loi Bài Câm Hoc Tâm Nguyên' [A Critical Review of the Article 'Origin of Musical Instruments']. *Nam Phong* 50: 175-6.

NGUYÊN NGU Í
  1964 'Dê Nhât Đai Hôi Văn Nghê cua Sinh Viên Âm Nhac và Kich Nghê Sài Gòn' [The First Music Festival of Students from the National School of Music and Drama in Saigon]. *Bách Khoa* 171:91.

NGUYÊN THUYÊT PHONG
  1989 *Thê Gioi Âm Thanh Viêt Nam* [The World of Vietnamese Sounds]. San Jose, California: Hoa Cau.

NGUYÊN VĂN ĐOI
1980 Sonata no. 1 for three *dàn tranh*. Manuscript.

NGUYÊN VĂN THINH
1963 'Bách Khoa Phong Vân Giói Nhac Sĩ: Nguyên Văn Thinh'
[*Bách Khoa* Interviews Musician Nguyên Van Thinh].
Nguyên Ngu Í (ed.). *Bách Khoa* 158:101-5.

PHAM DUY
1975 *Musics of Vietnam*. Dale R. Whiteside (ed.). Carbondale,
Illinois and London: Southern Illinois University Press.

PHAM THÚY HOAN
[1986] *Môt Sô Tiêu Phâm Viêt Cho Đàn Tranh* [Compositions for
Đàn Tranh]. Roneoed copy.

PHUONG THUY (ed.)
1986 *Âm Nhac o Thành Phô Hô Chi Minh* [Music in Hô Chi Minh
City]. Hô Chi Minh: Hô Chi Minh City Publisher.

SON NAM
1974 *Cá Tinh Miên Nam* [Cultural Identity of the Southerners].
Saigon: Xuân thu, reprinted in the United States.

TÂN VIÊT ĐIÊU
1961 'Tim Hiêu ca Nhac Cô Điên Miên Trung' [A Study of
Classical Music from Central Vietnam]. *Văn Hoá Nguyêt San*
60:361-80.

THÁI VĂN KIÊM (ed.)
1969 *Vietnamese Realities*. Saigon: South Vietnamese Government Publisher.

TÔ HUU
1973 *Xây Dung Môt Nên Văn Nghê Lon Xung Đáng Voi Nhân Dân Ta
và Thoi Đai Ta* [Building Great Arts for Our People and Our
Era]. Hanoi: Văn Hoc.

TRÂN THANH LONG
1987 'Nhât Phá Son Lâm, Nhi Đâm Hà Bá' [Life of South
Vietnamese Working in Forestry and Fishery]. *Ti Vi Tuân
San* 71:24-5.

TRÂN THANH TÂM
1964 'Bách Khoa Phong Vân Gioi Nhac Sĩ: Trân Thanh Tâm' [*Bách
Khoa* Interviews Musician Trân Thanh Tâm]. *Bách Khoa*
159:87-90.

TRÂN VĂN KHAI
n.d.   *Nghê Thuât Sân Khâu Viêt Nam* [Vietnamese Music-Drama].
            Houston: Xuân Thu.
TRÂN VĂN KHÊ
    1961   'Lôi Ca Huê và Lôi Ca Tài Tu' [*Huê* and Amateur Songs].
            Bách Khoa 101:67-9.
VUONG HÔNG SÊN
    1968   *Sài Gòn Năm Xua* [Saigon in the Past]. Saigon: Khai tri.

Discography

1. Tape D.39. *Huê* music and popular songs played by Buu Lôc and Tôn
    Nu Liên Thuy. One C-90 cassette. n.d. [pre-1975]. Private
    collection of Phuong Oanh.
2. Tape D.45. *Huê* music played by Buu Lôc and Phuong Oanh. One C-90
    cassette. n.d. Private collection of Phuong Oanh.
3. Tape D.59. Master Hai Biêu plays and talks about *tài tu* and *cai luong*
    music. One C-90 cassette. n.d. [pre-1975]. Private collection
    of Phuong Oanh.
4. Tape BM.73.9.1. Folk and *Huê* music played by Vĩnh Phan and Ngô
    Nhât Thanh. One reel-to-reel tape. Duration: 40'33". 1968.
    Document of the Musée de l'Homme (Paris).

Conclusion:
Music in an Age of
Cultural Confrontation

Stephen Blum

In his lectures of 1961-62 on the sociology of music, Theodor W. Adorno was willing to grant that 'even quite distant cultures (if we employ just once that loathsome plural) have the capacity to understand one another musically' (1962:165).[1] At first glance, it may seem strange to attach an expression of one's loathing for the plural, 'cultures', to a claim that mutual understanding through music is a real possibility. Yet all attempts to represent particular cultures or culture in general involve assumptions and decisions about what the representations exclude (as in the familiar oppositions of culture and 'nature', 'barbarism', 'anarchy', 'civilization' or 'society').

Adorno saw all culture worthy of the name as resistance to 'the world of exchange value':

> If material reality is called the world of exchange value, and culture is whatever refuses to accept the domination of that world, then it is true that such refusal is illusory as long as the existent exists. Since, however, free and honest exchange is itself a lie, to deny it is at the same time to speak for truth: in face of the lie of the commodity world, even the lie that denounces it becomes a corrective (1951:49; tr. 1974:44).[2]

Lies that 'do not in the least hinder the everyday routine of politics and social life' (1962:164) have no value as correctives. Reflecting on the construction and exploitation of 'national musics', Adorno saw these as 'brands of merchandise for the international market', manufactured from 'qualitative differences' that had not been assimilated into 'the general concept of music' (ibid.:173).[3] In his writings, 'the general concept of music' is unconditionally utopian: resistance to various types of domination increases to the extent that cultures exercise 'the capacity to understand one another musically', and vice versa. Adorno did not pretend that this is a realistic account of what usually happens or is likely to happen.

Many ethnomusicologists and music historians have proceeded on the assumption that 'the inherent value of music is use value' rather than exchange value (Qureshi 1990:343), most often without adopting these terms and without insisting on an absolute opposition between 'culture' and 'material reality' or 'the everyday routine of politics and social life'. As we compare various representations of 'musical culture', we find different ways of thinking about the use value of music and its relation to exchange value. If we attempt to clarify these with reference to 'the general concept of music' or 'the inherent value of music', we move from history or ethnography to philosophy or general theory – a justifiable move so long as we do not mistake one theory (or one utopian vision) for the 'substance' or 'essence' of history.

No appeal to an essence of history is needed to recognize that representations of cultures, and propositions about culture contact, are produced in circumstances marked by asymmetrical power relations of various types. Agawu, among many others, reminds us that no ethnomusicologist works 'in a world in which representer and represented inhabit the same socioeconomic and political spheres' (1992:250). This is so obvious that we may well ask how scholars can continue to discuss the 'essential features' of one or another musical culture, without reflecting on how these have been represented, by different parties, for different purposes. Unsatisfactory answers are readily available: it is a matter of convenience, it is the scholar's job to find unity rather than discord, the representation is not really affected by the motives of those who construct it, and so on. Yet neither musical life nor musical scholarship is an exception to the rule that '*conflict* can never be eliminated from cultural life. One can change the means, the object, even the basic direction and the agents, but one cannot do away with conflict itself' (Weber 1968b [1917]:517).[4]

Hence, we have good reason to be suspicious of those who claim that a culture 'speaks' through a single voice (be it their own or their master's voice). Any culture is better understood as 'a congeries of inner tensions' (Miller 1956:1), a site of arguments and negotiations. Observing, correctly, that the USA 'is in actuality not a nation of black people and white people', the writer Albert Murray adds that 'There are white Americans so to speak and black Americans. But any fool can see that the white people are not really white, and that black people are not black. They are all interrelated one way or another' (Murray 1970:3).[5] Of course, with minimal effort we can locate fools whose words and actions acknowledge few if any of the interrelationships; but this should not lead us to conclude that Murray is wrong. On the contrary, the capacity to 'see that the white people are not really white, and that black people are not black' is available to each and every fool (and to non-fools as well, if we can imagine such creatures). It is exercised in every perception and consequent action that do not presuppose a 'substance' or 'essence' of blackness or whiteness.

Murray's point holds equally well for many other pairs: rural and urban, settled and nomadic, indigenous and foreign, national and regional, believers and heathen, Malay and Chinese, to name but a few. Representations of 'rural musical culture' or 'Malay musical culture' imply complementary representations of musical cultures that are 'not rural' or 'not Malay'; yet few if any musicians can honestly claim to stand outside the interrelationships that make white people 'not really white' and so on. Inasmuch as every musician is 'an agent who participates in more than one social group' (Blum 1975:208-9) and is thus 'strangely composite' (Turino 1990:401, citing Gramsci), musical performance enables participants to discover and renew the connections between multiple aspects of experience. The identities of musicians are far more complex, and more flexible, than one might suppose from most non-musical representations of 'ethnicity', 'nation', 'race' and 'culture'.

An insistence on the purity or uniqueness of one musical practice is a sure sign of culture contact (which includes all efforts to avoid, abort or deny contact). To speak of a national music, for example, entails awareness of other national musics and of musics that are in some sense 'more than national' or 'less than national'. Questions about the nature of 'our music' can only arise when those who pose them are concerned with problematic relations between 'us' and 'them' (Picken 1975:609). As various answers are proposed and debated, it is easy to forget that such concepts as 'race and culture, people and nation' should be understood as 'questions, and not answers; not substrata of phenomena, but complicated phenomena in themselves; not sociological elements, but results; in other words: products and not producers' (Musil 1978:1366, tr. 1990:162).[6] The 'products' are put to use by actors, who offer competing answers — best interpreted, in turn, as new questions.

In other words, a concept of culture is misused, in scholarship as in other activities, when it points more to a substratum than to ways of questioning and reinterpreting certain results of prior actions. '"A culture" is . . . better seen as a series of processes that construct, reconstruct, and dismantle cultural materials, in response to identifiable determinants' (Wolf 1982:387), and these determinants always have something to do with contact: people construct, reconstruct and dismantle cultural materials when they know or suspect that other people have undertaken (or may undertake) such tasks in a different manner (frequently seen as a manner that 'does not deserve the name culture'). One who acts 'in response to identifiable determinants' has a *purpose:* 'the conception of a *result (Erfolg)* that becomes the *cause (Ursache)* of an action *(Handlung)*' (Weber 1968a [1904]:183).

Norbert Elias argued in 1939 that 'the French concept of *civilisation* reflects the specific social fortunes of the French bourgeoisie to exactly the same degree that the concept of *Kultur* reflects the German' (1978:49).[7] Comparing the very different histories of class conflict in eighteenth-century France and Germany, he showed how and why we should consider the internal conflicts within each nation together with their external relations as we examine the histories of these terms, which he outlined to the point at which the European nations 'see themselves as bearers of an existing or finished civilization to others, as standard-bearers of expanding civilization' (ibid.:50). 'The history of the German concepts *Zivilisation* and *Kultur* is very closely interrelated with the history of relations between England, France, and Germany' (ibid.:289-90), including of course their competition for colonies and the consequences of this competition.[8] Scholars concerned with both newer and older meanings of 'culture' in many parts of the world since 1939 can learn much from Elias's study of 'the civilizing process', beginning with the point that 'the culture concept came to the fore in a specific historical context, during a period when some European nations were contending for dominance while others were striving for separate identities and independence' (Wolf 1982:387; see also Williams 1958). Reading the papers on Ukraine and Croatia in this volume should remind us that the tensions of that 'specific historical context' have by no means played themselves out; nor have they been confined to Europe (as Tan's study of Malay and Chinese identities in Malaysia makes painfully clear). In every representation of culture, we can discover traces of what V.Y. Mudimbe calls 'the violence of the Same':

> We already have enough evidence to understand that accultura-
> tion is not an African disease but the very character of all histories.
> In the sequences, mutations, and transformations that we can
> read [and that we can hear, see and feel in performances], all
> histories deploy in effect the dispersion of the violence of the
> Same, which from the solid grounding in the present, invents,
> restores, or endows meaning to the Other in a past or in geo-
> graphically remote synchronic cultures. (Mudimbe 1988:196)

In order to live in a fully unified culture, one would need to be totally dominated by 'the violence of the Same', accepting all the consequences of the position criticized by Benjamin Constant in *De l'Esprit de conquête* (1957 [1814]:985): 'L'on immole à l'être abstrait les êtres réels; l'on offre au peuple en masse l'holocauste du peuple en détail'.[9] The fact that so many people have adopted this position in our century does not serve to justify it; quite the contrary.

A general theory of music deserving of the name will remain 'especi-ally sensitive to ideas that don't fit current doctrines' (Friedrich 1986:118). It would interpret what Adorno called 'the general concept of music' as 'one special concept of music', created and developed in relation to other special concepts. It should prepare us to reconstruct many histories of music, with attention both to 'dispersion of the violence of the Same' and to prospects for non-violent alternatives.

Interpreting Musical Cultures in Contact

From the late nineteenth century to the present, musicians and scholars in many parts of the world have faced conflicting demands made by spokespersons for cultures described as 'modern' or 'traditional'; 'élite' or 'popular'; 'international', 'national' or 'local'; and so on. People often act out these conflicts and explore possible resolutions in musical performances. Experience of such performances can help us to recognize how representations of culture result from competition between people with different styles of action, different ways of making and avoiding contact (see Lloyd 1990 on 'mentalities').

Those who write histories of concepts and representations of culture are also engaged in performance, through the act of writing for one or more groups of 'implied readers'.[10] The points at which writer and reader recognize or deny culture contact may or may not coincide. Perceptions of cultural distance can take many forms, and the only way to avoid false consciousness of 'cultural purity' is to examine the transactions through which individuals and groups reproduce cultural knowledge. We begin to understand something of what people mean by 'culture' when we hear them arguing about it — comparing one culture with another, or with something they refuse to regard as culture. Every culture is a site of encounters; all claims to the contrary notwithstanding, no culture can be reproduced as an unchanging essence with fixed locations and boundaries.

To avoid self-delusion we need to acknowledge multiple (and potentially incompatible) ways of experiencing and understanding music. None of us, however skilful and conscientious our writing and speaking, can do this without the active collaboration of our readers and listeners, the best of whom remain continually attentive to voices and positions that the writer or speaker has ignored or misrepresented, deliberately or inadvertently (or both, as is often the case).

Many of the respects in which musical scholarship is a long-term, collaborative undertaking are well illustrated by the seventeen essays in this volume. Three writers (Sumarsam, Mazo and Stockmann) look closely and carefully at the history of theoretical inquiry or research on a particular subject. They show us how general theories of music can develop, given enough time and relatively favourable circumstances. To insist upon quick results is to underestimate the complexities of music and musicology: 'much of what seems unordered eventually turns out to be ordered; rather than being diametrically and dialectically counterposed, order and chaos are overlapping, interacting, and mutually contextualizing' (Friedrich 1986:150).[11]

Sumarsam and Mazo describe different circumstances in which theoretical discussion of modal practices has become more refined during the past century; their papers enhance our understanding of the process that Harold Powers (1980:422) has aptly termed 'expansion and internationalization of the concept "mode"'. After assessing the strengths and weaknesses of the gamelan theories formed through interaction between Javanese and Dutch intellectuals, Sumarsam notes that Ki Sindusawarno and Martopangrawit, who did not belong to the Javanese intellectual élite, began to develop theories 'based on the musician's point of view' — no small achievement in any time and place. Mazo draws both on intensive interviews with village lamenters and on a substantial body of research carried out since the late nineteenth century. She argues that the terms *popevki* ('melodic gestures', from *pet'*, 'to sing') and *lad* ('mode', 'manner', from *ladit'*, 'to be in concord with') are appropriately applied to certain village practices, even though these terms were first used in Russian church musical theory. Mazo finds 'unequivocal modal relationships' that remain constant despite the (obligatory) instability of pitches in lamenting.

With respect to the *starinski pjevanje* or 'ancient singing' of the Dinaric Alps, Petrović also considers 'tonal flexibility' to be one of the most significant stylistic features — again within 'definite limits' which, in her view, have not converged with those of Eastern or Western modal systems. She argues that 'certain tonal concepts exist, but not in modal systems'; genres are not distinguished by modal differences but by the types and functions of ornaments. Perhaps this practice marks one of the limits to 'expansion and internationalization of the concept "mode"'. The concept is useful in circumstances where one can distinguish two or more modes. Musicians familiar with a modal system have been known to complain that an unfamiliar musical practice 'remains confined to one mode' — a sign that they have failed to hear the significant differences (which may not be modal in any sense of the term).

Stockmann rightly emphasizes the extent to which research on Sami musical practices is necessary both to 'a general theory of music' and to a basic understanding of European musical culture as a whole, not least because the approach to 'motivic development' in the Sami *yoik* is a unique and highly individualized manifestation of principles used by many other peoples. After reviewing the history of research on Sami music from the late eighteenth century to the present, she predicts that 'the Sami themselves will decide, on several levels, how to go on with their music'. Her narrative moves from the attempts of missionaries to suppress shamanism and yoiking to a 'not so distant future' when Sami musicologists will assimilate and criticize earlier efforts at notation, recording and analysis of Sami music. Stockmann's appropriate emphasis on 'the cultural differentiation of the Sami' is entirely consistent with her interest in 'a general theory of music'.

From the essays of Stockmann, Mazo, Petrović, and Sorce Keller, we can begin to imagine a comprehensive history of human musicality in Europe (as an ideal, not as a realizable goal). One can describe a particular configuration of styles and practices as 'Italian' without presupposing an underlying cultural unity, as Sorce Keller shows. The same is true of abstractions on a much larger level ('European', 'Middle Eastern') and of abstractions that pertain to villages, families and individual performers. Some of the motivations for differentiating a local or an individual practice seem clear enough: if a lament is 'not one's own, then it doesn't touch one emotionally', as a woman in Tot'ma district said to Mazo. In other words, too much convergence would eliminate the very possibility of meaning. Performers sometimes describe the crucial differences with respect to social class or stratum rather than locality: a peasant woman of Basilicata in southern Italy, asked whether or not rich people lament, replied 'Yes, the rich lament, but not as we *pacchiani* ["clods"] do. We who are *villani* [rustics], *contadini* [peasants] lament more' (De Martino 1958:77). Although ethnographers can pose questions about differences between rich and poor or between residents of one village and their neighbours, most of the answers rely on terms that were not introduced by that particular ethnographer (e.g., 'We [in Tot'ma district] lament with a very thin, very poor voice — not like theirs'). The connotations of such terms as *pacchiani, villani,* and *contadini,* or 'thick' and 'thin' voices, vary according to the interests and positions of speakers and writers. It is difficult to disentangle the various strands of meaning even in such simple statements as 'we *villani* lament more' or 'those *villani* don't know how anything's done'. Efforts toward comprehensive histories of musicality in specific regions are attempts to understand what was (and is) at stake for all who have made such statements.

Most of the essays in this volume describe changes in musical life that occurred as a result of culture contact. The authors find evidence of change in rituals and ceremonies, stage performances, festivals, films and radio broadcasts, notated compositions and recordings, treatises, pedagogical practices and government policies. Such changes can be seen as responses to identifiable determinants, in the sense outlined above. In many situations, however, the determinants are identifiable only in principle: actually to identify them we would need both additional evidence and further argument about interpretation of the evidence, making use of comparative studies. Disagreements among musicologists concerning the causes of change result from the culture contacts in which all of us are involved.

Schechter's account of the 1980 Corpus Christi festivities in one Ecuadorean village is set in an appropriately broad context: the long history of interaction between European and indigenous Andean practices. As Schechter notes, the various components of this syncretic festival occur in many different combinations over much of Latin America and the Caribbean — a situation that cries out for comparative studies. The numerous ritual observances that are somehow related to the history of colonization and evangelization in Latin America might also be compared with some of the Southeast Asian ceremonies that combine Islamic and pre-Islamic elements (see Kartomi 1986 and 1991 on Minangkabau performing arts).

Whereas Schechter's paper is centred on one festival held in 1980, Pasler focusses on a few works written by two French composers in the years 1909-14. She shows that careful transcription of recordings was crucial to the compositional process of Maurice Delage in writing his *Quatre Poèmes Hindous* and *Ragamalika*. It would be difficult to exaggerate the importance of transcription and other responses to recordings in the creative activities of many twentieth-century musicians in every part of the world (see also Malm 1991). Pasler looks at several factors that made it possible for Delage to hear many details in the recordings of Imdad Khan and Coimbatore Thayi. She suggests that 'the self-criticism of modernist aesthetics' enabled Delage to take some of his cues from recordings of Indian music; Roussel, ten years older, seems to have been comfortable with an aesthetic that made 'India' merely a source of local colour and, more importantly, of impressions that could be 'translated into our ordinary musical language' by the composer.

Not content to use an existing 'musical language', Delage turned the recordings he had acquired into texts, with the aim of producing new texts. Even in situations where transcription is not involved, recordings become texts when musicians hear them often enough to reproduce the features that interest them: the recording is vested with a particular type of authority, qualified by other types of authority. A recording or a score is construed as a text when performers treat it as a set of detailed instructions or guidelines for performance; in practice, no single text or collection of texts can fully determine the performer's responses.

One way of reading the papers in this volume is to compare the different types of 'guidelines for performance' described by the authors, and the various ways of responding to these guidelines. The yoiker's life story becomes a text as she or he improvises a 'complex yoik composition'. Lamenting in Vologda province also requires improvisation, with great emphasis on 'subtle relations between voice and text in establishing verisimilitude' — inasmuch as 'there are no tales [or yoiks, or laments] without implied narrators and audiences' and 'the social function of texts . . . consists of maintaining the metaphysical links' (Stock 1990:11). The texts that are enacted in Andean celebrations of Corpus Christi and its Octave likewise serve to maintain certain metaphysical links. In all three cases we can recognize that 'societies do not have to wait for official interpreters to come along before they make the political choice that leads to a preference for one type of retrospective over another' (ibid.:1). Performers tell themselves stories about themselves, which may be heard either as new stories or as new responses to old stories.

With sufficient knowledge of musical activity in a given set of circumstances, we can attempt to assess the extent to which one or another constraint has been decisive, and we can estimate the chances that musicians will continue to respect familiar sources of authority. Smith's paper carries out both of these tasks rather well with respect to the Australian bush band. For a few young musicians of the Australian folk revival, as he reports, Irish immigrants associated with the Melbourne chapter of the *Comhaltas Ceoltóirí Éireann* played the role that Delage assigned to recordings by Imdad Khan and others. Smith gives several reasons for the interest of young Australians in 'contemporary Irish models of performance', and he offers a generalization that holds for many other instances of culture contact: 'When learning music of technical difficulty such as Irish traditional dance music, a live model is of enormous help to demonstrate techniques and to suggest ways of achieving a certain sound, better than even the clearest recordings can do'.

Smith describes circumstances in which musicians felt a strong desire, which became a need, for a more elaborate performance idiom than that of traditional Australian instrumental genres. Overcoming the considerable social distance that separated them from members of the Irish immigrant community, participants in the Anglo-Australian folk revival learned to play Irish dance tunes and added these to the repertoire of the bush band. Smith concludes that the music of the bush band 'does not command a single interpretation' and that 'the coexistence of elements with diverse social meanings enables the music to become a site of social debate'. In this instance, constraints on the meanings of a 'public folk music' include both a unifying ideology of 'folk' and the circumstances in which a reinterpreted 'folk music' has attracted new performers and audiences.

The essays on Vietnam, Papua New Guinea, Fiji, Malaysia, Croatia, Ukraine, India and the midwestern USA depict other sets of constraints on the interpretive moves available to musicians and listeners. Lê's analysis of changes in *Huê* and *tài tu* music is a second case study of musical genres as 'sites of social debate'. For example, Lê notes the resistance of some musicians to the fashion for reinterpreting these genres in terms of a Confucian view of music. He indicates that *cai luong* ('renovation'), a genre of music theatre developed in the 1910s, remains popular but is now 'regarded as being non-progressive by many intellectuals'. As taught at the National School of Music in Saigon beginning in the late 1950s, *Huê, tài tu* and *cai luong* music seem to have become what (following Smith) we might call 'public classical music': students learned to reproduce fixed pieces, and improvisation was discouraged or prohibited. The Korean genre *sanjo* appears to have suffered a somewhat similar fate (Song 1986:199-200 and Howard 1989).

Several of the problems involved in reshaping traditional performing arts for festivals and shows attended by foreign visitors are treated in the papers of Niles and Saumaiwai (see also Shiloah & Cohen 1983). Niles reports that many Papua New Guineans were critical of Polynesian groups that performed at the Third South Pacific Festival of Arts in 1980, judging them to have made too many modifications in their traditional practices. Saumaiwai compares various attitudes toward performance of Fijian *mekes,* noting a greater interest in costuming than in details of musical performance during the past decade. It is clear that, both in PNG and in Fiji, the South Pacific Festivals of Arts have stimulated considerable debate on the subject of 'ancestral traditions'.

One of the enduring problems of nationalist movements is to create and sustain myths that can link a sense of 'ancestral traditions' to a sense of national identity. Even a brief glance at the lavish expenditure of energy on such projects during the past two centuries would reveal that this has never been an easy task, least of all with respect to music: the ancestors are not apt to ask for national music unless they are made to do so in new operas, shows, choruses and the like. Nationalists and champions of regional identity have never relied on musical means alone but have invariably subordinated music to literary and political discourse. As Lortat-Jacob observes (1984:28), 'There is no folkloristic troupe without discourse and speeches based on a more or less mythic history'.

Niles and Saumaiwai describe shows in which, on the whole, the claims of ancestors have priority over those of the modern nation. Although he does not rule out the possibility that stringband music might become the national music of PNG, Niles concludes that music has not been given a significant role in fostering a sense of national identity at the present time. Perhaps PNG and Fiji will be able to function as nations without musical emblems of a unified national identity.

Tan's account of government cultural policy in Malaysia shows one of the unintended consequences of many nationalistic endeavours: the very substantial Chinese minority has reaffirmed its cultural identity in response to policies favouring a 'national culture based on the culture of the indigenous people of Malaysia'. The official view that racial violence can only be prevented by imposing a common 'national culture' is a dangerous fantasy. The Home Affairs Minister's proposal that the Chinese lion dance should be changed to a tiger dance may seem risible to an outsider, but the lion and dragon dance troupes that formed a voluntary association to protect themselves from official harassment were responding to a very real threat.

The papers of Blazeković and Noll identify many of the motives and strategies that have produced institutions and networks of national music in many parts of the world. The creation of repertoires of national opera, Singspiel and related genres in many languages (including Danish, Swedish, Norwegian, Russian, Croatian, Ukrainian, Polish, Hungarian, Greek, Czech, Armenian, Romanian, Serbian, Slovenian, Azerbaijani, Bulgarian, Georgian, Latvian, Lithuanian and Slovak)[12] is a subject that warrants more scholarly attention than it has yet received, as does the larger topic of singing in 'national languages'. Blazeković notes that the success of the first Croatian national opera in March 1846 was quickly followed by other steps toward propagating the national language. Ivan Zajc, whom Blazeković calls 'the central musical personality in Croatia during the second half of the nineteenth century', is one of several prominent figures, in various nations, who composed national operas — works that were very often *by* as well as *about* men who had demonstrated their capacity for leadership.

Noll compares two cases of rural-urban culture contact in which convergence entailed many collisions: the musical practices of peasants in western and eastern Ukraine were altered in rather different ways by the political programs of urban élites. The voluntary associations active in western Ukraine did not seek to transform all aspects of rural musical practice, whereas the scale and intensity of the immense effort to impose a new 'mass culture' in Soviet Ukraine have rarely been equalled. Noll quotes the Soviet writer H.M. Shevchuk on the need for 'liquidation of the older primitive village culture', and he describes the immense influence exercised by the Central Training Compound through its numerous publications and directives. The idiom of 'Soviet music' was given priority over national as well as over regional idioms.

One of the distinctive features of what Noll calls the 'music network' of Soviet Ukraine was its heavy emphasis on competitions, including the 'musical olympics' of the 1930s. There can be little doubt that the prospect of receiving recognition from agencies of the state has motivated countless musicians to alter their vocal and instrumental techniques in order to approximate an accepted standard. Large industries such as the film industry of Tamilnadu provide similar incentives, as Venkatraman's survey of developments in Tamil film music over the past six decades reveals. Reading Noll's and Venkatraman's papers, we can imagine some of the ways in which musicians may have perceived and responded to changes in the demand for their services; such changes almost never benefit everyone indiscriminately but favour those musicians with the 'appropriate' attitudes and training.

Changes in the patronage of music are largely responsible for many of the most heated controversies among twentieth-century musicians, critics and scholars. The 'music networks' that Noll describes were created during a period when Eastern European peasants were increasingly involved in 'network markets' and 'music patronage based on cash transactions [became] a normal occurrence' (Noll 1991:370). Many studies of culture contact have compared musical practices that are heavily affected by government policies and/or network markets with older practices that depend on social relationships of 'compulsory interdependence' (Lortat-Jacob 1984:31) in small communities oriented toward sectional markets. Musicians accustomed to a particular type of rationalization in musical life can easily share Delage's reaction to Indian performers: 'It is amazing that they can play together with all these contradictions!' The meanings of 'playing together' cannot remain unchanged as processes of rationalization and bureaucratization proceed along the lines described in many of these papers (and elsewhere, as in the dissertations of Buchanan 1991 and Robbins 1990).

Nettl's study of music schools in the midwestern USA describes a tightly controlled environment: a market that offers consumers several types of music, presented in highly standardised formats. An ambitious student who could afford the necessary wardrobe might learn to perform in a number of large ensembles, travelling with some of them to participate in competitions. The student might learn little or nothing about the modes of social interaction that produced earlier versions of these musical practices, which were rarely if ever 'pure' by the music school's standards.

Alter's essay reports on two intelligent attempts at compromise: admitting that 'institutionalization holds certain benefits in an environment of government and private corporate patronage', teachers of vocal music at the Sangeet Research Academy and the Bharatiya Kala Kendra do not wish to see their authority undermined by curricula, examinations and degrees. It should be interesting to follow the subsequent careers of singers trained at these institutions. The extent to which governments and corporate patrons might begin to support musical instruction centred on oral transmission, in India and elsewhere, is difficult to predict.

Nietzsche's Culture of Comparison and Halm's Comparison of Cultures

Were it not for various incentives to make comparisons, musicologists would not have needed the term 'musical culture', or such related (and older) terms as musical tradition, idiom, style and taste. Culture, like tradition, becomes a topic of discussion only when people are concerned with contacts, conflicts and prospects for change.[13]

The authors of these seventeen papers examine several ways of recognizing and responding to cultural contact, conflict and change. The essays on Croatia, Vietnam, Fiji, North India, Malaysia and Ukraine deal with types of contact that occur as 'states, communities and individuals engage in direct interaction with one another' (Robbins 1991:viii), pursuing interests that are not easily reconciled. For over a century, some of the more hostile modes of interaction have been described with such terms as *Kulturkampf* (Franz-Willing 1971), the more recent 'culture wars' in the USA (Shor 1986, Hunter 1991, Gates 1992), or the all-too-familiar 'liquidation of the older primitive village culture' and similar slogans. Even when musicians have not been murdered in the name of the state (as happened in Soviet Ukraine and elsewhere), the effects of 'symbolic violence' are very real (Bourdieu & Passeron 1970), and nowhere are they more evident than in efforts to legitimize or to deny the legitimacy of cultures.

Much of what was to come in our century of cultural confrontation was delineated with appalling clarity by Nietzsche in the 1870s and 1880s. In paragraph 23 of *Menschliches, Allzumenschliches* (1878), he described and prescribed an 'age of comparison':

> . . . such an age receives its meaning through the possibility of comparing diverse cultures, customs and perspectives on the world, which can be experienced alongside one another — something that could not be done formerly, inasmuch as all artistic styles were constrained by time and place when control of every culture was invariably localised.[14]

This new 'culture of comparison' would supposedly enable a select few to rise above the 'isolated, original folk cultures'; Nietzsche predicted that it would be superseded in turn by a better way of life. More than a century later, what Nietzsche saw as the 'spiritualized cruelty' and the 'terrible energies' of every 'higher culture' show no signs of weakening.[15] Our world includes many cultures of comparison — some of them hegemonic, others subordinate.

Die Geburt der Tragödie aus dem Geiste der Musik (1872) concludes with a polemic against 'Socratic culture' ('the culture of opera') and a vision of the rebirth of 'tragic culture'. Many musicologists, sociologists, critics and novelists have adopted the literary device of comparing two cultures (or, going back well before Nietzsche, two styles, two mentalities, two nations, etc.). A notable example is August Halm's *Von zwei Kulturen der Musik* (1913), which (in a manner somewhat more Hegelian than Nietzschean) compares two approaches to musical composition — those of fugue and sonata, as developed by Bach and Beethoven with emphasis on style and on form, respectively. A culture of music, in Halm's sense of the term, exists as a set of 'productive energies'; to learn what transpires in both fugue and sonata, and what each genre demands, is to acquire two cultures (1913:28, 9). The art of a cultured composer resides in a 'well-honed frugality that husbands all energies, being well acquainted with them, taking them seriously, and knowing when to deploy them' (ibid.:178).[16]

Halm's perspective evidently allowed for about seven possibilities: 'lack of culture' (as in Handel's case, p. 157); partial or full mastery of the culture of fugue or the culture of sonata; and a preliminary or more advanced synthesis of the two cultures (adumbrated in the first movement of Bruckner's Ninth Symphony, p. 254). He was especially interested in the question of how to effect a synthesis of the two cultures, and he compared the questions or problems posed by fugue and sonata to the needs or demands of an individual and those of the state, respectively. The fugue 'resembles more an individual existence, a way of life, something like a tree'; 'it is the formula of an individuality', bringing to fruition the characteristics of its subject. The sonata, in contrast, 'is the formula of the working together of many individuals, an organism on a large scale. It resembles the state' (ibid.:32-3).[17] These metaphors are appropriate to Halm's understanding of a culture of music as a set of demands and limitations.

The metaphors express an opposition between 'individuality' and 'authority' that turns up again and again in writings on the subject of culture, as Raymond Williams pointed out in his pathbreaking study of *Culture and Society, 1780-1950* (1958:337):

> The idea of a common culture brings together, in a particular form of social relationship, at once the idea of natural growth and that of its tending. The former alone is a type of romantic individualism; the latter alone a type of authoritarian training. Yet each, within a whole view, marks a necessary emphasis.

Halm (not without cause) was initially more concerned with the dangers of 'authoritarian training' than with those of 'romantic individualism'. He described the culture of fugue in terms that were similar to those used by his brother-in-law, the educational reformer Gustav Wyneken. For Wyneken, an autonomous 'youth culture' was to serve as the 'germ of a new collective culture' (see Rothfarb 1988:5-6 and 1991:12-15), just as Halm's culture of fugue pointed toward the autonomy that would be fully realized in a 'third culture of music'. The program of Wyneken's Freie Schulgemeinde in Wickersdorf aimed to create a non-authoritarian environment in which the *Kulturwille* of the students might realize itself (not least through experience of music). Halm (1919:150) hoped that development of a 'musical youth culture' would provide a 'human music' as an alternative to the dominant 'bourgeois music' of his day. In his later writings he abandoned the idea of musical composition as a synthesis of two cultures; Halm was inspired more by Nietzsche than by Hegel as he imagined 'a music that is called to represent a whole way of life, to prefigure and perhaps to realize a life of a higher kind' (Halm 1927:72). Comparing his own perspective (suspicion toward most of what musicians had accomplished so far) with that of his friend Heinrich Schenker ('unquestioning belief in genius'), Halm acknowledged that either perspective could serve as a 'valuable heuristic principle' (1978 [1917-18]:273).

The perspectivism that Halm learned from Nietzsche heightened his sense of the 'narrowness' and 'exclusivity' of cultures (1927:20). A question posed in his book on Beethoven (ibid.:72) clearly articulates the dual meaning of 'culture' in his writings: 'How can music, without participating in an existing culture and without being symptomatic or representative of such a culture, itself become culture or lead to a culture?'[18] Lawrence Scaff formulates another version of the same question as he examines the responses of Max Weber and members of his circle to what Scaff (1989:191) calls 'the problem of modernity: How is it possible for us to rebel against the world, the culture, the civilization *we* have created, yet to do so in the name of our ideals of life? What does it mean for us to subvert ourselves, to counter culture with culture?' Halm's answer in his 1919 essay on musical youth culture was very close to Emil Hammacher's in his *Hauptfragen der modernen Cultur* (1914; quoted by Scaff 1989:192): 'the "only hope" for the future of a culture of "autonomous spirit" under current conditions is "the deepening of personality through its felt opposition to the ruling powers"'. The composite nouns used in these discussions of culture and counter-culture included 'female culture' (Simmel 1923 [1911] and Vroman 1987) as well as 'youth culture'.

Halm raised issues pertaining to what we now call *Wirkungsgeschichte,* the history of responses to literary, artistic or musical works (Iser 1974, Dahlhaus 1977). He argued that musical technique, properly understood, points to the appropriate response: 'a genuine artist's way of working offers direct testimony concerning his convictions, his attitude toward art, and also the kind of response that he wants!' (Halm 1927:199).[19] The limitations of our culture inhibit our ability to respond, but music lays the foundations for a new culture when it calls for a new way of hearing and understanding, 'a new self-understanding on the listener's part as well' (ibid.:19-20). A musician, like a politician, may succeed in declaring a 'state of emergency' (*Ausnahmezustand*), but his or her 'tyranny' eventually comes to an end. Such was the case of Wagner, who 'forced people to concern themselves with him, listen to him, reckon with him and adopt a position toward him' (ibid.:27, 48).[20] Halm found it necessary to recognize the numerous respects in which Wagner's 'tyranny' had resulted in false interpretations of Beethoven's music. Because he and his contemporaries 'involuntarily' interpreted Beethoven's symphonies as the 'symbol' of a certain way of being human, the process of reinterpretation would be analogous to the experience of psychoanalysis (ibid.:68, 16, 199).

This brief discussion of Halm's writings has touched on only a few of the respects in which they are relevant to current work in musicology. Musicians and musicologists participate in 'cultures' that are continually redefined in relation to one another: 'empirical reality becomes "culture" for us as, and to the extent that, we bring it into relation with evaluative ideas; it comprises those portions of reality that become *meaningful* to us through that relation' (Weber 1968a [1904]:175).[21] Every culture is a culture of comparison, shared and resisted in various ways by a population of individuals (each of whom may accept or reject a particular interpretation of 'our culture').[22] Only by appealing to a false taxonomy of cultures, understood as essences, can one pretend that the concepts and methods of ethnomusicology and European music history have little or nothing in common. The various senses of 'culture' in the writings of ethnomusicologists and historians of European music can be understood as parts of 'a complex argument about the relations between general human development and a particular way of life, and between both the works and practices of art and intelligence' (Williams 1976:80-1). The ways in which groups and individuals participate in this complex argument need to be carefully examined, without assuming that people are born and raised in the 'cultures' to which we have assigned them.

Many interpretations of cultural difference combine a number of factors — such as 'race', ethnicity, religion, class, gender, language, 'breeding', means of livelihood — often without spelling these out. The interpretations are inevitably false in significant respects. When one factor is taken as primary, the result is also a construct that is potentially misleading, such as 'black culture', 'female culture', 'youth culture', 'culture of poverty' (Lewis 1959), or 'working-class culture' (Thompson 1963). In Simmel's essay on 'female culture', as Marianne Weber observed in a sharp rejoinder, 'psychological analysis and normative philosophical thinking are . . . so closely bound together that one finds a prescription for woman's destiny contained within the description of her being' (cited by Scaff 1989:147; see also Vroman 1978). The same point applies to Halm's writings on youth culture: prescriptions contained within descriptions are just what one finds in deconstructing any interpretation of the essence of a culture.

Efforts at deconstruction notwithstanding, the fact that 'culture' is now a subject of continuous debate encourages participants in the debates to distinguish more and more varieties, and it is often useful to do so (especially if one can remember how and why the distinctions were drawn). Many of us can no longer even count the number of cultures and subcultures to which we have been or might be assigned by researchers, journalists and bureaucrats. The proliferation of cultures requires an intensification of critical reflection and historical consciousness – a task to which the papers in this volume make a modest contribution.

Notes

1   'Selbst einander sehr ferne Kulturen – wenn man jenen abscheulichen Plural einmal gebrauchen will – sind fähig, musikalisch einander zu verstehen'.

2   'Nennt man die materielle Realität die Welt des Tauschwerts, Kultur aber, was immer dessen Herrschaft zu akzeptieren sich weigert, so ist solche Weigerung zwar scheinhaft, solange das Bestehende besteht. Da jedoch der freie und gerechte Tausch selber die Lüge ist, so steht, was ihn verleugnet, zugleich auch für die Wahrheit ein: der Lüge der Warenwelt gegenüber wird noch die Lüge zum Korrektiv, die jene denunziert'. Fredric Jameson discusses this passage in his *Late Marxism* (1990:45-51,87).

3   'Dabei verwandelte sich das qualitative Verschiedene, nicht im allgemeinen musikalischen Begriff sich Erschöpfende der Völker in eine Warenmarke auf dem Weltmarkt'.

4   'Denn nicht auszuscheiden ist aus allem Kulturleben der *Kampf.* Man kann seine Mittel, seinen Gegenstand, sogar seine Grundrichtung und seine Träger ändern, aber nicht ihn selbst beseitigen'.

5   This point has also been made by other African-American writers, among them James Baldwin (1955, 1963) and Ralph Ellison (1964).

6   This passage occurs in an unpublished draft of 1923, edited as follows in the second volume of Musil's *Gesammelte Werke* (1978): 'Da also diese Begriffe Rasse und Kultur, Volk und Nation . . . augenfällig auf etwas Reales hinweisen, ebenso augenscheinlich aber nichts fest

Faßbares oder gar Einfaches bezeichnen, kann man von ihnen vernünftigermaßen keinen andren Gebrauch machen, als daß man in ihnen Fragen und nicht Antworten sieht, nicht Substrate der Erscheinungen, sondern komplizierte Erscheinungen selbst, nicht soziologische Elemente, sondern Ergebnisse, m.a.W.: Produkte und nicht Produzenten'.

7 Elias summarizes these fortunes as follows: 'The French bourgeoisie — politically active, at least partly eager for reform, and even, for a short period, revolutionary — remained strongly bound to the courtly tradition in its behavior and its affect-molding even after the edifice of the old regime had been demolished ... The German middle-class intelligentsia, politically entirely impotent but intellectually radical, forged a purely bourgeois tradition of its own, diverging widely from the courtly-aristocratic tradition and its models' (ibid.).

8 The political contexts of the terms are largely ignored in the well-known study by A.L. Kroeber and Clyde Kluckhohn, *Culture: A Critical Review of Concepts and Definitions* (1952), which does not mention Elias's book.

9 Constant's sentence serves as the epigraph to Isaiah Berlin's *Four Essays on Liberty* (1969).

10 In addition to 'implied readers' (in the sense of Iser 1972), musicologists are concerned with the 'implicit theories' of composers and with the 'implied listeners' of specific works or practices, as Carl Dahlhaus has noted in several publications.

11 William Empson made a similar point with respect to the analysis of poetry: 'It is a matter of luck whether or not you have in your language or your supply of intellectual operations anything which for a particular problem, will be of use; ... Things temporarily or permanently inexplicable are not, therefore, to be thought of as essentially different from things that can be explained in some terms you happen to have at your disposal' (1946[1930]:252).

12 The order in which these languages are listed approximates (to the best of my knowledge) the time sequence in which national operas or related genres were created in each language. The list is doubtless incomplete.

13 Many authors have made this point with respect to tradition. 'The Medieval Muslim thinker al-Ghazzali observed that the genuine traditionalist does not know that he is one; he who proclaims himself to be one, no longer is one' (Gellner 1988:208). Elsewhere Gellner

(1979:60) remarks that 'when the Lebenswelt really *was* a Lebenswelt, no-one called it by any such name'. According to Carl Dahlhaus (1973:177), 'reflections on tradition are foreign to its nature. Tradition lives mainly in what goes without saying, what is self-explanatory'.

14   'Ein solches Zeitalter bekommt seine Bedeutung dadurch, daß in ihm die verschiedenen Weltbetrachtungen Sitten Culturen verglichen und neben einander durchlebt werden können; was früher, bei der immer localisirten Herrschaft jeder Cultur, nicht möglich war, entsprechend der Gebundenheit aller künstlerischen Stilarten an Ort und Zeit'.

15   Nietzsche speaks of 'the terrible energies' of culture and compares high culture to 'a bold dance' in pars. 246 and 278 of *Menschliches, Allzumenschliches*; see also *Jenseits von Gut und Böse* (1886), par. 229: 'Fast Alles, was wir "höhere Cultur" nennen, beruht auf der Vergeistigung und Vertiefung der *Grausamkeit*' [Almost everything that we call 'higher culture' is based on spiritualisation and absorption of cruelty]. Walter Benjamin echoed this point in a text of 1940 (1969:271-72): 'Es ist niemals ein Dokument der Kultur, ohne zugleich ein solches der Barberei zu sein. Und wie es selbst nicht frei ist von Barbarei, so its auch der Prozeß der Überlieferung nicht, in der es von dem einen an den andern gefallen ist' [There is no document of culture that is not at the same time a document of barbarism, and the process of transmission is no more free of barbarism than is the document itself].

16   'Solche Gesichtszüge einer Musik deuten auf überlegenen Verstand, auf Wissen und Können. Es ist jene sichere Sparsamkeit, die mit allen Kräften haushält, weil sie alle kennt, sie ernst nimmt und an ihren Platz zu stellen weiß.'

17   '... die Fuge wird im Grund von einem Gesetz beherrscht: dieses ist eben ihr Thema; dessen individuelle Eigenschaften, seine Tugenden sollen durch jene zur Geltung und Entwicklung kommen; ... überdies sich bedeutenden Gefährten zu gesellen: sie sollen in ihr zum Wachstum kommen. Die Sonatenform weist dagegen mehr einen Gang der Handlung auf; diesem dienen die Hauptthemen und die Art, wie sie verarbeitet werden; ... kurz alles Geschehen ist hier viel mehr als in der Fuge, ja es ist in erster Linie eine Funktion im Ganzen ... Die Fuge hat mehr Struktur als Aufbau, sie gleicht eher einer gesonderten Existenz, einem Lebewesen, etwa einem Baum,

wenn man konkrete Vorstellungen wagen will; *sie ist die Formel einer Individualität.* Die Sonate dagegen ist die Formel des Zusammenwirkens vieler Individuen, ist ein Organismus im großen: *sie gleicht dem Staat'* (pp. 332-3). Adorno (1962:223) rejected Halm's 'hypostasis' of fugue and sonata.

18 'Wie kann Musik, ohne an einer vorhandenen Kultur teilzunehmen, ohne Symptom und Exponent einer solchen zu sein, selbst Kultur werden oder zu einer Kultur führen?'

19 '. . . die Arbeitweise eines echten Künstlers sagt ganz direkt etwas aus über seine Gesinnung, über seine Stellung zur Kunst – und also auch über die Art des Wirkung, die er will!'

20 Carl Dahlhaus, a close reader of Halm, applied the phrase *Ausnahmezustand* both to Schoenberg's 'emancipation of the dissonance' (Dahlhaus 1986:17) and to the new demands that Beethoven's music was understood to make on listeners in the early nineteenth century (Dahlhaus 1980:8-9). In speaking of 'Schoenberg's Aesthetic Theology', Dahlhaus (1986) was adapting the title of Carl Schmitt's *Politische Theologie* (1922), which is very much concerned with the implications of a 'state of emergency'.

21 'Der Begriff der Kultur ist ein *Wertbegriff.* Die empirische Wirklichkeit ist für uns "Kultur", weil und sofern wir sie mit Wertideen in Beziehung setzen, sie umfaßt diejenigen Bestandteile der Wirklichkeit, welche durch jene Beziehung für uns *bedeutsam* werden.'

22 The advantages of 'population thinking' over 'essentialism' are discussed by Ernst Mayr (1982) and, with respect to classification of musical instruments, by Margaret Kartomi (1990). Population thinking is greatly preferable to essentialism in discussions of musical cultures.

References

ADORNO, Theodor W.

1951 *Minima Moralia: Reflektionen aus dem beschädigten Leben.* Frankfurt: Suhrkamp. Eng. tr. by E.F.N. Jephcott, London: Verso, 1974.

1962 *Einführung in die Musiksoziologie: Zwölf theoretische Vorlesungen.* Frankfurt: Suhrkamp.

AGAWU, Kofi
1992   'Representing African Music'. *Critical Inquiry* 18: 245-66.
BALDWIN, James
1955   *Notes of a Native Son.* Boston: Beacon Press.
1963   *The Fire Next Time.* New York: The Dial Press.
BENJAMIN, Walter
1969   'Geschichtsphilosophische Thesen'. In Benjamin, *Illumina-tionen: Ausgewählte Schriften.* Frankfurt: Suhrkamp, pp. 268-79. Essay written in 1940 and first published in 1950.
BERLIN, Isaiah
1969   *Four Essays on Liberty.* Oxford: Oxford Univ. Press.
BLUM, Stephen
1975   'Towards a Social History of Musicological Technique'. *Ethnomusicology* 19:207-31.
BOURDIEU, Pierre & Jean-Claude Passeron
1970   *La reproduction. Éléments pour une théorie du système d'enseignement.* Paris: Éditions du Minuit.
BUCHANAN, Donna Anne
1991   'The Bulgarian Folk Orchestra: Cultural Performance, Symbol, and the Construction of National Identity in Socialist Bulgaria'. Ph.D. diss., Univ. of Texas at Austin.
CONSTANT, Benjamin
1957   *Oeuvres,* ed. Alfred Roulin. Paris: Gallimard (Bibliothèque de la Pléiade).
DAHLHAUS, Carl
1973   'Traditionszerfall im 19. und 20. Jahrhundert'. In *Studien zur Tradition in der Musik,* ed. Hans Heinrich Eggebrecht and Max Lütolf. Munich: Emil Katzbichler, pp. 177-90.
1977   *Grundlagen der Musikgeschichte.* Cologne: Hans Gerig. Eng. tr., *Foundations of Music History.* Cambridge: Cambridge Univ. Press, 1983.
1980   *Die Musik des 19. Jahrhunderts.* Laaber: Laaber-Verlag (Neues Handbuch der Musikwissenschaft, 6). Eng. tr., *Nineteenth-Century Music.* Berkeley & Los Angeles: Univ. of California Press, 1989 (California Studies in 19th-Century Music, 5).
1986   'Schönbergs ästhetische Theologie'. In *Bericht über den 2. Kongress der Internationalen Schönberg-Gesellschaft 1984.* Vienna: E. Lafite, pp. 12-21. Tr. in Derrick Puffett and Alfred

Clayton, *Schoenberg and the New Music.* Cambridge: Cambridge Univ. Press, 1987, pp. 81-93.

DE MARTINO, Ernesto

1958   *Morte e pianto rituale.* Turin: Boringhieri.

ELIAS, Norbert

1978   *The Civilizing Process, I. The History of Manners,* tr. Edmund Jephcott. New York: Urizen Books. First publ. in German 1939.

ELLISON, Ralph

1964   'Some Questions and Some Answers'. In Ellison, *Shadow and Act.* New York: Random House, pp. 253-63. Interview first published in 1958.

EMPSON, William

1946   *Seven Types of Ambiguity.* 2nd edn. New York: New Directions. First publ. 1930.

FRANZ-WILLING, Georg

1971   *Kulturkampf gestern und heute. Eine Säkularbetrachtung 1871-1971.* Munich: Georg D. W. Callwey.

FRIEDRICH, Paul

1986   *The Language Parallax: Linguistic Relativism and Poetic Indeterminacy.* Austin: Univ. of Texas Press.

GATES, Henry Louis, Jr.

1992   *Loose Canons: Notes on the Culture Wars.* New York: Oxford Univ. Press.

GELLNER, Ernest

1979   *Spectacles and Predicaments: Essays in Social Theory.* Cambridge: Cambridge Univ. Press

1988   *Plough, Sword and Book: The Structure of Human History.* Chicago: Univ. of Chicago Press

HALM, August

1913   *Von zwei Kulturen der Musik.* Munich: Georg Müller.

1919   'Musikalische Jugendkultur'. *Neue Musik-Zeitung* 40: 149-50. Repr. in Halm 1978:245-8.

1927   *Beethoven.* Berlin: Max Hesse.

1978   *Von Form und Sinn der Musik.* Gesammelte Aufsätze, ed. Siegfried Schmalzriedt. Wiesbaden: Breitkopf & Härtel.

HAMMACHER, Emil

1914   *Hauptfragen der modernen Kultur.* Leipzig: Teubner.

HOWARD, Inok Paek
    1989   'Review of Song 1986'. *Yearbook for Traditional Music* 21:139-41.
HUNTER, James D.
    1991   *Culture Wars: The Struggle to Define America.* New York: Basic Books.
ISER, Wolfgang
    1972   *Der implizierte Leser: Kommunikationsformen des Romans von Bunyan bis Beckett.* Munich: Wilhelm Fink. Eng. tr., *The Implicit Reader.* Baltimore: Johns Hopkins Univ. Press, 1974.
    1974   *Der Akt des Lesens: Theorie ästhetischer Wirkung.* Munich: Wilhelm Fink. Eng. tr., *The Act of Reading: A Theory of Aesthetic Response.* Baltimore: The Johns Hopkins Univ. Press, 1976.
JAMESON, Fredric
    1990   *Late Marxism: Adorno, or, The Persistence of the Dialectic.* London: Verso.
KARTOMI, Margaret J.
    1986   'Muslim Music in West Sumatran Culture'. *The World of Music* 28/3:13-30.
    1990   *On Concepts and Classifications of Musical Instruments.* Chicago: Univ. of Chicago Press (Chicago Studies in Ethnomusicology).
    1991   'Dabuih in West Sumatra: A Synthesis of Muslim and Pre-Muslim Ceremony and Musical Style'. *Archipel* 41: 33-52.
KROEBER, A.L. & Clyde Kluckhohn
    1952   *Culture: A Critical Review of Concepts and Definitions.* Cambridge, Mass.: Harvard University, Peabody Museum of Archaeology and Ethnology (Papers, 47/1).
LEWIS, Oscar
    1959   *Five Families: Mexican Case Studies in the Culture of Poverty.* New York: Basic Books.
LLOYD, G.E.R.
    1990   *Demystifying Mentalities.* Cambridge: Cambridge Univ. Press.
LORTAT-JACOB, Bernard
    1984   'Music and Complex Societies: Control and Management of Musical Production'. *Yearbook for Traditional Music* 16:19-33.

MALM, Krister
  1991 'Music on the Move: Traditions and Mass Media'. Charles Seeger Memorial Lecture, 36th Annual Meeting, Society for Ethnomusicology, Chicago. To be published in *Ethnomusicology*.

MAYR, Ernst
  1982 *The Growth of Biological Thought: Diversity, Evolution, and Inheritance*. Cambridge, Mass.: Harvard Univ. Press.

MILLER, Perry
  1956 *Errand into the Wilderness*. Cambridge, Mass.: Harvard Univ. Press.

MUDIMBE, V.Y.
  1988 *The Invention of Africa: Gnosis, Philosophy, and the Order of Knowledge*. Bloomington: Indiana Univ. Press.

MURRAY, Albert
  1970 *The Omni-Americans: New Perspectives on Black Experience and American Culture*. New York: Outerbridge & Dienstfrey.

MUSIL, Robert
  1978 'Der deutsche Mensch als Symptom'. In Musil, *Gesammelte Werke,* ed. Adolf Frisé. Reinbek bei Hamburg: Rowohlt, 1978, 2:1353-1400. Eng. tr., 'The German as Symptom', in *Precision and Soul: Essays and Addresses,* ed. & tr. Burton Pike and David S. Loft. Chicago: The Univ. of Chicago Press, 1990, pp. 150-92. Drafts written in 1923.

NOLL, William
  1991 'Economics of Music Patronage among Polish and Ukrainian Peasants to 1939'. *Ethnomusicology* 35:349-79.

PACINI HERNÁNDEZ, Deborah
  1989 'Music of Marginality. Social Identity and Class in Dominican Bachata'. Ph.D. diss., Cornell Univ.

PICKEN, Laurence
  1975 *Folk Musical Instruments of Turkey*. London: Oxford Univ. Press.

POWERS, Harold S.
  1980 'Mode'. In *The New Grove Dictionary of Music and Musicians,* ed. Stanley Sadie. London: Macmillan, 12:376-450.

QURESHI, Regula Burckhardt
  1990 'Focus on Ethnic Music'. In *Ethnomusicology in Canada,* ed. Robert Witmer. Toronto: Institute for Canadian Music,

pp. 339-44.

ROBBINS, James
  1990 'Making Popular Music in Cuba: A Study of the Cuban Institutions of Musical Production and the Musical Life of Santiago de Cuba'. Ph.D. diss., Univ. of Illinois.

ROTHFARB, Lee A.
  1988 *Ernst Kurth as Theorist and Analyst*. Philadelphia: Univ. of Pennsylvania Press.
  1991 'Introduction' to *Ernst Kurth: Selected Writings,* ed. & tr. Lee A. Rothfarb. Cambridge: Cambridge Univ. Press, pp. 1-33.

SCAFF, Lawrence A.
  1989 *Fleeing the Iron Cage: Culture, Politics, and Modernity in the Thought of Max Weber.* Berkeley: Univ. of California Press.

SCHMITT, Carl
  1922 *Politische Theologie.* Munich: Duncker & Humblot. Eng. tr. of 2nd ed. (1934) by George Schwab, Cambridge, Mass.: The M.I.T. Press, 1985.

SHILOAH, Amnon & Erik Cohen
  1983 'The Dynamics of Change in Jewish Oriental Ethnic Music in Israel'. *Ethnomusicology* 27:227-52.

SHOR, Ira
  1986 *Culture Wars: School and Society in the Conservative Restoration 1969-1984.* Boston: Routledge & Kegan Paul.

SIMMEL, Georg
  1923 'Weibliche Kultur'. In Simmel, *Philosophische Kultur: Gesammelte Essais.* 3rd edn. Potsdam: Gustav Kiepenheuer, pp. 268-311. First published 1911. Eng. trans. by Guy B. Oakes in *Georg Simmel: On Women, Sexuality, and Love.* New Haven: Yale Univ. Press, 1984, pp. 65-101.

SONG BANG-SONG
  1986 *The Sanjo Tradition of Korean Komun'go Music.* Seoul: Jung Eum Sa (Traditional Korean Music, 1).

STOCK, Brian
  1990 *Listening for the Text: On the Uses of the Past.* Baltimore: Johns Hopkins Univ. Press.

THOMPSON, E.P.
  1963 *The Making of the English Working Class.* London: Victor Gollancz.

TURINO, Thomas

1990 'Structure, Context, and Strategy in Musical Ethnography'. *Ethnomusicology* 34:399-412.

VROMAN, Suzanne

1987 'Georg Simmel and the Cultural Dilemma of Women'. *History of European Ideas* 8:563-79.

WEBER, Max

1968a 'Die "Objektivität" sozialwissenschaftlicher und sozial-politischer Erkenntnis'. Repr. in Weber, *Gesammelte Aufsätze zur Wissenschaftslehre*, 3rd edn., ed. Johannes Winckelmann. Tübingen: J.C.B. Mohr (Paul Siebeck), pp. 146-214.

1968b 'Der Sinn der "Wertfreiheit" der soziologischen und ökono-mischen Wissenschaften'. Repr. in Weber, *Gesammelte Aufsätze zur Wissenschaftslehre*, 3rd edn., pp. 489-540.

WILLIAMS, Raymond

1958 *Culture and Society, 1780-1950*. London: Chatto & Windus and New York: Columbia Univ. Press.

1976 *Keywords: A Vocabulary of Culture and Society*. London: Fontana/Croom Helm.

WOLF, Eric R.

1982 *Europe and the People without History*. Berkeley: Univ. of California Press.

Contributors

ANDREW ALTER received his Bachelor of Arts from Wesleyan University, CT and his Master of Music from the University of Adelaide. He is currently a lecturer in the Department of Music at the University of New England, New South Wales, where he teaches classes in Musicianship and Ethnomusicology. His current research focusses on issues in cross-cultural music education, with particular reference to aural training methods in Indian and Western music. Address: Department of Music, University of New England, Armidale, NSW 2351, Australia.

ZDRAVKO BLAŽEKOVIĆ, an expert on Croatian music, is a Fellow of the Institute for Musicological Research in Zagreb, Yugoslavia. Address: c/- Graduate School, City University of New York, 33 West 42nd Street, New York, NY 10036, USA.

LÊ TUÂN HÙNG is a composer-performer and musicologist who was trained as a traditional musician in Vietnam. He received his Bachelor of Music (Music History and Music Performance) from the University of Melbourne in 1985 and his Ph.D. in Ethnomusicology from Monash University in 1991. His compositions include *Composition for a Friend* (1988), *Reflections* (1990) and *Basho* (1991). He has published various articles on aspects of Vietnamese music and presented three programs on Vietnamese music for ABC Radio National and SBS Radio. He is the founding member of the Australian contemporary ensemble Back to Back Zithers. Address: 35/200 Dorcas Street, South Melbourne, VIC 3205, Australia.

MARGARITA MAZO is Associate Professor of Music History at Ohio State University. She was educated at the Leningrad Conservatory, where she later worked as Chair of the Division of Musical Folklore and conducted annual interdisciplinary fieldwork in Northern Russia. Since coming to the United States in 1979, she has taught at Harvard University and the New England Conservatory of Music. Recent publications include a critical edition, *Nikolai Lvov and Ivan Prach Collection of Russian Folk Songs* (UMI, 1987), and articles on Russian village music in *JAMS* and other scholarly publications. She initiated the Smithsonian Institute's joint Soviet-American research and representation project on the folklife of cognate groups residing in the Soviet Union and the United States, and is currently working on the musical traditions of Russian Molokans and Old Believers in both countries. Address: School of Music, Ohio State University, 110 Weigel Hall, 1866 College Road, Columbus, OH 43210-1170, USA.

BRUNO NETTL is Professor of Music and Anthropology at the University of Illinois at Urbana-Champaign. His publications include ethnomusicological studies of the Blackfoot people and of Iran, and books on the field of ethnomusicology. He has recently been concerned with ethnomusicological approaches to contemporary Western art music culture. His most recent book is *Blackfoot Musical Thought: Contemporary Perspectives* (1989). Address: School of Music, University of Illinois, Urbana, IL 61801, USA.

DON NILES received his Master of Arts from UCLA and began work in 1979 as ethnomusicologist at the Institute of Papua New Guinea Studies, a position he still holds. His work involves recording and commenting on all types of PNG music. In particular, he has focussed on filling in gaps in recording activity, archiving, organology, and seeking patterns in the musical diversity of PNG. Publications include the *PNG Music Collection* and the annual *Commercial Recordings of PNG Music*. He is the ICTM Liaison Officer for PNG and the Area Editor for Oceania for *RILM*. He became a PNG citizen in 1990. Address: Music Department, Institute of Papua New Guinea Studies, PO Box 1432, Boroko, Papua New Guinea.

WILLIAM NOLL conducted fieldwork in villages and research in sound recordings archives and manuscript divisions in Poland (1980-83), Ukraine (1989-90) and Moldavia (1990). Publications include 'Music Institutions and National Consciousness among Polish and Ukraine Peasants' in Stephen Blum et al, eds., *Ethnomusicology and Modern Music History* (1991), and 'Economics of Music Patronage among Polish and Ukrainian Peasants to 1939', *Ethnomusicology* 1991. He is currently teaching at Kiev University. Address: Kiev 252013, vul. Tabirna 44, Kv. 37, Ukraine.

JANN PASLER (Ph.D., University of Chicago) is Professor in the Department of Music at the University of California, San Diego. She also teaches each year in a doctoral program, 'Musique et Musicologie du XXe Siècle', in Paris, France. Her current research focusses on re-defining the origins of modernism in France as well as exploring post-modernism and interculturalism in contemporary music. Publications include *Confronting Stravinsky: Man, Musician, and Modernist* (1986) and a video documentary, 'Taksu: Music in the Life of Bali' (1991). Address: Music Department , University of California, San Diego, La Jolla, CA 92093, USA.

ANKICA PETROVIĆ is Associate Professor at the Music Academy, University of Sarajevo, and a Fellow of the National Humanities Center, USA, for 1993-94. She received her Ph.D. in Ethnomusicology at the Queen's University of Belfast. Her special interests are the polyphonic music of the rural regions of Yugoslavia, ritual Albanian, Muslim and Sephardic Jewish musical traditions, and women's musical expression in Balkan countries. Address: National Humanities Center, 7 Alexander Drive, PO Box 12256, Research Triangle Park, NC 27709, USA.

CHRIS SAUMAIWAI studied music theory and composition at Baldwin-Wallace College and the Cleveland Institute of Music. She went to Fiji in 1965 to record and document traditional Fijian music for archival purposes, and has lived there ever since, recording in Viti Levu, Vanua Levu and Ovalau. Her special interest is Fijian lullabies and games. Publications include an article on the music of Fiji in *The New Grove Dictionary of Music and Musicians*. Address: PO Box 1206, Suva, Fiji.

JOHN M. SCHECHTER (Ph.D. in Ethnomusicology, University of Texas at Austin) is Associate Professor of Music at the University of California, Santa Cruz. He pursued field research in highland Ecuador in 1979-80 and 1990. Publications include *The Indispensable Harp: Historical Development, Modern Roles, Configurations, and Performance Practices in Ecuador and Latin America* (Kent State Univ. Press, 1992). His articles on Quichua music-culture, Inca music-culture, the Latin American child's wake, and Latin American musical instruments have appeared in

Ethnomusicology, Current Musicology, and *The New Grove Dictionary of Musical Instruments.* Address: Board of Studies in Music, Porter College, University of California, Santa Cruz, CA 95064, USA.

GRAEME SMITH has been a performer within and commentator on the Australian folk revival, and on Irish traditional dance music. His Ph.D. thesis, undertaken at Monash University, analyzed the construction of social meaning of Irish accordian playing styles. He is chairperson of the Australian branch of the International Association for the Study of Popular Music. Address: 30 McCracken Avenue, Northcote, VIC 3070, Australia.

MARCELLO SORCE KELLER obtained a doctorate in Sociology from the University of Milan and a Ph.D. in Ethnomusicology from the University of Illinois. He taught at the University of Illinois and Northwestern University, and is now Professor of Music at the Milan Conservatory. He is a founding member of the Societa' Italiana di Analisi Musicale and editor of its journal *Analisi.* He has contributed to Italian and English musicological journals and reference works. A book, *Tradizione orale e tradizione corale,* was published in 1991. Address: Via del Sole, 26, 6963 Pregassona, Switzerland.

DORIS STOCKMANN taught at the German Academy of Sciences, Berlin from 1953 to 1989, lecturing at universities in Germany and abroad. She has been an active member of the International Council for Traditional Music, through study groups, chairmanship and publications. She has published works on the theory and history of traditional music, including *Der Volksgesang in der Altmark* (1962) and *Albanische Volksmusik* (1964), as well as numerous studies on transcription, classification and analysis, musical communication and semiotics, archeology and early history, and Medieval sources in Germany and other European countries. Address: Claudius-str. 12, 10557 Berlin, Germany.

SUMARSAM holds a Bachelor of Arts from the National Academy of Gamelan, Surakarta and a Master of Arts in Music from Wesleyan University, CT. He is currently a doctoral candidate in Ethnomusicology at Cornell University. He is the author of several articles on gamelan music in *Asian Music, Ethnomusicology, Indonesia,* and *Karawitan: Source Readings in Javanese Gamelan and Vocal Music.* He is Adjunct Associate

Professor of Music in the World Music Program at Wesleyan University, teaching performance, theory and history of Javanese gamelan. As gamelan musician and *dhalang* of Javanese *wayang kulit*, he has performed and lectured widely in the United States. Address: Music Department, Wesleyan University, Middletown, CT 06457, USA.

TAN SOOI BENG is a lecturer at the Arts Centre (Pusat Seni), University Sains Malaysia, Penang. She studied at Cornell and Wesleyan Universities, USA and received her Ph.D. (Music) from Monash University, Melbourne. She is the author of the monographs *Ko-tai: Chinese Urban Street Theatre in Malaysia* and *The Phor Tor Festival in Penang: Deities, Ghosts and Chinese Ethnicity,* and various articles on the Malaysian performing arts. In 1989 she received the Society for Ethnomusicology's Jaap Kunst award for her article 'From Popular to Traditional Theatre: The Dynamics of Change in *Bangsawan* of Malaysia'. Address: Pusat Seni, Universiti Sains Malaysia, 11800 Pulau Pinang, Malaysia.

S. VENKATRAMAN is a Ph.D. candidate in Social Anthropology at the London School of Economics and Political Science. He has carried out research on the folklore of Sugalis, a semi-nomadic tribal group from Tamilnadu, India, and the traditional Tamilnadu oral narrative form, *Villuppattu* (bow song), and is currently working on *Therukkoothu*, a Tamilnadu form of street theatre. From 1982 to 1985 he worked as joint secretary and as researcher/documenter at Sampradaya, an archival and research centre for all traditional south Indian music forms, based at Madras. Address: 2, Sreenivas Apartments, 6, Prakasam St, T. Nagar, Madras 600017, India.

Index